GRACE HAPPENS

An Awakening of Consciousness

Philip Weber

Copyright © 2023 Philip T. Weber

All rights reserved. No parts of this book may be reproduced without the written permission of the publisher. For more information, contact the publisher at info@elirecht.com.

2305 Camino Robledo, Carlsbad, CA 92009

ISBN 979-886814397-7

~ This book was written for all who are called to it ~

The Eternal Harvest

The primordial, omnipresent Impulse is the seed of Awakening
The fearless searcher is the soil
The Divine Hand is the wind, the sun, and the rain
Surrender to Life – the Unknowable Ocean of Infinite Conscious Energy – is the fertilizer
Through the descent of Grace, the mind-projected illusion of separateness dissolves
In Silent Awareness we Realize our Nothing-ness, Everything-ness, and Is-ness
Eternal, ever-deepening, and indescribable Liberation is the inevitable harvest

~ PW

Dedicated to:

Adyashanti

Without your impeccable, experientially-based teachings appearing exactly when they did, I cannot imagine how the post-awakening terrain could have been traversed. Thank you so much for being a guiding light in that extraordinary wilderness. *The Eternal Harvest* was inspired by Adya's epigraph in chapter ten of his book, *The Impact of Awakening: Third Edition*.

&

The Self-Realization Fellowship

Founded in 1920 by Paramahansa Yogananda, the organization and its fellowship of truth-seeking souls provided me with the teachings, techniques, and contextual field that were perfect for my spiritual unfoldment. It was a magical and blessed journey beyond all description, culminating with an "Undreamed-of Possibility."

*The only worthwhile change,
the only permanent advance, is the inner
evolution toward spiritual perfection.*

~ *Paramahansa Yogananda*

Once upon a time there was a puppet made of salt
who had traveled a long time through dry and desert places
until one evening he came to the sea
which he had never before seen and didn't know what it was . . .

The puppet asked the sea: Who are you?
I Am the sea it replied.
But the puppet insisted, What is the sea?
I Am.

I don't understand said the puppet made of salt.
The sea replied, that's easy, touch me.
The salt puppet timidly touched the sea with the tip of his toes.
At that moment he realized that the sea began to make itself perceptible,
but at the same time he noticed the tips of his toes had disappeared.
What have you done to me? He cried to the sea.
You have given a little of yourself to understand me, the sea replied.

Slowly the salt puppet began to walk into the sea with great solemnity as
though he were about to perform the most important act of his life.
The further he moved along, the more he dissolved, but at the same time
he had the impression that he knew more and more about the sea.

Again and again the puppet asked,
What is the sea? Until the wave covered him completely.
Just before he was entirely dissolved by the sea he exclaimed:
I exist!

~ Anonymous

Editor's Note

Dear reader, you hold in your hands the story of one man's journey of Self-discovery. It is a raw and honest report of the awakening of consciousness told from both a bird's-eye view and from the ground of everyday living. Although it is only about one person, this document reveals the divine truth about each of us and what is possible for humanity. While Self-realization is not exclusive to Phil (and for reasons unknown, it appears to be happening now more than ever), to my knowledge there are few accounts such as this one. This is primarily because his multi-year awakening process was being documented as it was unfolding.

Before we get into the details, I would like to tell you why I was chosen for the role. First, I have a background in academia, having graduated from two institutions of higher learning, in which I had rigorous experience with formal writing and editing. Second, I am intimately familiar with many of the concepts elucidated herein, not only due to my avid reading of various spiritual literatures over many years, but also due to my own spiritual living and practice. Third, I know the author personally, can vouch for many aspects of his story, and am able to authenticate his conscious awareness-experience, as best I can, by way of personal witnessing and attunement.

Let me share a bit about how the editing phase unfolded and the decisions that were made for the sake of consistency. We began with a bounty of raw materials: emails and journal entries that Phil had written (to himself and to friends and family) during his awakening process. They make up the meat of the first half of the book: chapters one through six. These source materials were not altered except in three instances: to preserve the confidentiality of Phil's correspondents, to add/delete a word or fix incorrect grammar/spelling for greater readability, and to [include supplementary information within brackets] when we felt more context, detail, or understanding was warranted.

Before I was on the scene, Phil had already chosen which communications would make it into the manuscript, distilled them to their essential parts, and deleted the often insightful and caring responses to them that he received. He also wrote brief commentaries before and after these materials to expound and expand on what was being presented. When I began proofreading, my primary focus, other than on grammar and syntax, was on flow and clarity of expression. I found the emails captivating, but I felt that the commentaries had fallen flat, making for a choppy and difficult-to-decipher story. Thus, my main contribution became encouraging Phil to expand on the commentaries, add some more human elements, and tell a more coherent and relatable story – so that you can know that awakening is possible no matter your past or present circumstances. Admittedly, this was difficult for Phil to do, as he felt that these aspects of his "outer life" were irrelevant. Yet, as we continued to shape the narrative together, and as I began to draw out (painfully at times) stories that were often humorous and/or profound, he came to feel that the final product contained more transparency and heart.

From these efforts, there persists a common thread through the entire narrative: two distinct voices working in tandem, one from the past (emails and journal entries) and one in the present (commentaries). You will recognize them, as we utilized fonts to denote their differences: the commentary voice is in Garamond, the journal entries are in Tekton, **and the emails are in their original Arial, dated and signed.** Via these voices, you are shown an unusual perspective on the awakening process and guided, as if by an old friend, along Phil's compelling adventure.

From our wonderfully intensive back-and-forth collaborations, each chapter proved to be a unique challenge requiring its own approach, almost mirroring the different phases of Phil's journey on which we were concentrating. The challenge was revising material from different time periods and from different places in consciousness! This required the author to sink into and relive those phases of his life, and it required me to join him. Needless to say, this was an opportunity to deepen into our spiritual awareness, and we are both better off as a result.

In the second half of the book, there is an extensive no-holds-barred Q&A interview, an epilogue reflecting Phil's deepest voice and insights, a compendium of the Masters and modern-day sages that profoundly influenced the author, and a list of books and recordings that he found most useful during his journey. These hindsight-based resources are designed to assist you with your ever-evolving awakening of consciousness, should you so choose. Overall, this book provides a summary of many helpful spiritual gems Phil encountered over the course of his lifetime.

Finally, throughout the book, you will notice that there is repetition of ideas. While we edited some out, we felt that keeping what we did provided an opportunity to deepen into key points often overlooked by the egoic perspective. "The hard core of egotism," wrote Paramahansa Yogananda, "is difficult to dislodge except rudely." Repetition, like a hammer to a nail, is one method to crack through its tough shell.

With these preliminaries addressed, you are now ready for Phil to lead the way. Assisting in the shaping of this narrative has been a sincere privilege and one of the most fulfilling experiences of my life. I am certain that his beautiful and inspiring story stands uniquely on its own, and let it be included in the annals of history as one more testament to the human spirit. Enjoy the ride!

Love,
Eli Recht
December 2021
Encinitas, California

Table of Contents

Introduction: Wanna Take A Ride? 11

Chapter One: A Brief History In Time 23

    Cutting The Final Knot 32

Chapter Two: The Kiss 33

Chapter Three: The Rebirthing Journey 41

Chapter Four: Entering The Marketplace 85

Chapter Five: Integration And Acclimation 97

Chapter Six: The Real Voyage Of Discovery 123

    We Are Already One 143

Chapter Seven: Q&A Interview 145

    Paradox 196

Epilogue: The Road Goes Ever On 197

Appendix: Soul Food 223

Appreciative Accolades 239

Question: What is our true identity?

Answer: In unmanifested stillness, our identity is the Absolute Unicity – Pure Awareness not aware of itself; manifested, functioning in duality, our identity is Consciousness Seeking Itself.

~ *Nisargadatta Maharaj*

INTRODUCTION:
Wanna Take A Ride?

Are you a devoted and determined seeker of Self-Realization? Hang on then, because this book suggests that being a "seeker" is just the last gasp of the illusory separate self. Are you unwavering about the goal of achieving enlightenment? Best be sitting down now, as this book also suggests that no one ever "achieves" enlightenment. How can one get something one already has? How can one become That Which One Already Is? How does anything *illusory* do anything at all? Alan Watts used a simile around this type of conundrum, saying it's "like trying to lift yourself off the ground with your own bootstraps!" The "you" that you may be thinking is doing the lifting isn't Real! To any spiritual ego-minds reading this, I'm sorry to be the bearer of tough news so early on here, but no matter how long or how diligently you try, attaining What You Are can't be done. What is there to <u>do</u> then? For Now, expand your assumptive horizons about awakening, and accept that the "I" is not steering the ship…and it never was.

Does your mind generate fear-based scenarios around the possibility that awakening might not happen for you in this lifetime? Alternatively, if it were to happen, are you feeling it will most likely take many more years of meditation, purification, study, or prayer? Or worse, that it will take countless more incarnations before you are finally worthy? Do you envision that enlightenment only materializes for cave-dwelling yogis, otherworldly saints, sages, mystics, cloistered monastics, and religious rock stars? My experience states the opposite, and that the type of approach that (un)consciously puts Self-Realization off to some future moment is just the ego's way of staying in control and intact. You don't need to study scripture for years. You don't have to change your religion or spiritual path, nor do you have to adopt one. There's no requirement from those on high to give up sex, meat, booze, weed, TV, Taco Bell, or anything else you occasionally enjoy. You don't have to walk around India in a loincloth or retire to an icy cave in the Himalayas. There is absolutely no need to renounce your job, your friends, your family, or your hobbies and interests – although you may end up choosing to do one or more of these. Awakening is beyond our ability to "make" happen (hence it taking as long as it will take), but we can still traverse the spiritual path in a manner that renders us more likely to receive the Grace that brings lasting transformation.

Grace Happens is my rollercoaster account of **Consciousness Awakening to Itself**. It documents and examines my experience of the critical, albeit narrow portion of the spirituality spectrum that awakening is. Undeniably, there are already excellent books about this in today's marketplace. Some of them are individual descriptions of the author's journey, others are comprehensive explorations of the before, during, and after phases of the realization process, and several are narrower looks at specific aspects, such as the psychological, neurological, and/or energetic ramifications of transcendence. This book falls into all of these categories to some degree.

For the purposes of this book, Awakening (i.e. Enlightenment, Liberation, Self-Realization, Moksha, Nirvana, Fanā, etc.) is the *annihilation of self*. You are not a skin-encapsulated, ego-centered body-mind organism known as {fill in name here} that confronts an objective, external world "out there." Stated another way, awakening is the destruction of every idea one has (or has ever had) about who one thinks one is as a separate "I." It is the complete, lasting loss of one's inner, self-referential world and, along with it, one's identity as a {fill in gender, age, ethnicity, nationality, occupation, marital status, sexual orientation, role as a parent/child/sibling, political affiliation, net worth, credit rating, hobbies, religious and/or spiritual affiliations, etc. here}. In the no-BS words of U.G. Krishnamurti, **"The end of the illusion is the end of you."**

Awakening is not a thing, it's not an event, and it's not a state. It's not something you get, and it's not something you'll be in the future. Simply put, awakening is unconditioned transparent knowingness. It is the Realization of your own True Nature – the intrinsic primordial essence as Nothing and Everything. It is Recognizing the Emptiness of All Things, and Being the Fullness of This Moment. It is no more and no less than radically Seeing and Accepting What Is…Just As It Is.

Our inherent divinity is our natural state. In some spiritual texts, we are told that we don't know our divinity because we are "ignorant" of the Unitive Nature of Reality. While this is true, it's also important to remember that *fundamentally* there is no real ignorance. If there was, we would definitely be caught between a rock and a hard place! Instead, realize that within Samsara (the dream state), there is just the *illusion* of ignorance.

Awakening happens naturally and inevitably when the illusory separate self has been seen through. Then, our real voyage of discovery begins. One's unveiled eyes see Truth, Beauty, and Love as indivisible, everywhere present. In one of his sermons, Meister Eckhart stated, "The eye through which I see God is the same eye through which God sees me; my eye and God's eye are one eye, one seeing, one knowing, one love." With our newborn vision, we see the Essential Unity behind and within the multifarious manifestations. However, we don't see this anymore as a hopeful concept or inherited belief system, but rather as Intimate, Direct, Luminous, Awareness-Experience.

The paradoxical nature of awakening is this: on one hand, it's an impersonal happening that flows from the evolutionary ripeness of an individuated modulation of consciousness. On the other hand, sincere effort and an unquenchable thirst for Self-Realization (i.e. Oneness, Unity Consciousness, Truth) are nearly always compulsory. As Nisargadatta used to instruct, **earnestness** about one's spiritual direction and practices is vital to awakening. While the transcendence of the ego-mind ultimately comes down to Grace, we still must do our part. Adyashanti calls this becoming "Grace prone." Based on how my sadhana (i.e. spiritual path) unfolded, I have concluded that we are far better off making a spiritual effort through whatever practices or teachings resonate with us instead of just sitting around waiting for a burning-bush level epiphany to fall into our laps. Although there are no absolutes about this, I do feel that sitting in the stands, eating snacks, and watching the game ain't gonna cut it. Even standing "on deck" for a closer view of the game (spiritual-seeker identity) is almost never enough. With determination and devotion, we must stand in the batter's box each moment and take our fearless swings. **Who's** swinging, and **What's** pitching? Conscious Awareness – You! While on this puzzling and sometimes contentious topic, I feel the following quote from Dorothy Hunt's book, *Ending the Search: From Spiritual Ambition to the Heart of Awareness,* really nails it: "Nothing you do can create enlightenment. Then why are there spiritual practices? To encourage your mind to be open and still long enough to receive Truth's gift."

While there are extensive spiritual resources offered herein, this is not a "how-to" book filled with techniques. It seems as if there are already enough of those in the world, and it doesn't feel like my mission to add any more. Additionally, no effort is made to encourage you to embrace a specific teacher or practice. While I deeply respect and honor all paths, this book is simply a document of my experience and not meant to promote any ideology or methodology.

The methods one adopts and utilizes aren't everything, and neither are the teachers and organizations who espouse them. From my perspective, the *attitude* with which we approach our spiritual journey is also key. Moving forward, I suggest beginning with the central assumption that the most expeditious way to extricate yourself from the cage of egoic-based delusion is to Realize that **there is no cage**! The path and methods you choose aside, just keep subtracting and releasing what is false. Once everything false is gone, whatever remains must be True. As my dad used to say, "A cup must be emptied before it can be filled."

The best of all possible news is that we are always playing with the house's money. In other words, the concept of enlightenment-unenlightenment is just that: a concept. From the "awakened" perspective, there is no (un) enlightenment. Moreover, Life and the spiritual path are synonymous. Utilize all of Life to abidingly transcend the illusion of the separate self. By living in this way, we are reminded of our Absolute Interconnectedness with All Things. One of the tasks that's particularly troublesome for longtime spiritual seekers is to navigate the strange and sometimes "pathless" path without becoming attached to the methods used. That, and not identifying with/as anything while doing it! One's identity as a "seeker" on a "spiritual path" is always shifting (i.e. consuming books, audios, videos, or attending seminars, retreats, workshops, kirtans, satsangs, convocations, etc.). What's hot, what's not, it's all a part of the process…until it isn't. Regardless of the road home, as the Event Horizon is approached and finally crossed, our Soul way forward becomes **surrender** – letting go of all attachments. While this is simple to say, in my case it wasn't easy to do. Fortunately, Life perfectly conspired for and as my highest good, just as It is continually doing for and as yours. What else could It possibly do?

History is replete with stories of awakenings that defy all logic and understanding. If you were to ask some of the people who know me, they might well include me in this group! There are many examples of awakened individuals and, somewhat astonishingly, I've become yet another embodiment of those who've Realized their True Nature. Undeniably, you can be too, but perhaps the foremost impediment to this is not **trusting** that you already are it.

If awakening is the primary objective of your life, or if this is the inevitable outcome that you are willing to embrace as the result of beginning a spiritually-centered life, then this book may be for you. However, if the eradication of the egoic-self feels like a spiritual bridge-too-far, or worse, utter madness, then don't fret; to everything there is a season. You, my friend, are perfectly fine just where and as you are! Continue being "a dancer" in The Dance, with as much *joie de vivre* as you can possibly muster. Nisargadatta Maharaj said that there are two types of karma – the kind that can be mitigated by Grace and the kind that must be burned away experientially. Burn this second type by living authentically, trusting that The Universe unfolds perfectly. Just remember: The Buddha taught that separation-based living necessarily includes suffering. Eventually, when one has suffered enough, regardless of how many years or incarnations it takes, all of this will sound appealing, and more importantly, it will become your life's primary objective. Strange as it may seem, when you arrive at this juncture, you will realize that your suffering was Grace. But don't take my word for it; always let your own direct experience be your guide. Between the turned-inward searchlight of discernment and the whispers of the intuitive heart, one always finds the way to their highest good. If you are on the fence about any of this, my question for you is: *have you finally suffered enough?* If yes, then please keep reading!

The contents of this book are not based in philosophical erudition. I am no scholar, nor am I exceptionally learned in fields such as metaphysics, epistemology, esotericism, psychology, or religion. Furthermore, I'm not a professional writer (thank God for my editor!), nor am I a spiritual teacher. And while The Universe may have other plans for me, I currently have no desire to become either. Instead, I think of myself as a "sharer." Simply, *Grace Happens* was written for these reasons:

1) To provide some experiential, real-world inspiration to dedicated seekers, especially to all my sisters and brothers who have journeyed on the spiritual path for many years.

2) To be a resource, both for when one is "circling the drain" of awakening, and then after when one is "being flushed" into the Realization of Oneness (Phil-speak...you'll get used to it). No two people experience an abiding transcendence of the ego-mind the same way. However, as there are often many overlapping challenges and characteristics of awakening, these types of books can prove useful beyond measure. Before awakening happened for me – and it is a *happening,* not a doing – I possessed many years of spiritual study and practice, combined with all sorts of spiritual experiences, but **none of it** prepared me for the actual awareness-experience of awakening! I had some nebulous ideas about the death of the ego but that was about it. As I was being flushed, I longed for any resource I could find to help me, and I realized how scarce accounts like this are in the world. Thus, one of my main motivations for writing *Grace Happens* is so that your awakening might be easier!

3) To kindle an awakening for you here, now. Short of this, my hope is to provide a confirmation of your own experience(s). As the spiritual path abounds with events that are mystifying (to say the least!), knowing that something you have faced has also been encountered by somebody else is often reassuring. If neither of these is the case, then my final hope is that my sharing here provides a measure of conceptual understanding, through which you may then be better prepared for when a transcendental leap does happen. *And it will!*

4) To offer my deepest gratitude to God and Guru for the immense blessings I have received.

There are numerous accounts in publication today in which the author writes something to the effect of: "this was never intended to be a book." While I'm a bit sheepish to admit this, it is true; I never originally wrote about my awakening for widespread dissemination. Back in 2014, I composed a rather lengthy PDF document that detailed my sadhana, including all the sometimes-strange spiritual experiences that punctuated it. It was shared with a small group of friends and family, and while there were several revisions over the next few years, that was the end of it.

Then, the awakening happened in September 2017, and the emails contained in this book came into being. First, I had to try my best to communicate what was happening to *someone* or I'd have probably flipped my wig. Having a few friends who had the spiritual understanding to comprehend what I was going through, at least to the degree that they could, was an enormous help. Second, by writing down everything, I was able to better contextualize it all. These new emails were then added to my original PDF and it was all revised again (and again, and…you get the idea), but I still never intended to publish it. For a time, I was sorry I'd created the dang thing, and I'm relatively certain that some of my friends were sorry too, as they'd come across yet another new version in their inbox. For all the kind souls who endured one revision after another and are reading this now, please accept my sincere appreciation and apologies.

You may be wondering then how this book ended up in your hands. Well… Life Happens! In January 2019, while on a forty-day solitary retreat at a Tibetan Buddhist center in the Southeast Arizona Mountains, an unmistakably powerful energetic Impulse arose. The Impulse was to take the relevant parts of what had already been documented and add to it whatever came up from and out of the modulation of consciousness writing (that would be me, Phil). The Impulse also provided the title *Grace Happens* along with the unexpected intention to disseminate it publicly. My never authoring a book before was completely beside the point! I'd gotten used to flowing this way over the previous two years, so rather than question the flow, I simply went with it. As for my about-face, I have taken shelter in Mahatma Gandhi's clarification to his followers when he unexpectedly decided to cancel important plans that were in place. When asked how he could justify changing his mind, he aptly stated, "My aim is not to be consistent with my previous statements on a given question, but to be consistent with truth as it may present itself to me at a given moment." Yep, ditto. That works for me…sans the loincloth. I'm more of a Levi's, T-shirt, and baseball cap guy.

Like most everyone else, prior to awakening I found myself believing something so deeply that I would view it as "the truth." In our world, these beliefs-turned-truths are generally known as facts, common sense, or my favorite…**reality**. As my awakening unfolded and my identity as "Phil" dissolved, there was a growing realization that the clearer, more expansive my awareness-experience became, the less I really knew – until eventually the only thing I could verify was my existence. This was one of the earliest insights that was revealed. In the spirit of transparency, I want to go on record as to *everything* I now know: I AM. Clear enough? I hope so, as I cannot be more succinct than that. Truly, "I AM" is all I can state that I unequivocally know…about myself or anything. One of the most famous examples in history of somebody exemplifying this Truth comes from Socrates. In what's been designated as the "Socratic paradox," he affirmed, "I know that I know nothing." All of this is about as counterintuitive and objectionable a concept to the ego-mind as there is, but when dispassionately analyzed, it's impossible to come to any other conclusion. And anyway, after ego-transcendence happens, investigating this is pointless, as it becomes Self-evident. This may have been why Friedrich Nietzsche was quoted as insightfully observing, "There are no facts, only interpretations." Is there, then, any wonder at all those *alternative facts* out there?

How then do we determine the relative truths that guide our lives? Direct experience is always the first, best measure. This means that there is no guru, teacher, book, religion, belief system, or conditioned mind that can tell us what is true. We come to know for ourselves. Other than this, the only other measure that can be used is inference (i.e. from the above-mentioned sources and others). We can say, "I know about this or that," but it is only ever an approximation of the truth. In the final analysis, we never know anything other than the knowingness out of which experience arises.

In this book, I express my insights from direct experience, from my lived truth. As a result, what is written may not fit in with your truth or your experience, and I take no issue with that. When something written is not from my direct experience, from the ground of I AM, but rather from how it appears and/or feels to me in that moment, I will make it known by prefacing it with something like, "I don't know, but my sense is…" What's more, I have no qualms about calling a spade a spade, even if it's not politically correct. My intention is never to disparage anyone or anything; I do this only to shine light on issues that I feel could benefit from it. Regarding this, I take heart from the following quote by the renowned Trappist author, monk, and mystic Thomas Merton: "If a writer is so cautious that he never writes anything that cannot be criticized, he will never write anything that can be read. If you want to help other people you have got to make up your mind to write things that some men will condemn."

Before we begin, it's important to mention a few points about language. Both written and verbal communication are like everything else in manifestation: they are embedded in duality. Non-duality literally means "not two." Thus, the Unitive Beingness that awakening foments is outside of a dualistic framework. As it turns out, non-dual awareness-experience Realizes that duality is nothing more than a concept (i.e. the mind's superimposition of the finite onto the infinite). It also turns out that this Realization extinguishes other taken-for-granted concepts such as causality, karma, reincarnation, and even time and space. Like countless others, I have found that the ineffable nature of all of this is challenging to communicate! At best, language only serves as a pointer. What's more, words always fail to convey *suchness* or, if you please, the complete feeling of the Timeless Moment. Therefore, moving forward let's excuse them for their innate clumsiness!

For the sake of ease, "I" have not relinquished the use of personal pronouns, either in this book or in how I talk. Linguistic gymnastics such as "the mind-body organism known as Phil" or "this psychosomatic apparatus" or referring to myself in the third person are occasionally employed for effect, to remind the reader of Who/What We Really Are. I have noticed in certain non-dual circles that there are those who don't appreciate the use of personal pronouns. Well, to any undercover agents of the non-dual police out there, I lovingly have three words for you based on sagely counsel from The Eagles – Get Over It. Additionally, I've heard that some people in certain spiritual circles loathe the word "Process." Humbly, I now see Life as *a mysterious and miraculous process,* so I pray that I'm allowed to use this term without too many objections.

As you read on, you may notice that I use the term "awakening" much more than "enlightenment." The first reason I don't use the "E" word a lot is that there are so many preconceptions, misperceptions, and downright fantasies about it. It has been used for millennia, so the concept has more baggage than a cabal of career politicians! If you put together a group of one hundred dedicated spiritual aspirants and asked them for a definition of enlightenment, you would likely get one hundred variations on the theme, *even if they all shared the same spiritual teaching or Master*. In this vein, if you were to ask me, "Are you enlightened?" I would need to understand what *you* mean by "enlightenment" before formulating my answer. Like other aspects of religion and spirituality, the notion of enlightenment would perhaps be best served by retiring it for a few hundred years, so that it could be heard again with fresh ears and considered anew. For me, the term "awakening" simply has less baggage. The second reason is that "awakening" is a useful pointer: just as we wake up from a dream in the morning, so do we wake up from the dream state of Samsara. The third reason I differentiate between "awakening" and "enlightenment" is that, through my own journey, my understanding of the terms has changed and I don't view them as synonymous anymore. A more nuanced discernment and awareness-experience of these two places in/as consciousness has arisen, and there will be more on that later. Lastly, when The Buddha was asked, "Are You Enlightened?" his reply was, "I Am Awake" (reportedly, I wasn't there; at least I don't remember being there). Well fine, if it worked for The Buddha then it works for me!

More importantly, the experiences of awakening and enlightenment are both prior to and beyond the intellect. How can the human mind understand something that is beyond it? The short answer is: it can't. So even if everyone somehow magically agreed on the definition of enlightenment, what would that do for us? If our understanding of awakening is not derived from our living awareness-experience, then it's just a *concept,* and one constructed mostly by people who are forming best-guess theories of their own. In science, it is considered a demonstrable maxim that a subsystem cannot fully comprehend the metasystem of which it is a part. As this appears to be scientifically verifiable, how do we expect the intellect to be able to grok anything beyond itself? The bottom line is – it is impossible to completely describe or intellectually grasp the Unitive Beingness of our Natural State. We can only Be It.

With all my heart, I wish I could tell you <u>how</u> to wake up from the dream state, but I can't. All anyone can really do is point you in the direction of what will ultimately be a process unique to you. If you are currently on a spiritual path that appears to be working, steadfastly stay on it and dive in deep. *Make it your own.* If you are still looking for your path, explore the Soul Food section, or don't be shy about investigating any of the other teachings that may call to you, which are beyond this book's scope. Paraphrasing Dr. Wayne Dyer, I encourage you to be open to all untried possibilities but without becoming attached to them. Trust The Process, and know that The Universe <u>has</u> and <u>is</u> a can't-fail, loving evolutionary purpose. You are not only in it…YOU ARE IT!

Please accept this book as another sincere testament to the ever-growing body of evidence that awakening does indeed happen. Recognize the fact that "you" cannot "achieve" awakening, and then make the most earnest effort that you possibly can toward that goal. Then, when you in and as This Moment are sufficiently ripe, Grace *will descend*. My dear, divine friend – you are not the performer in the picture show called "your life." You are the Screen of Consciousness on which the movie is projected. You're not a separate-self dancer. You Are The Dance Itself. Please, never succumb to fear, uncertainty, or doubt. Be the Loving, Awakened Spark of the Divine that You Are! If you only remember one message from this book, make it this one: awakening can and *inevitably* does happen to everyone, and that includes you.

And so, dear reader, with all that said…wanna take a ride?

> The Starting Point is the Path, the Path is the Goal,
> and the Goal is the Starting Point.
>
> ~ Dzogchen Proverb

Hold on to nothing.

~ Neem Karoli Baba

CHAPTER ONE:
A Brief History In Time

This snapshot of pre-awakening personal history was not in the book's original draft. While one's "story" may be interesting to some, I find it impossible to experience much enthusiasm for mine. Possibly, this is because I lived it and realized that it was all spent in the dream state. Perhaps, the original omission of my early life stems from a sense that it's all fairly ordinary and thus of little value in relationship to the transcendent events that followed. Nevertheless, I was convinced by my editor-in-chief to, at minimum, add a few more details of my life. His logic seemed, well, logical, in that I am a first-time author and not a public figure of any kind. With at least *some* knowledge of my journey before awakening, you won't be dropped into the meat grinder of my transformation process without any idea of how I got there or who is relating this amazing adventure. And so, in the hope that it will clarify the overall story, I'm providing this biographical sketch of what led up to my Realizing the true Nature of Reality one month after my 57th birthday.

I came into this world on August 10, 1960 in the beautiful Rose City known as Portland, Oregon. Born to a blue-collar father and a stay-at-home mom (at least while they were married), I was raised with one sibling, my beautiful sister Marilyn, who is twelve years older than I am. It wasn't until a 2019 genetic test revealed what Marilyn and I had already suspected: that she was actually my half-sister. While the circumstances are unknown, mom got pregnant from someone other than her husband and I was the result. Discovering that my father was not biologically related, however, meant (and means) nothing to me. Ya gotta snag a body somehow. It was like finding out that my favorite longtime jacket (i.e. body) had been made in Idaho instead of Oregon. I mean, who cares...unless you think you are your body! In any event, by the time this discovery was made, my parents had transitioned. On top of that, it's impossible not to cut my mom some slack, as her marriage wasn't good to begin with, mainly due to my dad's PTSD stemming from his service as a U.S. Marine in the south pacific during WWII. My dad was a member of the invasion force at Guadalcanal, which was one of the pivotal battles in the war against the Japanese. As it was and is with so many veterans, war left an unseen wound on my father that was never fully healed before he dropped his body. Despite this, I always felt that he loved me a lot. We always had a great relationship, so I can't ask for more than that. I had two wonderful-beyond-words parents, and I miss them both very much.

Near the end of my mother's life, I asked her if she was disappointed that I had not given her any grandchildren as my sister had. She told me that she always felt it was my life to live as I saw fit, that she just wanted me to be happy, and that she would never try to saddle me with her desires. She then reminded me of an event that transpired when I was seven, which apparently made an indelible impression on her. She related that I was in the living room playing, while my mom and one of her friends were chatting about their children and family life. Mom said that at one point I took notice and began listening attentively. Seeing this, my mom's friend smiled and asked me, "How many children do you want to have when you grow up, Philip?" My mom stated that, for a moment, her little boy vanished and with a look and voice of what she could only describe as a very old soul, I reportedly replied, "I don't feel that I need to have children in this lifetime to make it complete." Mom said there was a stunned silence in the room, after which I was a seven year old again. She then asked me to go outside to play and never mentioned this event until she was nearing her transition. After relaying this, my mother confided in me that she always believed I was "destined for something very different and special." Amazed, I asked her what she thought that special destiny was. Gazing out into the distance, she whispered simply and thoughtfully, "I don't know."

At age eight, I eagerly tagged along with my dad and his best friend for the dedication of the new Vedanta Society Temple in Southeast Portland (September 29, 1968) just a few miles from where I grew up. While touring the facility, the Hindu decor and Indian vibe felt very natural and even familiar to me. The moment that stands out most in my memory was when the three of us were outside in the parking lot watching the procession of monks and disciples solemnly walking into the temple for the Durga Puja.

Seeing them file in, I watched **in awe**, feeling that they were going to be "discussing the secrets of The Universe," as I described it then. As the last monk in the procession was about to enter, he stopped for a moment, turned his head to the left, and looking right at me, smiled in a way that I have never forgotten. His look seemed to say, "Your day to enter will come" and then he went inside and the doors closed. I yearned with all my heart to be in there with them.

It was also during my grade school years that my dad and I used to enjoy visiting The Grotto, formally known as The National Sanctuary for our Sorrowful Mother. Located a few blocks from where we lived, this 62-acre shrine and monastery operated by the Roman Catholic Church is a beautiful and peaceful place for meditation, contemplation, and prayer. I remember how comfortable I felt around the monks and on the monastery grounds, and this affinity for monastic and spiritual sites of all persuasions never left me. In fact, it continued to strengthen as I got older, which tied into my inborn ecumenical outlook. The Grotto has only gotten better over the years, and I make it a point to visit anytime I am in Portland.

During these formative years, I also discovered the magic and artistry of the *Revolver* and *Sgt. Pepper's Lonely Hearts Club Band* albums by The Beatles. As it was with most of the kids I knew during that era, The Fab Four were my favorite band. Their influence and importance in the world went far beyond the music they created. Two songs from these albums affected me very deeply, but in a way that I did not understand at the time. In retrospect, these songs were kindling my affinity for eastern mysticism and esoteric spirituality. *Tomorrow Never Knows* from Revolver and *Within You, Without You* from Sgt. Peppers laid a connection to India, Tibet, and Japan that would blossom during my teen years, and then again in my adult years. Moreover, I used to stare at the image of Sri Yukteswar (Yogananda's guru) on the cover of Sgt. Peppers, even though back then I had no idea who he was. The other Self-Realization Fellowship (SRF) Masters on the cover are harder to see (and at that age I wouldn't have known them anyway), but Sri Yukteswar's image always captivated me in a way I couldn't explain.

At age ten, my parents were divorced, and by age twelve, my mother was remarried to an unconventional but nevertheless generous and loving man (i.e. my step-dad). Except for a six-month stint in a middle school during the early stages of my mother's second marriage (a wonderful thing by the way, as she found her soulmate and was able to live the life she wanted), I spent my entire school-age years at the K-8 six blocks from our home. This was followed by four years at the high school just five blocks from my dad's house, where I lived from the mid-7th grade on. I loved learning and was a good student, but I lacked the necessary ambition and prodding from my dad to attend college.

During my early teens, innate interests flourished and I began deeply immersing myself into the martial arts, music, and chess, the latter two lasting throughout this lifetime. These early passions were primarily fueled by Bruce Lee, The Moody Blues, and Bobby Fischer, respectively. The music and martial arts fed my burgeoning interest in eastern spirituality and philosophy in general. Much of The Moody Blues music is unapologetically mystical, and their *In Search of the Lost Chord* album in particular moved me further into my exploration of "the other side of life." Through Bruce Lee, my affinity for Zen and Taoism developed, but far more importantly, his writings introduced me to Alan Watts, who became my first spiritual teacher. I fondly remember listening to Alan's Sunday night lectures on Portland FM radio. His famed book titled *The Book: On the Taboo Against Knowing Who You Are* was the most profound spiritual book I ever read, until the *Autobiography of a Yogi* found me many years later.

Growing up in humble surroundings, we didn't have a lot, although I never went hungry or lacked the basics. Still, the opportunity to travel out of state for something like a vacation wasn't possible until my sister married in 1972 and subsequently moved to the Boston area when her husband was accepted into Harvard for a Ph.D. in biochemistry. My first time visiting them was at age twelve when I flew across the country by myself to stay for the month of August. It was the trip of a young lifetime for me, as we traveled all over, seeing many historical sites in the New England area, not to mention New York, Philadelphia, and Washington D.C. I was able to visit Boston again in the summers of my 14th and 15th years and for two weeks when I was 16. With each trip, I grew increasingly familiar with the Boston area, much more so than could be explained by my short visits there. By the summer of my 15th year, I was confidently taking the bus and subway alone, hanging out in Cambridge Square, and hustling the locals playing speed chess for money. It was during this trip that a spiritual *maha* event happened, although it would not make complete sense to me until twenty-three years later. Little did I know back then that there was already an SRF link in place, as their apartment was located in *Waltham*, the site of Yogananda's first ashram.

During that momentous trip, we were sightseeing in downtown Boston and went to the observation deck at the top of the Prudential Building. This event is still unbelievably vivid in my memory. I wandered around one way while they went the other. As I looked out at the city, I began fixating on a building a few blocks off to the left. Suddenly, everything around me fell away. I was not cognizant of anyone or anything nearby, and my vision was drawn telescopically to the building. In my mind, I heard the faint sound of a drone from an Indian instrument of some sort (now, I would say a tambura). In a flash, I immediately knew that I had lived in that building in the 1920s, that I'd been a white male, and that I had not lived to see 1930. I was practically shaken to my knees by the power of the experience, but I knew that I could not say anything to my family. We met up later and walked around a bit, but just to test it again, I left them for several minutes and went back to the same spot. The experience repeated itself, albeit not as forcefully.

It wasn't until the age of 38 that this powerful experience finally came full circle. I was lying in bed reading the chapter in the *Autobiography of a Yogi* that recounts Yogananda's first years in the U.S. when again, the same drone could be heard in my mind, and the unbelievably intense memory from that day came back full force. I immediately knew then that I had been one of Yogananda's early disciples in Boston, and that prior to his arrival there in 1920, I had been a friend of Doctor and Mrs. Lewis, early and lifelong devotees of Yogananda. In a historic photo of that first group, I am standing on the left, behind Minot and Mildred Lewis. It's not lost on me that this sounds somewhat fantastical, and I'm pointing this out here *so you don't think I don't know!* All the same, in my heart there is an intuitive certainty that this is true, and words cannot express how **odd** it was (and still is) to see my prior physical form in a photograph. More than anything else, I am astonished by the physical resemblance to how I looked this time 'round in my 30s. When seeing the photo for the first time a few years ago, my beloved "Indian mom" in the Atlanta SRF group thought my face had been pasted into the image. It's strange! I have no doubt that this past-life connection was why it was effortless to find Yogananda again as my guru when I was ripe.

After high school, I got what jobs I could and moved out at 19. I'm afraid my ambitions didn't extend beyond partying and chasing girls, which was fine until five years had flown by and suddenly, an inner alarm started ringing. I realized that I needed to find some direction, and during a particularly rough stretch at a job I hated, I prayed for something that I liked and could grow in. A couple of months later, my mom and step-dad were attending a Christmas party at the Red Lion Jantzen Beach Hotel, which overlooks the Columbia River and Vancouver, Washington. The story, related to me by my mother, was that while they were there, my step-dad sauntered up to the hotel's banquet manager and asked if they had any job openings. Surprised, the manager asked if the job was for him but the reply came, "naw, it's for our good-fer-nothin' kid." He didn't actually feel that way about me; it was just his um… rather unique way of communicating with people! In any case, it worked, and the manager told him to have me come in and fill out an application. Given my 35-year career that followed, it is impossible for me to imagine how my life would have turned out had that three-minute conversation not taken place. This vividly illustrates that The Universe (a.k.a. God, Spirit, Source) is working for our long term highest interests always…and in all ways. Given my step-dad, it points to God working in mysterious ways too!

At the age of 23, I began my career as a hotel porter. For those not in the business, my primary function was setting up meetings and banquets, endlessly hauling tables and stacking chairs, and vacuuming the carpets before and after the functions. Carpet this hotel had aplenty, as the ballroom was nearly 20,000 square feet, could host 2,000 people seated for dinner, and at the same time host 1,000 people downstairs in the secondary ballroom. During the summer, we hosted Amway picnics outdoors, the largest being for 7,000 people. While the hotel only had 320 guestrooms, it was an enormous convention facility and…I absolutely loved it! Everything just seemed to go right for me during those early months and years, and by the time I was 28, I was a fledgling hotel General Manager with another company. Located across the road from Washington State University in Pullman, at 90 rooms with a newly renovated restaurant and bar, it wasn't a starship by any means, but it was mine…and one never forgets the first ship they captain. I was always blessed to have great professional mentors who must have seen something promising in me, for as they grew in their careers, they helped me in mine. This important practice of "developing talent and promoting from within" became a part of my ethos too, always endeavoring to nurture and advance the careers of my subordinates. A mere two years and two more assignments later, I was recruited into the "big leagues." In what can only be described as a meteoric rise, within six years of starting as a know-nothing banquet porter, I found myself in the role of Executive Director of Food and Beverage for the Sir Francis Drake Hotel in downtown San Francisco. From there, I had the good fortune of more than 25 years in senior property management and/or corporate positions, which included being an integral part of the corporate team that ultimately became Starwood Hotels, for years the largest hotel company in the world. By my late 30s, I had made a very successful name for myself and was well on my way to becoming an industry icon (or so I thought). Unnoticed at first, however, there became a growing dissatisfaction with the corporate world and my life in it. This continued until there came a life-changing night in mid-December 1998 while living in Atlanta. Dr. Wayne Dyer used the term "Quantum Moment" for what happened to me that evening. From that day forward, I called it "The Shift," and many years later described it this way in my journal:

During most of my 30s, I was very focused on my career, still partying (although less than in my 20s), and very much looking for "Miss Right." Although I had success in my career, many wonderful relationships (both romantic and platonic), and lots of "fun" (as the majority of the world defines the concept), there was something deep within that wasn't right. I was dissatisfied with my life's direction and yet, on a conscious level, I wasn't fully aware of this rapid, downward spiraling trend. I didn't understand why I was falling into an existential malaise. One evening, I was at home channel surfing, looking at each station for no more than a minute, as it was all utterly inane. I felt terrible (physically, emotionally, and spiritually) and had hit rock bottom, although from all outward appearances I seemed to be doing well – a nice house, a sexy BMW convertible, and all the rest. I **never** could have imagined how much my life would change as I hit the "next" button on the remote control for the umpteenth time. The channel and screen changed, and I saw a bald man in a sweater giving a PBS lecture titled *Wisdom of the Ages*. He would have lasted less than a minute too, if he hadn't mentioned someone long set aside in my mind – Alan Watts. I was instantaneously engrossed by Wayne and his message. He referenced Alan, saying that *the wake of the boat doesn't determine its course*, and in a moment of illumination, the last twenty years were set aside for good. I was once again at a place within where matters of the Spirit were a priority in my life. Only this time, I had an additional 20 years of life experience in the equation that apparently was unavoidable. Otherwise, those years would not have transpired in the way that they did. While spirituality was important in my early life, for most of my 20s and 30s it was all but forgotten (the occasional mystical experience notwithstanding). I was busy, you see, feverishly burning my worldly karma and wandering, deeply at times, in the egoic illusion of Maya. I sometimes refer to this twenty-year period as my "tantric period," which should not be construed negatively. It just was what it was.

The very next day I exploded back onto the spiritual path. Not surprisingly, many things (but certainly not all) quickly changed for the better. I went to the Barnes & Noble near my house, purchased two of Wayne's books, began immersing myself in metaphysical studies, and started working out and getting the body healthy. A couple of months later, I went to the Borders bookstore in search of something deeper and found a book that would completely change my life. I was walking down the aisle that contained books on eastern spirituality, not knowing what I was looking for. There was just an openness and inner stillness that, if it could have spoken would have said, "Don't worry; there is nothing to find, what you need will find you." I looked at a couple of books but nothing grabbed me. Then, about halfway down the aisle, on a shelf just above my head, I saw a hardback book with a picture of an Indian man on the spine. I suddenly recalled that it was the same picture and man that was in the book titled *Metaphysical Meditations*, which I found when I was twelve! Taking it down off the shelf, the magnetic pull I felt was so strong that later I joked that if I hadn't reached for the book, it would have flown right off the shelf and hit me between the eyes! The book was none other than the *Autobiography of a Yogi*, and after looking in silence at the covers and inside flaps for a few minutes, I knew I had found what I was looking for. My soul's script was planted into the fabric of The Universe and once again, my life was about to transform in a way that still seems so miraculous and full of Grace that it's difficult to recount the day and moment in which it happened without becoming tearful. Like the instant Wayne came on the TV, this is still indelibly clear in my memory and I'm sure it always will be. A well-known aphorism states, "When the student is ready, the teacher appears." Nothing describes these events more aptly than that. Within three months of beginning the book, I was receiving the SRF lessons, meditating twice a day, and attending the Atlanta SRF group in Dunwoody. With these, my spiritual unfoldment moved into the fast lane. While it was a sometimes confusing and wild journey, I can still only view it as miraculously and unfathomably perfect.

Although my hospitality career continued, the thrill was never the same, as my primary objective in life had radically shifted. More importantly, deriving my identity from what I did (and what I had) mercifully began to crumble. Between this point in my life and the blessed awakening, 18 years passed by. As these "sadhana years" are covered intermittently throughout the book, I'll finish this little trip down memory lane with the following observations and suggestion: While **everything** in our life is a necessary part of our spiritual unfoldment, it is also critical to remember that, as Wayne alluded to, our past does not determine our future. Whatever happened in the past had to happen and the proof for this is that it did happen, but this does not mean that we're trapped in any given trajectory that we may seem to be on. My twenty years of corporate climbing and the excesses that went with it did not preclude me from The Shift in my consciousness that happened at age 38. These "quantum moments" don't have to take months or years of analysis, consultations, and action plans. Fundamental shifts in Life only happen NOW, so never feel trapped by what's come before. In This Moment, there is infinite potential to choose our direction in life, because ultimately there is no past or future. Time and causality are simply creations of the mind and therefore not Real.

Cutting The Final Knot

"The final task in the spiritual quest is to overcome this last difference: the distinction between the goal and the way; the goal and he who is heading for it must finally disappear. In fact the man in search of the self is seized by a real onset of dizziness when he reaches what seems to him, from his point of view, to be the last bend in the road. He then realizes that he must henceforth renounce forever, without any possibility of turning back, everything which up till then has seemed to be the ground of his existence, which gave him being, his idea of self and his own consciousness bound to this idea of self. In the abysses of the heart to which he feels himself inexorably drawn, there is absolutely nothing he can grasp hold of or hang on to, nothing solid on which he can, so to speak, put down his foot, no air from outside in which to draw breath. It is the pure akasa, infinite space, where no point can any longer be perceived, which is not bound by any horizon. . . . It is no longer even the milieu in which a man feels secure, for it has carried off the one who sought to dwell in it into the infinitude, limitlessness, and solitude. . . . As the Upanishads often reiterate, a man must never give up before he cuts this "final knot in the heart," hrdaya-granthi, the bond which binds the Self to the conditionings of time and matter and prevents it reaching its unconfined and sovereign nature."

~ A Christian Pilgrim in India: The Spiritual Journey of
Swami Abhishiktananda (Henri Le Saux) by Harry Oldmeadow

This thing called satori ... is a state that one can understand only through experience. It cannot be grasped or explained through words alone.

~ Soko Morinaga

CHAPTER TWO:
The Kiss

Beginning in 2014, I was employed as a GM of an iconic all-in-one restaurant, bar, art gallery, and live music venue in Idyllwild, California. My team and the local Idyllwild residents were all fantastic people, and I very much enjoyed living and working in this charming mountain hamlet. After several years, however, I felt that my time there had reached its end, mainly because I had completed the turnaround project I was hired for. I was ready for a new challenge. In September 2016, I relocated to Temecula, California for a promising new job opportunity at a fine dining restaurant and winery, but that turned into the worst experience of my career.

In October, I had a lucid dream that left me feeling that I might be dropping the body (physical death) by the end of the next year. In the dream, my front door opened and a beautiful light streamed through, and I knew that Brother Death was waiting on the other side of the light. I ran toward the door excitedly anticipating my astral sojourn. As I crossed the threshold, Brother Death was there waiting, his hands looking like ancient withered tree roots. I floated into his arms and was overcome by the beauty of what I saw – an in-between state between the physical and astral realms. Then I woke up.

Of course, there was no way to know, but the possibility of impending death could not be ignored, especially as health challenges started manifesting shortly after the dream. One month later, while working the Thanksgiving holiday, I suddenly collapsed onto the floor with heart pain. I sought medical advice and was told that, among other issues, I had a blockage in one of my heart valves. Unfortunately, there were conflicting opinions regarding treatment options, so I decided against any operation. I was placed on temporary disability and could not work anymore. Stuck at home, I started feeling washed up as a person, depressed, and concerned for my future.

In early 2017, thanks to the caring and frank honesty of a dear friend, I realized that I could keep sliding into oblivion and perhaps die, or get off my pity-party ass and get going again. I finally decided that if I was going to go down, then I was going to go down swinging. Getting moving again was a day-by-day thing and not easy. With depression, it usually never is. For anyone out there facing a similar challenge, my advice is simple: 1) Don't isolate yourself, 2) Take advantage of all the resources you have at your disposal (this is no time for pride to get in the way), and 3) Find someone who is worse off than you and be a light unto their darkness.

Building momentum in a positive direction again, I began volunteering every week with a wonderful organization called Interfaith Community Services (ICS) located in Escondido, California. They provide a multitude of services to the homeless and disadvantaged, and I must say that ever since my year there, the very real and serious plight of the homeless has been in the forefront of my consciousness and philanthropic efforts. Each week, I had in-my-face reminders that, given what some of those souls were going through, I still had things pretty damn good. In my free time, I created my twelfth and last fine art photography book. All of these were coffee table-size hardcover books, self-published with Blurb. Never made to sell, these were gifts for my family and friends. The book was a closing retrospective of my ten years as an amateur shutterbug and, as I consciously intended from the beginning of the project, it was an "affirmation of life." The first person who got a copy was my abovementioned dear friend who thankfully called bullshit on me when I was at my lowest point and in denial. All of this is yet another example of extreme duress being a perfect catalyst for spiritual growth.

With my retrospective complete and the summer months approaching, the annual lease on my house in Temecula was mercifully running out. Even though I was still unsure about my health and possible time left in the body, I decided that if 2017 was going to be my last year, then by God *I was going to live it!* I resolved to lighten my load, donating approximately 75% of everything I owned to ICS for their temporary housing program. I'd been living in three-bedroom homes for the last twenty years and had been talking about downsizing for the last ten; this was the moment to do it. By the time everything was donated, my house had been turned back over to the property owner, and I had arrived at the SRF Hidden Valley Ashram (HVA) in Escondido to spend some time anchoring in the spiritual vibrations there. During my stay at HVA, I was on top of the world – free, fearless, and open to all possibilities yet attached to none – the best I felt in years!

By this time, it was mid-September 2017. The nadir of the descent and spiritual crises had passed, and having no idea what life now had in store for me, I trusted that The Universe had my best interests in Its Plans. From this place of uncertainty and total freedom, I surrendered completely to What Was in That Moment. My surrender was not done reluctantly, nor was it even conscious. It unfolded naturally and joyously and became an expression of my Being. Six months later, I ran across this beautiful quote in Roy Melvyn's book, *The Lost Writings of Wu Hsin*. It reminded me of this magical, two-week period when, authentically and wholeheartedly, I was laying all that currently was and had ever been "My Life" on the altar of the Infinite.

"True courage brushes aside
Everything experienced,
Everything felt, and
Everything known.
The soil is then ready for
The arrival of the unknown."

On Saturday, September 30th, 2017 at approximately 2:15 in the afternoon, my 18 years as a dedicated spiritual seeker came to an unexpected end. I had just finished lunch in the ashram refectory and went back to my room, when Grace Happened. In the following email written the next day, I shared my satori (i.e. sudden awakening) with two of my closest friends.

October 1, 2017

… I was in my room listening to the [Sounds True] audio talk I have on Meister Eckhart. Between his message and the way this person [James Finley] reads and comments on Eckhart's sermons, I find it resonating in my soul in such a direct way; it'd almost be frightening if it weren't so beautiful. The same can be said of what happened next.

The message was so simple and beautiful, that the eyes started to tear up some and then gently cry as all I could feel was gratitude for "The Beauty" which I found myself saying aloud over and over. This ebbed and flowed for approx. 20 minutes – I've had to guess the time, as clock watching wasn't remotely on my mind [or possible] – and then, what I am now calling "The Flood" as in a **Flood of Love** came over me and I just fell apart. Again, I can't gauge the time very well but for approx. 45 minutes I was in an alternating state of uncontrollable sobbing and near hysterical laughing. I was lying on the bed, I was staggering around the room, the hall, the bathroom, DRUNK with Love and I kept seeing glimpses of all the beauty I've noticed since coming here – snapshots of the sun on the wings of the butterflies in the garden, the hawks gliding in the air, the flowers, [the retreatant sharing his story at the Friday satsang and] making himself vulnerable to everyone, the clouds in the sky…*everything*…more beautiful than they've ever been before. It was like being plugged into a 220-watt socket of love when my whole life I'd never known anything but 110-watt. I could write a book and never be able to describe the intensity. All I remember saying out loud as it unfolded was "Take Me," "I Am No One," and "I Am Falling Into Love." As I write this, I feel the energy inside welling up near to the surface again and I have to stay inwardly still and as focused on what I'm writing as best I can, lest it overtake me again, which I don't feel physically ready for.

I can't express how grateful I am not to have had anyone in the next cabin, or even in the corner room opposite to me given the thin walls, as anyone hearing that would have thought I'd gone off the rails and would probably have been blowing an air horn for as many monks as possible. Being an extremely private person, the last thing I ever want is to be some sort of spectacle …

Finally, I was lying on the bed, no thoughts, feeling tired beyond belief. After some amount of time, I intuitively felt that fresh air might be helpful, so I staggered out and sat in the chair outside my room for what must have been an hour, before I started feeling "normal" again. I was determined to go the commemorative service and did. Internally I was near the "bottom of the ocean deep" [virtually no thoughts] but physically, I barely made it through, as there was a very slight bit of nausea but more importantly, the physical heart didn't feel right. While lying on the bed right after the episode, I truly thought it might give out, as it was violently pounding for a long time and the body was exhausted and limp. My prayer to Lahiri Mahasaya [paramguru of Paramahansa Yogananda] while casting the rose petals was simple – "Lahiri, help me fall into Love." I immediately went back to the room and went to bed, sleeping nearly 12 hours and after which, I'm feeling better.

If someone wrote all this to me, and even assuming I'd had an experience like it, I'm not sure I could recommend much more than telling them to "Trust The Process" and to remind them that Master [Yogananda's devotees often refer to him as "Master," which is a title customarily meaning "Master of Oneself" – and awakened being] is always with us and to, if all else fails, just hang on to Him. So with that, please know that I'm not asking you for a comment but naturally, the forum is open if you want to. Mostly, I just wanted to keep you up to date. This feels like the most remarkable time in this life, which is saying something given the personal history I've written about. I'm done asking God and Master for anything (for me), as there is no lack in The Great Way. My whole focus is very simple now – I am calling forth that I Am Falling into Love and Surrendering All That I Am. The illusory feeling of separation between me and anything and everything feels very thin...and things seem so simple and clear now.

Thank you so much for listening my friends; everyone needs someone to talk with and it's hard to imagine getting through these last 12 months without you.

Phil

It has been quite a while since I last read this email, and given the beyond-intense experience of it, along with all that it presaged, I must say that as I write this the emotional impact is still immediate, deep, and visceral. While not all awakenings are as earth-shaking as this was, they are typically abrupt and unmistakable!

As people hear or read about someone else's amazing spiritual experience or, in this case, awakening (typically not the same thing), they sometimes try to emulate what that individual was doing at the time figuring, "hey, if it worked for them, it might work for me!" While this is not a hard and fast rule, I will venture to say that anyone attempting to recreate someone else's experience will not only fail, but will be doing themselves a disservice by trying to limit the infinite. Why not fearlessly and trustingly invite The Universe to provide you with a wondrous, never-before-in-the-history-of-the-world Self-Realization? You may as well invite it, because that is what It is going to bring to your spiritual doorstep anyway. Everyone's process is unique. If it weren't, where would the fun and surprise be in that?

Along these lines I have been asked, "All you were doing was listening to a spiritual audio series?!" Well, not quite. In the name of total pellucidity, there was one more highly esoteric (and until this moment, secret) spiritual practice that was being utilized concurrently with the Meister Eckhart audio. Are you ready? I was playing spider solitaire on my laptop. I know it sounds bizarre but you may as well get used to it, as there is more bizarre-sounding stuff to come. The reason I share this is simply to illustrate that these things almost always happen when we least expect them. I realize that's a worn-out old cliché, but that is how clichés are made — they usually seem to be the case.

Do you remember your first kiss? Who doesn't?! While the kiss itself might be brief, the memory of it, and sometimes its ramifications, can last for a long time. In the same way, this satori event was lifechanging, so I subsequently christened it "The Kiss." Drunk on bliss, I wasn't exactly looking for a catchy moniker; it just flashed across the screen of my consciousness one day and felt right. Besides, if I kept calling it "The Flood" as I did in the email, down the road people might become confused, thinking that my water heater burst, or maybe that the local levy broke and everything I owned, possibly including me, was washed away. Now that I think about it, the latter isn't far from what really went down.

While there are any number of ways in which awakenings begin, I describe mine as a Descent of Grace. Upon reflection, The Kiss was the nuclear bomb that activated my Self-Realization. I say *activated*, as my awakening was an evolution that took about two years to come full circle. This Epiphany was like a missile hitting a skyscraper in that it dealt the skyscraper (the ego-mind) a mortal blow. However, the collapse of the ego-tower was not immediate. Awakening is rarely, if ever, instantaneously complete. In my case, there were core attachments that still had to be released and kundalini energies that seemed to need time to rewire my body and brain. Moreover, there was the loss of egoic personal will that I struggled mightily to adjust to. Perhaps the most difficult hurdle of all was the complete surrender of my identification as a separate self (the "I" known as Phil). **Nothing** passes The Gateless Gate. **Everything** must be surrendered…and "you" cannot fake it.

While I still wasn't certain at this point, the dream I had one year prior about Brother Death did not seem to be indicating *physical* death, but rather *metaphysical* death – the end of the ego-mind – the "Real" or "Big" Death, as some eastern spiritual traditions refer to It. In retrospect, the ambiguity of the dream was beneficial, since my anticipation and acceptance of physical death is what brought me to a place of total surrender, ultimately paving the way for the Process to unfold.

For those on the spiritual path, it is important to realize that awakening *is a death*, but like all deaths, it is also a rebirth. Viewed through the lens of duality, death and birth are two processes, but in Consciousness, they are simply One Process. The Death of the separate self is the God-given Rebirth into the Unitive Self that the spiritual path inevitably leads to! As we die to the old, so we are born to the new. And that is exactly what happened to me beginning with The Kiss. From soup to nuts, this specific transition that I call the rebirthing phase took about nine months (quite a time frame for a birth, don't ya think?). There were some incredible twists and turns along the way and it was, by far, the wildest part of the entire ride.

There can be no rebirth without a dark night of the soul,
a total annihilation of all that you believed in and thought that you were.

~ Vilayat Inayat Khan

CHAPTER THREE:

The Rebirthing Journey

In this chapter, my journey continues at HVA and within a month finds me heading off to Texas and Georgia in what I jokingly referred to back then as "my first and last farewell tour." It's a little intimidating to articulate and share what can never be fully described but there's the rub — the ineffable nature of the mystical cannot be communicated to the degree we all wish for. Due to my health challenges and the feeling that my time in the body was coming to an end, I planned this trip to visit family and friends before the wholly unexpected happenings of September 30. With this new turn of events, the tour was far stranger than I imagined it would be, in part due to the fact that at this point I really didn't understand what had happened or what was happening. Once the trip was completed, I traveled into the desert (the crucible) for six weeks as things began to get serious. From there, a shakedown period began, culminating with an unforeseen pilgrimage to Mount Shasta where everything stabilized to the point that I was able to reenter the world and begin to learn to embody the non-dual awareness-experience that The Kiss brought. Bear in mind that my experience may be different than the one you will have. However, if this chapter shows anything, it's that transcending the ego-mind is almost always messy and sometimes downright awful. That said, it's always worth it in the end, as what we think we are losing is an illusion — *we never had anything to lose other than our ignorance of the true nature of things* — and what's even stranger, there was *no one* to lose it.

This follow-up to my first email describing the next three days after The Kiss is an early (and therefore awkward) attempt at relating the wondrous and dizzying events that unfolded. Unbeknownst to me at the time, the world I'd known throughout this life was ending and with this, the birthing of a living experience devoid of the egoic separate self began to unfold.

October 4, 2017

As a few days have gone by since the weekend, I wanted to add the following updates to my last email, as writing helps me contextualize these recent happenings.

The following two days were spent in deep internal stillness. As I walked around the ashram Sunday, there were moments when the subject-object awareness would vanish. I wouldn't experience it when it happened, as obviously there was no "I" there to notice it. This is a first for this outside of a sitting meditation and even then, it hasn't been a frequent happening. There's nothing to report about it as "I" wasn't there but there is a pointer I will use. At the end of the movie *Peaceful Warrior*, Dan was asked "Who Are You?" His inner voice replied, "This Moment."

Through the eye of a photographer, I was able to see and share the beauty here that is often missed but with this, it was as if I was experiencing HVA for the first time, now with the wonder and amazement of a child. The sounds of the birds were a symphony against the underlying backdrop of the silence. Often, I'd see something and stand still for many minutes, lost in it. I've always loved desert sand dune images filled with simple form, light, and shadow and for the first time, in the light of the setting sun, I saw countless dunes in the sand of the volleyball court. Other than scale, they're no less beautiful and just as magical. [I was completely lost, gazing at the sand for at least thirty minutes. The same would be true when I'd see birds in trees, water flowing in the pond, etc. I must have been a rather odd-looking sight for anyone who happened to notice me!]

On Sunday night, the Crown and Ajna [third eye] chakras were incredibly active, with the energy at the top of the head surging and spinning like I've never felt before (and, not in quite a while). Unlike in years past, I didn't attempt to "do" anything with it. I just thanked it and said "Take Me." I wasn't able to sleep until 2am or so and again, the body was tired the next day, even with ample sleep.

On Monday, there was more of the same but less intense. No "Floods" but there were several, what I'll call, "sweet, warm, gentle spring showers." The mind generated a concern about being too spacey to head back to ICS in the morning, but that too was surrendered. It turned out more than fine!

On Tuesday, I had a few errands in addition to the volunteer seva [service]. Driving in traffic and normal daily activities was what I needed to settle back into a more "normal" state of being.

However, qualitatively, there was a big difference. I'd still be frozen here and there with the beauty of the everyday things we see. I was briefly lost in the little children playing outside the church at the bottom of the hill, as well as with the dogs romping in the animal park. While having lunch, I watched a man helping his little boy with a shoe that had come off. In that moment, with no thoughts, I saw in that act the entire cycle of life, much as I did with the little leaf in the snow that became the image on page 58 of *Ten Years Gone* [My photography retrospective book that was created in May 2017] with the added Zen proverb: "One falling leaf is not just one leaf: it means the whole autumn." In these "ordinary" moments is indescribable **Holiness** for those with eyes to see.

An amazing experience with a very troubled young man took place while I was training a new volunteer at ICS. The specifics aren't important (and would take a lot of time to put in writing) but what was relevant was that in this space of awareness, Spirit came through in such a direct way that afterwards the trainee said he'd never seen anything like it. Much more importantly, a heart connection was made with this young soul. As gentle tears formed in his eyes he knew it too [maybe not consciously but at some level he knew he'd made a Shift] and through it, I have no doubt that an important breakthrough was made. I may never know when it will translate into action on his part but those details are irrelevant. The key is, when it counted, I was...**not there**...completely "out of the way" for Spirit to say the right things in a way that allowed for his Shift. Afterwards, in a deep way never before experienced, I REALIZED that I am not The Doer. Deeply humbled to be utilized by God in this way, all I could feel was gratitude. It was an experience I will never forget and I'll always feel that he [the young man] gave me the greater gift. [This was the first momentous experiential recognition that "I" *wasn't the doer*. It wasn't a thought but rather, a deep inner knowing that flashed through my entire being.]

There is more pain in the physical heart. Whatever happened on Saturday, Brother Donkey [Saint Francis' nickname for the body] paid a price, and I deeply thank it for all its service so far.

Regardless of all the struggles, this has been a wonderfully transformative process and one that I am profoundly grateful for…which includes everything that is to come, whatever it looks like.

Phil

And so the rebirthing began. As you read the emails in this chapter, keep in mind that along with the confusing yet exhilarating energies and overall disorientation, new satori-level insights were coming in as well. You will certainly come across things that might make you think, "Hey, that's not how Phil described it in the Introduction or in the Q&A" (in the event you might have peeked at the latter section early). These contradictions are a part of the uniqueness of this book. Through these soul confessionals, you are along for the ride *as it was happening*. In my correspondences, you will see me working through the process of comprehending many heretofore-unconsidered truths about the Nature of Reality. There are certainly instances where these insights come in fragments, so in one email I may understand something in one way, only to express it differently at other times while the "processing" was unfolding. Along similar lines, I suppose this is why many music lovers enjoy outtakes from their most loved musical artists or albums, as they are able to witness and more fully appreciate the creative process that went into their favorite songs as they came into being; almost as if one were sitting in the studio with them all those years ago.

Reflecting on this chapter's first email, the initial thing I want to address is the absence of "I." I had gone from being a seemingly separate subject perceiving seemingly separate objects to Realizing the Unity of All Things. The illusion of separateness fell away, which left me with no "I." The *outside* had become my *inside,* so to speak. What, then, was perceiving? It was and still is Consciousness perceiving Itself or, if you please, an undifferentiated awareness-experience. You may be wondering whether awakening means we see things that others don't see. Well, we do and we don't. On the surface, I am still aware of my individuality and the multiplicity of manifestation. For example, it's obvious that one tree is different from another. Moreover, I am seeing the same tree that you or anyone else would see. The difference is that, with non-dual consciousness, there is no filter, no cognition, and no preconceived bias to categorize and label the world. Awakening means seeing without any conditioning in the way. While the everyday world is ordinary on one level, it's also quite wondrous and miraculous on another level, and permeated with a palpable feeling of sacredness. To this day, I find immense delight in the littlest of things for no other reason than they are as they are. Perception is immediate and direct. Seeing is pure and clear. This leads to a deep, visceral, unmistakable knowing that everything is One and that I Am that Oneness. You can't miss it! This new, intimate perception that I was experiencing, reportedly called Clear Seeing by The Buddha, became my new "normal." It's simple, ordinary even, yet beautiful beyond words. What's more, it is so beautiful <u>because</u> it is beyond words or, maybe I should say, beyond thought. Just as Douglas Harding wrote about many years ago, it was and occasionally still is at times…like having no head!

True meditation has no purpose. However, one of the many benefits of meditation is stilling the mind and getting in the gap between thoughts. Imagine that gap being permanent: that gap is the Now! This typifies my awakened experience. Rather than seeing an object and recognizing, cataloging, and judging whether it is good, bad, or indifferent (all of which happens in a fraction of a second), I simply observe it as it is, without any commentary and, maybe more importantly, without judgment. *Nothing has any inherent meaning except the meaning we give it.* Another example is that when I am listening to somebody speak to me, I don't have any mental activity regarding what they just said, what I might say, or anything else. I am right there listening to them, fully present in the moment. It's the difference between looking and seeing, or hearing and listening. This is what Ram Dass referred to when he famously said, "Be Here Now." This is the Natural State.

For months after The Kiss, and especially during the first couple of months, I was having rushes of bliss. It felt like an overall body high; euphoric, with a pronounced sense of well-being. These rushes would last for hours at a time, and if I had no responsibilities to take care of, they would often last for days. While I don't know for sure because I am no expert on the subject, I'm speculating that the bliss was, at least in part, due to sister kundalini doing her thing. But also, a part of it was certainly the *newness* of the intimate Direct Perception which, up until that point, I had never known. As I said in the above email, it really was as if I was seeing things for the first time and I am extraordinarily pleased to say that this never went away. Of course, I'm used to it now so it's (thankfully) not such an overwhelming thing.

When I first read Eckhart Tolle's *The Power of Now*, I learned that he'd spent the better part of two years sitting on a park bench just Being, and back then I thought, "How dreadful." Suddenly, I found the idea of that incredibly inviting. One might think that being in bliss is a wonderful thing and it is… to a point. However, when trying to function in the world, it can be darn challenging and even wearisome after a while. I discovered that if I really *needed* to do something, like drive my car somewhere or do my volunteer service at ICS, much of what was happening internally would subside, maybe not completely but enough to get by. I attribute this to Divine Intelligence.

October 19, 2017

My Friends, it's been quite a ride here so far…I'm so blessed. I've found over the years that just as with methods, spiritual experiences also have to be surrendered; otherwise, we're not in the Now but instead, trying to relive or recreate the experience again.

The Process knows what to provide and when, so while I'm deeply grateful for the experience I wrote to you both about [the October 1st email], it also has to be surrendered. Experiences, like methods, can be a trap and it appears to me that egos love both. Therefore, once they've served me and I've grokked them as best I can, usually through sharing them in writing, I drop them like a hot potato.

There's been a bit more unfolding since my last email and intuitively I feel the next few days could be interesting from a physical point of view. As a pragmatic person, at least to some extent, I have all my affairs in order as best I can. FYI, there's an envelope in the desk of my room with emergency info and also one in the glove box of my car that includes a DNR and a Living Will. I've been asked for an emergency contact list and I am sending one out to everyone that may need it. If I were a betting man and assuming my physical demise is going to happen at all, *which I'm not*, I'd guess I have until the end of the year before dropping the body. However, the "Flood of Love" … took a real heavy toll on an already compromised heart and intuitively, *something* feels very close. Regardless, I remain open to all possibilities with no attachments or aversions.

PW

As one can tell from this email, when I said that I was truly living as if this was going to be my last year on Earth, it wasn't an exaggeration. My physical heart was in rough shape, but as events unfolded and the kundalini subsided eight months later, the heart got a lot stronger. My devil-may-care attitude didn't play well with my family and friends but they also knew that, come what may, "Phil's gonna do what Phil's gonna do." In the event I did croak, at least I had all my affairs in order, so as to make things as easy as possible for those I would leave behind.

Regarding the first paragraph of the above email, while I wasn't able to make the following distinction at the time, I want to be clear that one can be in the Now without having to surrender one's methods. Eventually we surrender everything, but in the interim, our spiritual methods (such as meditation) facilitate access to the Now.

Three weeks in, I went to a talk given by my longtime friend who was the abbot of HVA. As The Universe would have it, his talk was about the very place in consciousness I was now living from. For the first time, the subject matter resonated experientially rather than intellectually. During the talk, the bliss was intense and I felt as if I was floating an inch off the chair. I thoroughly enjoyed the talk and then went back to my room and started surfing the internet. I was intuitively led to a website that had writings about the same subject matter as the talk, except it was couched in non-dual semantics, Zen terminology, and metaphors taken from quantum mechanics. Never before this moment had I studied Zen or non-dual teachings, yet somehow this way of speaking seemed to be the only thing that resonated with my new insights. Moreover, the vocabulary on the website became very useful, as it made my awareness-experience more easily explainable to others. Unfortunately, I was unable to find the website again, but I did copy some excerpts from it and send them in an email to a friend.

October 21, 2017

The scientific term "event horizon" used in black hole theory recently came to mind. I pulled this off an interesting website that literally just found me:

"In Zen the term 'gateless gate' is used, which describes this paradox very aptly: the tan t'ien is a gate, in the sense of being a boundary separating us from the higher reality, but it is also a 'no-gate' in the sense of being a wide open passage into the beyond. When the door is open, it is not a door any longer – it becomes an opening. The concept of a door is valid only in regards to it being open or closed. When it is truly open, is it still a door or is it a passage? Or is it just the beyond? One thing is certain: when we pass completely through the inner door, that door is transcended. But the paradox of the human soul is that she lives on both sides of that door simultaneously. She is the true bridge, including the consciousness of unity, between the outer and inner realms."

"The issue of whether we realize our true self within the context of the body or need to go beyond identification with the body has puzzled many spiritual thinkers. This question cannot be answered by the simple, linear mind. To solve what seems to be a contradiction in terms in this question, it must be viewed from a higher perspective."

"When Ramana Maharshi spoke about the spiritual heart, he pointed to his chest, but also said that it is not in the body. Was he just confused? He was not confused in a spiritual sense, but his seeming mixed message could be misleading conceptually. While he felt the doorway to the self in his physical center, he was also experiencing his true self beyond the body as a point of reference."

"His preconceived non-dual notions led him to believe that the physical body is inert and insentient and that we need to root out the idea of it being the self. He said, "The foundation for all miseries is the impure vasana [mental tendency], the belief that holds the body to be 'I'." How does the entry of the soul into the absolute affect our identity? Does our human identity also cross the event horizon? Our human identity, or personality, is the base from which we live normally in the world and the start point for our spiritual journey. When we have awakened to our pure me, or soul, that then becomes the new center for our identity. Our human identity, with all its memories and ability to manage in the world, is not lost, but becomes subservient to our soul, the new home and identity from which we live. It is in our center as the soul that we cross the event horizon into the unmanifested and absence."

"It could be said that, once properly crossed, the event horizon becomes like a transparent window between the two realms, now looking from absence to presence. What we call the 'sealed state' represents the maximum transfer of the soul's energy into the inner reality, leaving behind just the minimum remaining energy of our human identity to continue operating within the laws of the dimension of presence."

"The much more profound, primordial absolute is the universal root-foundation of all of the dimensions of creation, both inner and outer. It is not merely a reality at the bottom of the pyramid of creation, as it has no location and exists beyond the dimensions of the inner and the outer. It is the supreme isness, the primordial core of the original light of I am. As far as human life as we know is concerned, it is the bedrock of our isness: our final deliverance."

When it comes to the dissolution of the ego a.k.a. "Edging God Out" (a great Wayne Dyer expression that I have adopted and sometimes use), the term "transcending" resonates most with me as a pointer to the process.

There now is an Awareness of being at a demarcation point or, if you please, an "event horizon" and beyond or through it is The Void. From here, it appears that the Void is Love as that, ultimately, is All There Is. It is <u>this</u> that I Am Falling Into and with this, a deepening knowing that "I Am No One."

Phil

Looking back on this period, there was a definite "evangelical fervor" in Phil that must have grated on some with whom he was sharing. It eventually caused a couple of friends to walk away. I couldn't see it at the time, and since then I've come to know that this is common among the newly awakened, as the immediacy and power of the Directness of Perception is, at times, overwhelming. It's as if one has been blind their entire life and then suddenly given sight. Is it likely that such a person wouldn't want to zealously tell those closest to them what they're seeing? Fortunately, this didn't extend to strangers on the street! While it did subside over time, it took about two years to get fully under control. This is another possible result of awakening that one should be mindful of.

October 23, 2017

This body clearly has its physical issues but the "death" that I foresaw might possibly not be physical but rather, the Real [metaphysical] Death. It'll be what it'll be, as The Process unfolds in me (and in all things) in the way that It Will.

It unfolds so perfectly when this "I" is "out of the way" that the **joy, love, gratitude, child-like wonder,** and **beauty** of it is becoming so great that this physical vessel isn't able to contain it, which **is** taking a heavy toll on the body. Describing the indescribable is impossible, hence the reason so many Masters and mystics use pointers. If I were to use any pointer now, I could only say this – *I am dying into Love.* If Brother Donkey gives out due to the full experience of my inherent divinity, then I'll quote Pete Townsend from one of his songs about Meher Baba: "I call that a bargain, the best I ever had. The best I ever had."

With all my heart, I thank you for listening, for your understanding, and for your support. Without the caring and love that you and others have given me, it is impossible to imagine how this unfoldment process could be survived! [Having even one confidant is very important during major Shifts in consciousness. Don't go it alone unless there is no other choice, but also don't be indiscriminate about who you share with. Trust is incredibly important here!]

For me, whether the body lasts 2 more months or 20 more years is beside the point, as there is no preference or attachment to any outcome. Who would there be to have the preference? Can you understand this? My knowing is that the illness is, at this point in the unfolding, a critical part of the sadhana. Last year I feel I was given a look into a possible 12-15 month future that, *if embraced and trusted,* would be the very best possible vehicle for my spiritual growth. Longevity isn't the key – Liberation is. When and how this incarnation ends is irrelevant, as The Great Way unfolds as It Will. The illness, facing possible bodily death, acclimating to an amazingly wonderful new state of consciousness, and most of all *surrender* are my path right now.

Based on how the body's been the last two days, I am a bit surprised I'm here typing this and not in the hospital. It has been a rough time physically and yet inwardly, the depth of stillness, the love for everything, and the gratitude for things just as they are has been at times overwhelming, which tells me what's happening is Right Action. *If Spirit doesn't need to use this body, then it won't and there won't be* ANY *loss to the Universe or the Divine Plan.* Only the hubris of the ego and its inability to let go of dogmatic concepts that usually accompany spiritual paths and disciplines could possibly think that it knows what and how things (*anything*) **should** unfold, hence the adage "Never should on people!"

It has become my knowing that ALL spiritual paths and methods are traps and in the end, they too must be surrendered. The paradoxical thing seems to be that we have to be trapped by them first, in order to truly surrender them! When I entered the Guru-Disciple relationship…it was forever. That said, while my loyalty to Yogananda as my spiritual Master remains, I've surrendered my SRF path and its techniques, and it's incredibly liberating, as then whatever method is helpful will happen in harmony with The Tao. It's easy, it's simple, it flows.

Perhaps this is where the way of the mystic and the path of the occult [esoteric teachings] irreconcilably split. There is room in my heart for all paths, for all decisions, and for all outcomes. There was a time when I used to hope that my path, however it looked, would be similarly respected but that too has been surrendered. Saint Francis said seek to understand, and not seek to be understood, and that is where I live now when I'm Still and Present.

It is in this conviction that I embrace and trust the experience that I was given last year [the lucid dream portending death] and whatever is to come over the next few months. It feels like freedom to me and nothing anyone can argue will gainsay that now. My direct, personal experience of The Divine is the only compass I need. That's freedom, at least as I perceive it.

God Bless and again, thank you for allowing this type of authentic sharing between us over the years…it means more to me than I could ever express!

Phil

These recent emails illustrate that the path I had taken to this point had worked (there's no higher praise than that!), but it hadn't at all prepared me for what an awakening brought with it or a vocabulary to explain it. While I was certain that a Shift of some sort had taken place, I wasn't sure what was happening. Taking a "step back" from the Beingness of it and analyzing it in a logical manner was simply not possible, as the mind wasn't working in that way or well, for that matter. The only thing I was confident about was following my intuition for guidance. From here on out, the non-duality teachings of Adyashanti, Nisargadatta Maharaj, Ramana Maharshi, and a few others down the road, became critical to the unfolding.

On October 26th, due to the thoughtfulness and concern of two of my SRF friends, I was incredibly fortunate to be introduced to Adyashanti's teachings about one month after the initial awakening. They loaned me *The End of Your World* and *The Impact of Awakening,* two of his books about where I had unexpectedly found myself, although as things unfolded I was not able to read them for about one year. The energies flowing through me were so intense that it was almost impossible to read anything deeper than the sports page! However, the books did lead me to his audio recordings (talks, satsangs, and multi-broadcast courses), which proved to be priceless, as comprehending spoken teachings was something I could do, even while the bliss was raging. While perusing Adya's website, I found a chronological compendium of his audio recordings, each with a detailed outline of topics that were addressed. From these, I was able to target recordings specifically on awakening, during and after. In the Soul Food appendix, I have listed the ones that helped me most.

On October 27th, I left California to visit my family in Texas. There, I began month two of the rebirthing process, and I should say that the change in location had no effect on the bliss and energies that continued to pervade my consciousness.

November 6, 2017

I wanted to let you know the trip is going well and the time spent with family has been wonderful. As writing to you both helps me grok newer/deeper levels of *consciousness* and *awareness,* I want to share this email. Thanks to the pointers that Nisargadatta Maharaj left us, they are deeply and indelibly resonating with me since last month's "Kiss from God" as I'm calling it now.

Nisargadatta's teachings finally clicked and the impact has been profound. They always registered with me on an intellectual level but never on an experiential level until now.

As I perceive it, Consciousness lies within Awareness and while many use the two terms interchangeably, Nisargadatta made an important distinction between them. While it may be the Ground of Being in all that is manifested, Consciousness is also ever changing; it ebbs and flows, it expands and contracts and it is, as it were, *an experience,* as there must be an "I" there. Even in the concept of "witnessing consciousness" there is an "I" there to witness. Drilling down further, if we are not the witness but simply the process of witnessing itself, then that still requires a subject-object relationship, which is still within duality. At the deepest level is Awareness, which for me at this moment is perceived as an underlying Presence that is simultaneously everywhere and nowhere. When asked what is real, Swami Muktananda precisely replied, *"What is real is that which never changes."* It appears therefore, at least on a qualitative level, that the consciousness within any given mind-body organism is always changing and therefore, it is only **relatively** real and not **absolutely** real. Thus, unchanging Awareness is the only Absolute. [One can see that I was beginning to grok the dualistic aspects of reality, that there could be an absolute and a relative working together. What I failed to grasp at that point was that I was overlaying duality where there is none. In Truth, the absolute and relative are concepts.]

In a previous email, I described the feeling of "I Am No One" and while true, it is still a subset of consciousness. I also stated there was a feeling of "Dying into Love" and that, it appears, is what Nisargadatta was pointing to with "Awareness." This cannot be described in words as obviously language is within duality and consciousness. As Lao Tzu said, "The Tao that can be expressed is not the eternal Tao." It does appear that "**Awareness**" as Nisargadatta used the term, is the same pointer as "**The Void**" (the Zen term I've been using), which is the same as "**The Godhead**" (used by Meister Eckhart), which is the same as "**No Self**" (used by Adyashanti). Therefore, as God is synonymous with **Life** and **Love**, then these two are also the equivalent of "**Awareness**." Understanding this on an intellectual level only may or may not be useful in fomenting deeper realizations of this seemingly abstract conceptual consciousness-awareness differentiation.

However, at the level of intellect only, it doesn't provide a shift (expansion) in one's consciousness, which seems to have recently happened within the mind-body organism known as Phil. I am not writing any of this from any place other than my current, direct experience. In an infinite multiverse, there must be infinite levels of consciousness to "evolve" or "fall" into. The notion of "remembering" resonates deeply with me, as we are already that which we are falling/evolving into. However, the Realization of Awareness is where the sense of "I" and all these concepts fall away. It appears to me now that there cannot be an "I" that is Realized but rather, that Realization *"happens"* **out** of the sense of "I" identifying itself as anything within consciousness…including the witness and/or the act of witnessing itself.

The Kiss, while transitory as all experiences are, has brought forth a marked shift in the understanding of Nisargadatta's teachings, which may be the narrowest and most direct I have ever come across. They are not for the faint of heart, as they bypass most everything that is customarily associated with a spiritual path, drilling directly to the core of the issue, in some ways even more than Zen or Advaita Vedanta. Just as it was with Meister Eckhart, it is wondrous and very humbling that these teachings have come along at precisely the time I've become truly ready to hear them.

This was also experienced with Nisargadatta's quote on sadhana, which is the truest definition that I have found and fits my current Process perfectly. [He said, "Sadhana is a search for what to give up. Empty yourself completely."] I had mentioned in another email that my Process felt easy, simple, and that it flowed. While that is still true, I now understand that even the experience of Process, however blissful, still falls within the duality of consciousness – inescapably *a part of,* and yet *apart from* "The Void" which could, it would seem, be described as The Field of Pure Potentiality, whereas Consciousness could be defined as The Field of Pure Actuality. Two sides of the same coin as it were or, as Yogananda put it into chant, "Spirit and Nature dancing together."

God/Self-Realization or, Dying into Love, if you please, cannot be accomplished by the "I" (the ego), as it has no fundamental, independent reality of its own. It appears that all we need to do is be loving, compassionate, and serviceful. Then, through Surrender, we adopt, as James Finley pointed to, an inner attitudinal stance of least resistance to

The Process. Doing this, we rest in the I AM – the Still Presence of This Moment. From there, it appears that it all comes down to The Grace of God/Guru/Self. How much simpler could it be?

Adyashanti has stated that the essence of Nisargadatta's teaching can be distilled into two words – **Be Still** (or, as Nisargadatta also put it, rest in the Awareness of I Am That). <u>Be</u> <u>Still</u> were the two words that God spoke to me over eighteen years ago. It appears that only now I am Self-Realizing what His simple yet incredibly profound and direct message actually meant… and it's more beautiful than I could ever hope to express.

Nisargadatta's astonishingly accurate quote expresses *exactly* what I Am Now experiencing: "Love says, 'I am everything.' Wisdom says, 'I am nothing.' Between the two my life flows."

Phil

One begins to perceive the influence of the teachers and teachings I mentioned in the previous commentary. While I still had no clear inkling of what exactly was happening, I was at least able to start verbalizing it, albeit in a somewhat unclear manner…I was a bit of a mess after all! Looking back and given everything, especially in the first nine months, it is a wonder that I could write, let alone coherently. I've ascribed most everything written to muscle memory and, of course, to Grace.

Regarding the passage about "Being Still" and God speaking to me, it feels important to expand on that now, as actually *hearing* God's voice isn't a normal thing for me. The ensuing journal entry, written in 2014, describes one of my first meditations in 1999:

> There have been many times that I felt I was in communication/communion with Spirit and never heard a sound. While God only knows why, He did speak directly to me this time, along with two other times. The one thing I know for sure about my experience of hearing God's voice is that, to this day, with each of the three instances, I can hear the voice exactly as I did at the time – the intonation, volume, everything – just as if I had heard it a moment ago.

I had recently received the first SRF lesson that talks about meditation and was a little disappointed, since more than anything I wanted a meditation technique to practice. The first lesson was, from my viewpoint, light on details and specifics. Later, of course, I found that the subject is addressed in great detail with many definite techniques, but at the time I was doing what I could with what little I knew. I'll never forget meditating in my home one afternoon, when suddenly I heard a voice that filled the room and seemed to come from over my right shoulder, and yet it also seemed to originate from everywhere. As before, I cannot say that I perceived it with my ears but rather, *in my mind*. It was the *exact* voice that I heard twice before and it simply but powerfully said, "Be Still, My Child." I was stunned, in part due to the fact that one doesn't (or at least I don't!) hear God's voice very often. But more than that, unlike the other two instances, I could not comprehend the message. All I could infer was that it had to be important, otherwise (presumably!) God would not have said it. Although not for a few years, Stillness would eventually become very important and ultimately, deep inner Stillness – no-mind – would become my primary [our natural] state of awareness.

The other two occasions of hearing God's voice aren't relevant to the overarching theme of this book, and as such I am not including them. Suffice to say that the other messages were as succinct as this one was. To this point, God's loquacious side (as seen in one of my all-time spiritual favorites, the Conversations with God (CWG) books by Neale Donald Walsch) hasn't been shared with me. What is important is that the message was finally understood, but not until 2019 after the awakening was mostly integrated. God's message to me echoes what Ramana told his devotees in the following: "All that is required to realize the Self is to be still. What can be easier than that?" and "The whole truth can be summed up in one verse from the Jewish/Christian scriptures, 'I am that I am.' And the entire method for realizing this truth is found in another of those scriptures, 'Be still and know that I am God.'" Here now, **Be Still** appears to me to be the most single-pointed spiritual teaching and technique there is. It is in deep, internal Stillness that we Realize our Oneness with God, and Silence is Her language. Knowing, so to speak, only comes through Being. And it is in the forever-unfolding unknowing that we come to know.

In this next email, we see that the kundalini was still storming, and that deepening insights continued to manifest. This message also pointed to an important consideration to remember – if you are experiencing intense energies and/or having penetrating, ongoing realizations, then stay as grounded as you can. This is almost never the time to be meditating for hours on end or doing a bunch of Kriyas! Instead, try walking barefoot on the grass, earth, or sand, do some gardening, or just spend time out in nature. These energies will eventually dissipate, but as they can be overwhelming, it's best not to amplify them even more. Remember, kundalini is intelligent…just let it do its thing.

November 8, 2017

… I'm actually not feeling spacey or "otherworldly" at all, although some additional/excess energies have been affecting sleep patterns since last month, as well as a lot of activity (off and on) in the ajna and crown chakras. My family lives such a "normal" life that this is actually a great spot to "ground" to, which was a part of my decision to visit.

Realizations never end, or so it appears. There's no finish line when we're done and we don't just hang out in the clouds playing the harp. Thankfully! As it appears now, only Realizing The Absolute does not equate to "enlightenment" anyway. It's wonderful and awe-inspiring based on the taste I've had but as best I can tell, it is the integration of The Absolute and The Relative that comes with deeper states of enlightenment, which is why I loved Nisargadatta's quote [being nothing and everything] so much. Experientially, I'm tasting this unfolding now and it's comforting to know that The Process is an infinite one, as it eliminates all sense of caring as to how and when The Process develops. The perfection of it all is really beautiful and humbling.

Phil

I've been asked about why I am so thankful that, as best I can tell, there is no finish line that we cross at the time of awakening. First, that would imply a static place in consciousness and I know of nothing static (i.e. unchanging) in Consciousness, so being "done" does not seem possible. As all of manifestation appears to be eternally evolving, why then would anything stop progressing? Second, where's the fun in stopping?! Maybe it's just the wanderlust in me, but dang…*forever* is a long time! I can't help but think we'd eventually get bored and want to start the process all over again. All of this aside, my insight that we (individuations of consciousness in physical form) are always evolving came very early on. While I don't know this, my feeling is that even if a localization of consciousness (Soul) maxes out the in-form experience as a human, in an infinite universe there must be many other forms through which It can evolve, with each form having its own unique challenges and opportunities. This understanding immediately felt both obvious and comforting, hence my thankfulness for the eternal nature of the Cosmic Dance.

The following email finds me beginning to appreciate how our spiritual experiences, powerful and transformative though they may be, might also become stumbling blocks. Additionally, I realized that <u>all</u> egoic identities, especially that of a spiritual seeker, are impediments to awakening.

November 12, 2017

… I understand how/why spiritual "seekers" are enamored by extraordinary experiences of The Absolute or The Relative, as they're amazing to be sure. Fortunately, my seeking days are long over and it seems that I am not stuck in attempting to recreate an experience such as I had while at HVA. If we're truly in The Now, we can't be holding some (any!) experience up in comparison to This Moment, wondering why it isn't happening more, or when it will happen again, or where it went, or…it goes on and on – such is the way the mind works. Whatever IS seems *enough* now and when it doesn't, that's OK as well; just old karma running off it would seem. The Kiss from God remains though, like the scent of perfume in a room after the person that was wearing it has left.

The way I'm experiencing This Moment is that of it being very ordinary but also wondrous and holy. Immense love wells up in me for the simplest of things and yet, well, "ordinary" is the only word I can come up with. It seems some awakenings to whatever extent they happen, are at the level of the mind or at the level of the heart. They can be both at once too obviously, although I suspect that's comparatively rarer. Each can be intoxicating but as I see things now, whichever one happens has to be surrendered so that the other may happen. Once both have opened us to a sufficient degree, it's all about integrating the two, which seems to be where I find myself.

It flows effortlessly in the way it will, leaving me feeling free and at peace – keenly caring about the world (heart awakening) and yet with a sense of non-attachment that comes with the I Am No One (mind awakening).

Phil

I'm sure you can tell that writing was a significant aspect of my awakening process. After my first email, I received a strong intuitive urge to save them all, and here now I am very pleased that I did!

November 22, 2017

Energies continue to flow in very intensely, with the crown and ajna chakras very alive. Additionally, immense feelings of love continue to well up off and on, specifically in the gut (middle of the body). Like anything, it's an experience (transitory) so while it feels wonderful, there is no desire for it to do anything but what it will. With that, further/deeper understandings of Awareness continue to happen, and as there's no one here that I can talk with, I write.

Phil

Despite the encouraging developments I described in the email above, lamentably my brain felt mushy and I was having a tough time focusing on details. Especially early on, my short-term memory was, let's just call it... suboptimal. Moreover, any semblance of normal sleeping patterns went out the window, and there was random pain in and around the heart. Making it all worse were the frequent third-eye headaches, presumably due to hyper-stimulation of the ajna chakra.

On December 9, 2017, I continued my journey east from Texas to Atlanta to visit my SRF family there for a week. It was wonderful to see everybody again after almost seven years, but it was difficult for me because I was so disoriented. Furthermore, some of my closest friends and family were concerned about my physical health, urging me to seek medical treatment. In most cases, this advice would be prudent and something I would probably encourage a friend to do as well. In my case, however, there was a knowing in my core that I needed to let the process play out unimpeded in an effort to maximize my spiritual growth. To be safe, I approached my trip to the South feeling that

I was going to say goodbye to everyone and set my affairs in order. The divergent views between my friends and family and I understandably gave some closest to me great pause and subsequently created distance between us. Naturally, this distance made authentic sharing with them problematic, as they did not want to stand idly by while their loved one was potentially going to die in the near future. Perhaps I didn't allow some of my friends enough time to come to terms with the ramifications of The Kiss, but at the time (correctly or incorrectly) I felt they were less than genuinely receptive to the awakening that had just taken place, as I was no longer the very-together, high-functioning fun guy they remembered. On some level, it might have seemed that they had already lost me. To any of my dear friends and family reading this, please know that I own the decisions I made, I have placed no blame, and I love you even more now than I did back in the day.

Needless to say, my time in Georgia did not go entirely as hoped. The following journal entry, written in February 2018, is an indication of what I encountered during that trip and what I struggled to deal with afterwards:

Typically, we avoid allowing ourselves (the ego) to become vulnerable. For whatever reason(s), I have been intuitively guided to do so over the last eighteen months, although not in an indiscriminate fashion by any means. The initial outward results from this authentic sharing were predictably mixed. Many relationships truly became deeper, but one, by my heavy-hearted choice, culminated in an indefinite hiatus. [A couple more followed over time.] Regarding the latter, it only ended from an interpersonal standpoint, at least for me. While these beautiful souls are currently no longer constant companions on my journey (at least for the foreseeable future), *they remain forever in my prayers and in my heart*. Fortunately, it all provided powerful "grist for the mill" in totally accepting What Is. Conceivably, that was one of the reasons I was inwardly led to share what I did in the way that I did. Unavoidably, *we all function from the state of consciousness that we are*, hence the adage from Jesus to not judge.

My understanding of why people enter into and maintain relationships, generally speaking, falls into three predominant categories, although there can certainly be overlapping motives. 1) One person wants something from the other person. 2) A "trade," as it were, takes place, consciously or unconsciously. Each has a mental checklist of sorts they are looking to fill and if/when both decide enough boxes are checked, the relationship happens. This appears to especially be the case when the budding relationship is romantic in nature. In my experience, the first two are by and large the most common. 3) One or both of the individuals enters the union with one central purpose – **their intention to give**. What they give to the other and to the relationship as a whole can be anything, but in my case the foundation is always love. If the giving is unconditional, with no expectation of reciprocity, then this is, as I view it, the highest form of relationship, *as long as what is given does no harm*. The greatest example of this that I am aware of is in the way a true Guru (Avatar, spiritual Master, jnani-sage, jivamukti, etc.) **embodies** perpetual and unconditional love and compassion, not only towards his or her disciples but for <u>all</u> sentient beings.

My decision to step away from some of my friends wasn't due to them not believing what I've written about or any disagreements regarding my direction in life and/or the decisions I've made over the last year and a half. These are ultimately between God and me, not anyone else. My pullback was based solely on my observation that our discussions were, and possibly had been for years, actually making them uncomfortable…both the subjects shared as well as the specific act of deep, authentic discourse itself. It became clear in a non-judgmental way that if what I was giving wasn't beneficial, then the most loving thing I could do was to back away as quietly and gracefully as possible. For me, this comes naturally and it is also an archetypal response for most people with Myers-Briggs INFJ personality profiles.

Ending a valued long term relationship is hard for anyone, and especially so for those who process these things in the way that the INFJ often does. While I don't *identify* as one, I do recognize many of the INFJ traits in my personality. Living a spiritually-centered life does not mean that one ceases to feel! Indeed, one's feelings, especially love and compassion, become deeper. *How one demonstrates one's humanity is an expression of one's spirituality.* An aspect of my sadhana during this period was working through the hurt, anger, and sadness that was felt in what could be thought of as a grieving process. Based on my experiences and current understanding, it is critical that we completely work through whatever negative feelings are arising, regardless of what prompts them to come up, so that they are permanently released and closure is found. If this doesn't happen and they get buried inside (usually because we are **afraid to feel what our heart is expressing**), then anger, resentments, guilt, and all other manner of unhealthy energies can be, and most often are, trapped. Eckhart Tolle refers to this as "the pain body." Not surprisingly, this usually leads to many types of dis-ease including physical ailments and mental neuroses that, once triggered, unexpectedly manifest themselves weeks, months, or even years later. Extraordinary spiritual experiences aside, it is in this very important facet of life that one nearly always reaps the benefits of a regular meditation and introspection practice.

As I have never been one to deny my humanness (an important quality that Ram Dass and Neale Donald Walsch have exemplified impeccably), I have no problem admitting that even with all the spiritual experiences and blessings that I have had and have written about, these feelings and relationship challenges do occasionally arise. One aspect of Grace and becoming more awake is that it assists us in processing these types of situations in a healthy and consciously loving way. I've always been fond of what Dr. Wayne Dyer used to say on this: "Circumstances don't make the person, they reveal the person." For someone like me who profoundly values deep long-lasting friendships, such separations do not come easily or without a large amount of reflection beforehand. Fortunately, with all that has happened recently and throughout my life in general, I find myself at peace with my decision to pull back from some who I truly care about. It's healthy to remember that being a loving, understanding, and compassionate individual does not mean that one has to put up with being treated in an (un) consciously hurtful or unloving way. Given the very significant nature of my difficult but necessary decisions in this area, I felt that it was mandatory to expound on them here, as much of what fomented these changes was The Kiss and the intuitive push for authenticity with those closest to me that accompanied it. Importantly, it has also not been lost on me that by reacting in the way some have, it has actually been powerfully beneficial to my spiritual growth, which, in its own way, makes it all a blessing. As the great Vietnamese monk, interspiritual author, and peace activist Thich Nhat Hahn so aptly stated, "No Mud, No Lotus."

For those who are having or will have an awakening, one thing to remember is that the process is often disconcerting and difficult, if not impossible, to comprehend for close friends and family. Why? I don't know, but regardless, I was not expecting this. Perhaps, it was this that Jesus was pointing to when he reportedly said, "A prophet is not without honor except in his home town and among his own relatives and in his own household." Unfortunately, and as is often the case, those nearest to us may see or appreciate our shift the least.

The period between mid-December 2017 and late January 2018 was an extremely important time. After six days in Atlanta, I came back home to California to watch my destiny unfold and to discover whether I would live or die by the close of the year. Around Christmas, I received a deep intuitive sense that I was not going to drop my body. With the realization that my incarnation was apparently going to continue, I left for a one-week stay in Joshua Tree followed by five weeks in Borrego Springs. I certainly did not know what to expect when venturing out into the desert; I only knew that I felt an intense urge to go and to be open to whatever The Universe offered. Upon reflection, this time in isolation allowed me to: 1) Introspect on my recent trips to Texas and Georgia, and 2) Further integrate the awakening. In the subsequent journal entry, I touch upon the transcendent aspect of my desert sojourn:

"Emptiness,
Silence,
Stillness.
This is not a void to be feared but
A sanctuary to be sought."

~ The Lost Writings of Wu Hsin: Pointers to Non-Duality by Roy Melvyn

Since The Kiss, there has been an ongoing ebb and flow of alternating between the Sturm und Drang immanent experience of humanness and the transcendent Merging into Oneness. Adyashanti maintains that while there are certainly exceptions, this is most often how it flows, due to karmic runoff I suspect. As I understand it, this was how it unfolded for him as well. As I have mentioned before, the dualistic nature of language makes narrating what basically isn't even an experience very challenging, but regardless of the difficulty, I'm once again giving it my best shot.

Previously, I have written about the inner stillness that is now primarily my natural state of being. I would posit that a lack of endless mental noise and a quiet mind *is* our **natural state**. However, with the never-ending stimuli encountered in modern day life, along with people's seeming addiction to every type of distraction possible (much of which is available at the touch of the ubiquitous smartphone), most assume the mind's constant chatter is normal. Indeed, many of us at some level find the idea of spending time alone in silence to be an uncomfortable and avoid-at-all-costs proposition. Blaise Pascal, a highly regarded seventeenth century mathematician, inventor, and theologian insightfully pointed to this when he stated, "All of humanity's problems stem from man's inability to sit quietly in a room alone." It is no wonder that many are exceedingly frustrated when attempting to meditate, even after years of diligent practice, as their mind goes into overdrive with thoughts! Adyashanti likened this to the withdrawal symptoms associated with addictions. In this instance, the addiction is to incessant sensory input along with the mind's thoughts running amok.

The inherent stillness of the desert is like nowhere else in nature that I have found, and I am sure it is one of the reasons that it has been an attractive destination for those doing deep inner spiritual work for millennia. The processing of the feelings that I had, while introspective in nature, was essentially a "doing." However, the Merging into Oneness was simply "Being." This Beingness is really not a describable thing, as that would require a subject-object event and relationship, hence the use of pointers, as otherwise it is like trying to grab the wind; one may feel it but never actually hold it. I would point to it as an *undifferentiated state of being* where subject-object, along with the sense of there being an "I" that is separate from anything and everything, <u>dissolves</u>. Moreover, this also includes there being no sensation of an "I" at all. "I" only recognized that I was in the state after Pure Awareness subsided. In the Hindu and Advaita Vedanta philosophies, this is sometimes referred to as Turiya.

Philosophy aside, nothing in my experience prepared me for Being Pure Awareness. The transcendence of intellect, which is tied to the ego, cannot be remotely understood by the mind. The ego doesn't find the slightest hint of value in the idea! Also, this Immersion into what has been termed Primordial Awareness, The Void, or The Godhead (to name a few) is close to the concept of no-mind (i.e. Mushin) but with a much deeper, more immediate quality that brings with it a **Directness of Perception** unlike anything else that I have been. Dr. David Hawkins called this, if I understand his terminology correctly, "Radical Subjectivity – The Eye of Self." Meister Eckhart reportedly stated, "The eye with which I see God is the same eye with which God sees me." Adyashanti has described this as "seeing as God sees," as there is no judgment or labeling. It is, very simply, **Seeing What Is** without any attachments or mental filters in the way. Things just are as they are. **Reality just Is**. This Pure Perception isn't like the high states of Self where the siddhis [extraordinary spiritual abilities] manifest. No astral lights, no music of the spheres, no cosmic insights. It doesn't sound particularly sexy to the mind, does it? And yet, I wouldn't trade it for any of those things, amazing and transformative as they may be.

Given the ongoing vacillation in and out of these states of awareness, the transcendence that came with The Kiss was not abiding, and so there's still work to do in integrating and **embodying** it into my humanity and everyday life. This Process is, as the old saying goes, where the rubber meets the road. My desert journey allowed me to Process and to Be, to Feel and to Realize Oneness, to Embrace the Immanent and Merge with the Transcendent. It was yet another miraculous example of "being done" by my sadhana. Stated another way, when open, trusting, and authentically surrendered, Divine Intelligence Awakens our individuated wave of Consciousness in physical form...to Itself. It bears repeating that this wasn't anything that "I" did or could have done through effort [personal will] alone, which imparts *immense gratitude* and *profound humility*.

I suspect that anyone reading this would probably have a brain that hurts and wonder what on earth these states are good for. Like, "Phil, what does one *do* with it?" Well, the Process is still ongoing and therefore I cannot provide a definitive answer, if there even is such a thing. For now, about all I can say is that, in a *worldly* sense, there is no value in this Being. It hasn't gotten me any job offers or any discounts at Chipotle. No one congratulates me on all my cool sounding no-self stuff. Most likely, roughly 99% of the world's population wouldn't even care about what is being written here, let alone understand it by way of direct experience. Be that as it may, I would not trade it for any worldly thing, as everything in experience is transitory and therefore, *ya can't take it with ya baby!* One of my all-time favorite quotes from my guru, Paramahansa Yogananda, is: "The only worthwhile change, the only permanent advance, is the inner evolution toward spiritual perfection." If this process makes things more challenging in the short term, and so far it most definitely has, then I'm OK with it. Since my initial Shift at age 38, I've always had my intention set on what has been my **primary objective**; complete Awakening – Moksha. Moreover, as The Process has unfolded to this extent, I have absolutely no doubt as to what the result will be. <u>When it happens is irrelevant as Liberation, like everything else, only happens in This Moment.</u> As I began this note with an aphorism from Wu Hsin, I will close with one more.

"Silence is not the absence of sound.
Silence is the absence of you."

During my time in the desert, there was an immense deepening of non-dual awareness-experience. But what may not have been apparent from the above journal entry is that, at the same time, there was a crushing feeling of aloneness. There are no adequate words to express what it felt like to be on my own there. Like Matt Damon in the movie *The Martian,* I felt like the only person on the planet. Not only was I feeling estranged from some of my closest friends, but at the core, the ego-mind felt naked, trapped, and vulnerable as all its remaining attachments were falling away; everything that had ever propped it up was being ripped out. In sum, the ego-mind was deathly afraid. We must cross the Gateless Gate alone. It cannot be otherwise. That said, on the "other side," we see that we are never alone, but from the ego's illusory point of view, we feel as if the aloneness of the journey is so heavy it will kill us. Day in and day out, the desert acted as a clear and unsympathetic mirror for this desolate portion of my post-Kiss shakedown, just as it was meant to.

To add insult to injury, what few possessions I had left were literally dying alongside the ego. For instance, my trusted laptop had hard-drive failure, my iPod started malfunctioning (on which Adya's spiritual talks were about the only thing keeping me going), and even my folding chair that I left next to my car was stolen! The icing on this crappy cake was that, a few days later, my SUV (out of which I was living), suddenly wouldn't start. It was nighttime in the desert and I wanted some heat. I turned the key in the ignition and… nothing. There was nowhere to go, nobody to call, and I literally gave up. At that point, I recalled a long-forgotten moment in Swami Vivekananda's life. I had read that in the beginning of his renowned 1893 trip to Chicago, he missed his connection with the people who were supposed to pick him up and take him to his accommodations. Being in a foreign land, he didn't know what to do and had no way to get help. Showing complete trust in God, he found an empty boxcar in a railroad freight yard, curled up in it, surrendered his plight, and went to sleep. The next morning, as he wandered the streets of Chicago, he was miraculously found and taken to his destination. In the desert, I found myself in a similar predicament, which I now call my "Vivekananda moment." I realized, being stranded in the desert, that this was my opportunity to demonstrate the same profound faith in and surrender to The Universe. I did just what Vivekananda did. I laid down in the back of my car, and as I fell asleep I said with all my strength, "Dear Lord, I know you'll take care of me." The next day, I was delightfully surprised to find that my car started right up and never gave me a problem like that again.

This story of deep surrender illustrates a couple of things. First, the old adage is true – when it rains it often pours. In other words, when things go bad, they sometimes go really bad. Second, when it's pouring rain and the world seems to be failing us, we can be challenged to plumb the depths of our soul to find a level of trust and surrender that we didn't know we had in us. To anyone who is awakening or anticipating one, bear in mind that this is something that could happen to you. When everything appears to be falling apart and there is seemingly nowhere to turn, just give it all up to God. These are the trials that The Universe arranges for us, and it is this depth of surrender that helps us to awaken.

As one can see from the previous emails and journal entries, this was a very challenging time for me. When I was a teenager in the late 70's, *The Lord of the Rings* was my most prized book. Surprisingly, a section of it came back to me during the above "worst of times" bringing me some measure of solace. In the last book of the trilogy, Frodo and Sam are in one of the darkest parts of their journey through Mordor. During their conversation, Sam starts imagining the tale that someday might be told of their trials, and how the lowest parts might be the most meaningful and therefore the best parts to read. I won't ruin how their journey ends for anyone who hasn't read the book, but I will say that the pep talk they gave themselves came back to me, and there were more than a few times when remembering it gave me the same encouragement.

All of that aside, take heart my awakening friend; this next email illustrates that my desert pilgrimage and rebirthing wasn't all doom and gloom. As I had been traveling and then stumbling through the integration process, this is the first email I'd written in a couple of months. In it, you'll find me cognizant of the many positive aspects of the rebirthing, in part due to the understanding that the death that I'd felt was on my horizon was a metaphysical transcendence and not a physical transition. Always remember that the moments in life that appear to be the worst often hold the greatest potential for spiritual evolution, and that regardless of how these times may feel, we **never** face these moments alone, for God is always with us. In fact, She *is* us!

January 20, 2018

Hey there…Happy New Year! It's great to hear from you and thanks so much for all the kind words in your last email. I too am immensely grateful for your friendship and support over the many years. If we look, it isn't usually too difficult to identify the souls that we have known before and I have no doubt that you and I have shared this Cosmic Dance on other stages, in other times and guises.

Please forgive me in advance for the length of this reply but there's a lot that came with last year and with The Kiss and its ongoing aftermath. I don't want to respond to your thoughtful email in a hasty or casual way, as *authenticity* and the resulting *vulnerability* that often comes with it are helpful tools in one's spiritual growth and evolution and I am no exception in this. Furthermore, I haven't deeply written since the end of my stay in Texas. (Gasp!) So, I can respond to your comments and questions and in doing so, put some digital pen to digital paper, which is a process of sharing that often helps me to introspect and (re)contextualize the happenings in and as Life. My sincere hope is that by disseminating my Process in this way, it might be beneficial for others.

While I appreciate how one can be conflicted about the possibility of a friend or loved one dropping their body, simply, there is nowhere I or any of us can go! You know [from previous correspondences] that since the age of ten, I truly have had no aversion to the possibility of death, after "remembering" that I am not the body through a spontaneous astral projection. [See Q&A for details of this out-of-body experience.] Conversely, I certainly have no wish to die either! In one of James Finley's talks on Thomas Merton, he insightfully stated, "The person who is afraid of death and the person who is afraid of life both have the same problem – neither has yet learned how to live." *We are all awakening, and that necessarily happens through form, not in spite of it.* Besides, as Alan Watts used to point out, "It's the only game in town!"

Somehow, given the very sobering nature of what this last year has meant physically and financially, along with my current inability and lack of desire to work in the context that I used to, through God's Grace I remain in Acceptance of This Moment. And in that state of surrender, all concerns drop away…except when they don't! I add that last part not in an attempt at humor but as a reminder (to myself as well) that the feelings of concern and being conflicted that you mentioned are natural, understandable, and a part of our humanness. If you died tomorrow, part of me would be in complete peace with it, understanding the Transition Process and "bigger picture" (to some degree anyway!). However, that would not preclude a sense of personal loss, sadness, and grief – not only for me but also for all who love and depend on you – and I do recognize, understand, and appreciate this with those who know and love me as well.

I honestly felt there was a very good chance that I might not live to see the New Year and yet here I am, so I'm joyfully putting all of that talk, and the preparations that went with it, behind me now! Generally speaking, spiritual/mystical experiences are at best ambiguous, so there's no ignominy or anything unusual about misunderstanding one, if that even happened. Couldn't it simply have been an opportunity to express my faith and ability to surrender in a way perfectly designed to foment The Kiss and bring me to this current Now point? As this is what I choose to make of it, the answer is yes. From the beginning of my experience with Brother Death, I acknowledged four possibilities: 1) That my take on it was literally correct, 2) That I had the correct interpretation but the wrong timeline, 3) That I had an incorrect interpretation of death, thinking it physical rather than the "real death" stemming from an abiding loss of ego, or 4) That it was just a wild, subconscious-fed lucid dream. After a few months in early 2017 of struggling with some measure of fear, uncertainty, and doubt, I was finally able to surrender deeply and authentically enough to embrace the opportunity that I, in part, was giving to myself. The resulting Shift in consciousness was obviously completely unexpected (how could it be otherwise?) but nonetheless, as far as I am concerned, my faith and trust in The Process that was shown to me in that experience was rewarded.

Not surprisingly, opinions on this vary depending on who you ask. As I enter 2018, I have no problem concluding that it must be numbers 2, 3, or 4 on the above list. With that, and after extensive introspection and talking with friends, I feel very at peace and grateful with how I lived it. So pilgrim, the question now is…what happens next?!

My friend, **everything has changed** as I have fundamentally changed. Not at the level of personality, but instead at the level of consciousness and the directness of perception that is caused by it. While there was some prior level of intellectual understanding of No Self, it in no way prepared me for the experience of transcending the ego, and since then I have been left with the highly unique and unaccustomed procession of integrating the ebb and flow of it all into my moment-to-moment reality. I am certainly not complaining, as Realizing our inherent Oneness and Nothingness is a rare and precious thing, coming totally unlooked for as well. That said, there's still work to do on my part, as without the ability to completely embody it here in the physical plane, one lacks total Awakening. It isn't about having grand insights, profound and true though they may be, but rather *Where We Are Living From.* I am reminded that evolution never ends as we are manifesting in and as the infinity of consciousness. The Process **is** Divine Intelligence Itself so if we're open and "out of the way" through trust and surrender, evolution happens naturally and therefore quicker and easier. Without the miraculous discovery of the teachings of Meister Eckhart and Adyashanti, coupled with the reintroduction of Nisargadatta's teachings, I'd truly have been in a tough spot. Even for those with extensive spiritual and metaphysical resources, it can be challenging to find clear, accurate, and trustworthy *experiential accounts* of this extremely specific portion of the awakening process, along with that which often goes with it; during and maybe more vitally, after. The Kiss from God and all that has manifested since has left me feeling immensely humbled and grateful beyond words, as it wasn't anything I did or could do. I know now beyond all doubt that at the core of all spirituality and love for God is **surrender**. Simply being OK with What Is…which is always This Moment. Again, it's easier said than done, unless of course it isn't.

This leads to your questions as to where I am living and what has been happening over the last six weeks. I find myself yearning for *simplicity* more than anything else, along with solitude and silence, and I know of no better place in nature for all of these than the desert. There's quietude in the desert that is unmatched by anywhere else that I have been. It's just about the only place in the "outer world" that almost equals the inner Stillness that happens within. The silence here can be deafening and as odd as it may sound, I find it comforting and soothing. I've primarily been camping in Borrego Springs but I also spent some time in Joshua Tree. There is a stripped down essence to the desert that, while beautiful, can also be harsh. Throughout the millennia, this combo seems to call to some who do deep inner work and I am one of them. I remember telling one of the SRF monks some years ago that I had a desire to one day head off into the desert, much as the desert Fathers did in ages past. He correctly warned about how the ego can co-opt spirituality with desires such as this, but I responded that it felt like more than that. Given that it did indeed come to pass, it appears now that it was actually a "future pull," to use a fashionable new-age term. Remember, time isn't linear! Of course, unlike the desert mystics of old, I chose to eschew living in a cave and wearing a hair shirt, substituting these with a decidedly more comfortable method, which shows that even timeless practices for Self-Realization fall in and out of style!

These last six weeks have flown by incredibly fast and have been blessed in all respects, but all things must pass eventually and there are serious practical matters that need to be addressed; specifically finding a job and place to live. The disability insurance has run out and the large reduction of income over the course of an entire year has left most of my financial resources depleted. Could I have done more in the fall to find work? Yes. [In retrospect, probably not.] However, my reasoning was that if I were to die late in the year, it wouldn't be fair to the employer or for me, as I didn't want to spend my last days learning some new job. The trip to Texas and Georgia was very important to the Process and my commitment to it. Once a job and a place to live are out of the way, I'll need to get health insurance and address the physical issues that haven't gone away. Keen insights and transcendent states of consciousness aside, Brother Donkey cannot be put on hold indefinitely.

This Monday, I'll be returning to my beloved HVA through the end of February, so my prayer is that I am able to locate work in that amount of time. If I have to sleep in my car awhile until getting a place...well, I've proved I can do it these last six weeks and many deal with much worse. **Everything** is a blessing and an opportunity to evolve, regardless of what it looks like at the time, and I still deeply know that this is happening *for me* and not *to me*. Karmically, this just seems to be my Process right now. It is what it is and therefore I refuse to overlay any meaning onto it other than that of a blessed and perfect opportunity to awaken even more.

The last thing I would add is that, over the years as introspection has happened, *I have put an absolute premium on looking for any possible way that ego is acting in a self-delusional way.* In addition to authentic discourse with close friends such as you, I do my best to think critically and turn the searchlight of discernment inward, to ensure that the ego doesn't highjack the spiritual process. If or when a spiritually superior ego happens to people, most unfortunate results typically occur. Reassuringly, after The Kiss there's not much ego structure left and when I witness it trying to reconstitute itself around something, I notice that it appears to lack the energy required for me to identify with whatever it's latched onto. It is still "in the room" so to speak, so vigilance is still required. But whereas before it stood nearby, now it seems diminished and sent to sit in the corner. Obviously, I am speaking metaphorically but I'm not sure how to be any clearer.

And so, my friend, if you would like to talk more about any of this, or anything else of course, please *never hesitate* to let me know. Starting in kindergarten and 52 years later, everything is all on the table between us anyway! If your youngest has a game schedule, then perhaps she could email it to me. It would be great to see her play rugby and just maybe I could inconspicuously trip one of the other team's players from the sideline during a crucial play. Hey – just kidding! God knows (and you'll remember) that once upon a time I relished doing much worse, but I don't want any more of that karma! I'll join in your lament for the Steelers and include the Blazers in that as well. I have never seen a Portland team that perplexed me more! I do thank God that I don't take it all as seriously as I did back in the days of our youth but we all start somewhere. As I have been wont to say now and again – if Grace can happen to me, It can happen to anyone…and It does…and It will. Expect it when you least expect it!

Phil

My desert trip over, I found myself back at HVA, four months after The Kiss. It was a difficult transitional time, with a lot of anger and vile language erupting for no apparent reason; it would have made a salty old sailor blush! I was keenly aware of what was happening, and so to avoid worrying others at the ashram, I did all I could to keep these primal utterances to myself. Fortunately, for the most part, I was able to limit these outbursts to times when I was in my car, in my room, or pacing the grounds for hours at a time. On top of this, feelings of unworthiness arose, as I no longer felt "ashram appropriate." These feelings were preposterous, but it does show that the ego-mind will latch onto any identity possible. Fortuitously, the monk in charge had been intimately involved in my spiritual unfoldment, knew what was happening, and therefore wasn't too concerned with this stage of my awakening. In hindsight, my sense is that there was a purification process that transpired in the desert and for whatever reason(s), it was all now being expelled.

January 29, 2018

Dear Friends:

The mind-body organism known as Phil has not been well. After nearly no food or even going outside of my room here at HVA since last Wednesday, I'm starting to get around today.

There's been a processing of what remains in me and, "me" *being processed,* somewhat unceremoniously and unflatteringly at times. God's Grace doesn't always look or feel good (why should it?) hence our need for absolute surrender, trust, and humility. My attendance at this weekend's activities is, as they say in sports, a "game-time decision." [Adyashanti had scheduled two speaking engagements in Encinitas that weekend.]

You mentioned "Transmission" on a couple of occasions. Soak up all you can from Adya but please, I encourage you to not be <u>attached</u> to him (or *any* specific form) as all form is transitory, and to remember that The Transmission is in, and flows from, **All Things**. I sense It in the desert and in the mountains. It is in the forest and in the ocean. It's in the golden warmth of Brother Sun, and in the soft glow of Sister Moon. It is in the wagging tail of a happy dog and in a kitten's purr. It is in the smile of a newborn and in the embrace of a loved one. It is in me…and in YOU. It is in Everything…and in Nothing.

Staying open to everything and attached to nothing, with the wonder-filled eyes and heart of a child, we **see**, and **feel**, and **know** It *everywhere* always, and in all ways.

I have found that as "seeking" naturally and authentically ends, the identification of one as a "seeker" falls away. What's left is simply What Is…and we find God there waiting, to Embrace us into Her Infinity.

PW

January 30, 2018 – Follow up reply to the previous email

Thank you for your wonderful reply. There's certainly nothing wrong with a "boost" now and again. We all need them (until we don't) and as you both know, I too have been immensely assisted by Adya and his teachings. I consider you introducing him to me no small miracle and blessing. By all means, soak up all you can! It's important that we avail ourselves of all the blessings The Universe offers/provides. It may very well be that as I am so non-attached to things, due it would seem to the aftereffects of The Kiss, that even the *possibility* of becoming attached to *anything* is seen/felt as a barrier and a potential ego trap. Of course, that doesn't mean I don't care about anything – quite the opposite! It's just that in my experience I have seen so many on the spiritual path become convinced that what they are seeking is only in {fill in the blank} that they forget that it's also All Around and even more importantly, Within. [Ultimately, one sees *no separation* between what is all around and what is within. The Unicity of Beingness becomes One Living Reality.]

I hope to see you both on Friday but right now, I just don't know. Having Adya here so close and at this point in time seems like an unusual and potentially helpful opportunity, but given everything lately, I likely won't know until the day of the event. Such is my world right now it seems, and all I can do is roll with it.

Finally, I pray that I never come across as preachy or pedantic. I like sharing and my only goal in doing so is to be authentic and of service. In truth, I really don't know much at all, *especially* when it comes to what is best for another. My default recommendations usually boil down to trusting The Process, looking within for guidance, and then surrendering it all.

Phil

As events unfolded, I did make it to one of Adya's two talks in Encinitas. While there was nothing specific to my awakening journey that was touched upon in his Friday night lecture, I was deeply captivated by his energy and presence.

The next two months were a blur and I have very little recollection of them, as I wasn't writing or emailing. In February, my stay at HVA ended, and in March, I rented a room at an Airbnb in nearby Valley Center. I was looking for jobs but found nothing suitable. Even if I had, I was in no condition to work. I felt adrift and directionless, as if my life was put on hold. I found myself watching every minute of March Madness (a first!) along with playing copious amounts of spider solitaire. How is that for depressing? It was like I was existing in a bubble while The Universe was finishing dismantling me.

During this time, another "disaster" occurred. On one fine afternoon, I received a frantic knock on my door, and upon opening it, I found the owner of the Airbnb looking horrified. He said, "Phil, I've gotta show you something. There's been an accident." He took me outside and showed me a 20-foot long cherry picker resting atop my car. He had been pruning his palm trees and after not setting it correctly, the cherry picker slid down the driveway and landed on the rear of my car, crushing it in the process. This was the last series of events in which the few possessions I had left either broke or were completely lost, and this was a particularly bitter pill to swallow for two reasons: one practical and the other personal. The practical kick-in-the-teeth was that I knew if push came to shove, I could sleep out of my car. The heart-punch was that I was only able to buy my car brand new (a Lexus hybrid SUV) because of money from my mom after she passed. With my beloved ragtop BMW getting on in years, she wanted me to have a really nice, reliable car, and while she never saw what I picked out, I felt her presence when I did. Losing it "before its time" hurt in a very personal way. Despite the shock of seeing it crushed, I actually ended up comforting the owner, as he was truly distraught; I know that I would have been if the situation was reversed. This led to a month-long process of dealing with his insurance company, the repair shop, and ultimately having to find a new car. While none of this would have been an issue for me under normal circumstances, especially since I wasn't working and had plenty of free time, I found all this to be taxing in the extreme, as the loss of my personal will had yet to be resolved. This also felt like a culmination of the last of my attachments being ripped away, leading to the following email that shows me in a deeply vulnerable yet surrendered state.

March 24, 2018

Dear Friend,

"Many times has Wu Hsin been asked:
'What is emancipation?'
Emancipation is
Freedom from attachment;
Attachment to people,
Attachment to things,
Attachment to ideas and beliefs.
With all attachments cut,
One trusts that one will float
Rather than fall."

~ *The Lost Writings of Wu Hsin: Pointers to Non-Duality* by Roy Melvyn

Things all came together tonight. It seems the attachments are cut and now, I Am Learning to Float. All this life…it all comes down to this. It feels inevitable and yet, who'd have guessed? I don't know why tears are falling. No sadness, no happiness. Just feeling like I'm on the doorstep of my home, my hand on the doorknob turning it, and beginning to finally open the door…knowing I never left.

Phil

While I didn't know it at the time, at this point I was nearing the end of the rebirthing stage. The final surrender of all attachments and rapidly crumbling remains of the ego-mind were so utterly devastating that it is beyond my ability to describe. I was still unemployed and going further into debt and yet, the process was not finished. It felt as if the hand of God was on my shoulder, with Him saying, "You're not ready yet, and you're not going back into the world until you are." The next two months were uneventful, other than the fact that I purchased a new car. By May, an unanticipated trip manifested to the New Camaldoli Monastery in Big Sur and then further north to Mount Shasta. By June, I was back at HVA to continue my job search. This pilgrimage and the events that happened after would turn out to be the culmination of the death of the ego-mind known as Phil and the beginning of the next stage — reentering the marketplace of the working world. Incomprehensibly, there was no immediate impulse to write about the experiences that took place during and directly after the trip, so the following journal entry detailing my adventures was written almost eight months later in January of 2019:

In May of 2018, I attended a public lecture in Santa Barbara by H.H. Swami Vidyadhishananda Giri of the Hansavedas Fellowship. Stemming from a comment he made about spiritual centers in the western U.S., I received a strong push to visit Mount Shasta in northern California. This area has had a well-known mystical reputation for many years, dating back to the Native Americans and continuing up to the present, with all sorts of myths and legends about UFOs and ETs, ascended masters, Lemurians, and even Bigfoot. None of these were why I went and I hold no position on any of these either way. Interestingly, as of the time of this writing, I still do not truly know why I was called there and frankly, it doesn't matter. Logically, I needed to be utilizing my time looking for work and not spending money in this way and yet, I knew that logic shouldn't win the day. Until the post-Kiss work was done, a job was not going to come my way no matter what. All that was clear was that I was supposed to spend time with the mountain.

The adventure began by fulfilling a desire from back in 2013, when I first visited the New Camaldoli Hermitage. Since that visit, I'd really wanted to spend a couple of nights there, as the vibe is amazing and...what can I say...I love monasteries! While there, I purchased a book about the poetry and sayings of mystics and sages across the years and from all traditions. In that book, I saw the following quote by the eighth century Taoist poet Li Po and immediately felt that it encapsulated the reason for my journey to Shasta: "After the birds have left for the day, and the last cloud disappears, the mountain and I sit together until only the mountain remains."

I spent about ten days on Shasta, alternating between camping and staying in motels, as the weather fluctuated between mild and sunny, and cold, heavy rain. When traveling north on I-5, the mountain can be seen from a long way off and based on my experience, it has a potent and palpable energy that is unmistakable. While this is true of many things in nature, especially the majestic mountains of the Pacific Northwest's Cascade Range, Shasta nonetheless energetically grabbed me and pulled me in hard.

Interestingly, during my time there nothing "spiritual" or unusual happened. Nothing that is, except for a visit from a large-sounding, hard-sniffing local outside my tent that woke me up in the middle of the night. Assuming it was a bear and with only a few millimeters of nylon between it and me, I am not ashamed to admit to having felt a hefty quantity of "oh…shit" surge through the body-mind. My first reaction was to make some noise, so I hurriedly turned on my iPod speakers and what came blaring out was what I had last been listening to – Adyashanti! Thankfully, my furry friend continued on its way, proving that Adya is not only helpful with awakenings but also with scaring off wild animals! There was one odd thing that happened I suppose, at least odd for Phil. There were several nights while camping out on the mountain (at an approximate elevation of 7,000 feet) that I slept so deeply there were no dreams, no waking up, no nothing – just dead gone. Maybe it was the fresh air or the mountain's spell but this almost <u>never</u> happens to me. And yet, it transpired on Shasta with regularity. I mention this only because when I left Shasta, I felt *different*, or perhaps a better description would be *grounded*, and deeply at that. Given all the intense and dizzying energies that ebbed and flowed during the months after The Kiss, this was a relief. It was subtle, and I couldn't quite put a finger on it, but there had been a change at some level, as if a stabilization of some sort had taken place.

Back at HVA in June, two things happened almost immediately. The first was that a job posting caught my eye and straightaway I felt like, "Yep, this is most likely the one." As things turned out it was, although due to their lengthy hiring process it took two more months before I was on their payroll. It was as if The Universe was manifesting employment for me only after giving me the time required to stabilize and acclimate to this new place in consciousness, and I must say that if I had started working earlier, it'd have been dicey as to how it would have gone. These Shifts can and most often do take months or even years to settle into. In hindsight, the initial phase took about nine months to complete.

The second thing that happened can only be described as *truly extraordinary*. It seemed a "bookend" as it were, to the first happening (The Kiss) even down to its physical location, as I was in the far east corner room of cabin 3, while the former occurred in the far west corner room of the same cabin. It also felt as if the Mount Shasta sojourn was somehow needed in order for this to precipitate. Whether Shasta had a causative effect or not, I've never been able to shake the sense that these events occurred in an essential and scripted way. Anyway, they did happen, and that's all that counts!

During my time at HVA as a resident volunteer, Kriya yoga [the meditative technique given by Yogananda for channeling kundalini up and down the astral spine, i.e. the sushumna] was by far the primary aspect of my practice. Karma yoga [selfless service, i.e. seva] was *(seemingly)* a distant second. Spending an average of eight hours a day every day in formal meditation, I was doing, with monastic approval, 360 Kriyas per day. While I am not at liberty to discuss the exact technique here, suffice to say that this is a lot by almost anyone's standards. And yet, having surrendered the direction and illusory control of my sadhana, in Idyllwild, Kriya almost wholly fell away. It felt as if Karma yoga had become my path, along with deep surrender, which is sometimes called the "pathless path." Upon returning from Mount Shasta, almost immediately the impulse to do Kriyas again manifested, which struck me as both intriguing and exciting.

After only a few days of Kriya, a long-forgotten conversation from seventeen years prior with a close friend in Atlanta unexpectedly came to mind, which centered on a variation on how one channels the energy through the sushumna. I immediately knew this wasn't a random memory, so I changed the Kriya to this method and the results were instantaneous and astounding. The energy seemed to be double, even triple what it had been, especially with the downward current. This continued for another week with a little more potency every day. On June 14th, a very ordinary-looking Thursday morning, Kriya took on a whole new, mind-boggling dimension.

From the beginning, each Kriya was as potent as I have ever felt, and I was totally locked in with an unwavering mind and focus. Unlike the past where I had a set number to do, I restarted my Kriya practice leaving the quantity up to my guru, as I've always felt that we were doing them together. In the early days, I would sometimes rank the individual Kriyas on a 1-10 scale, with a 10 knocking me off my meditation chair/bench, losing myself in a bliss-rush for a time. [And yes, this can and does happen, as kundalini is a powerful force and not one to be played with or taken lightly.] Every Kriya was an 8 or 9 for the first 108, the number of beads on a mala. [For non-Kriya practitioners, 108 Kriyas takes about an hour to do.] With them being this potent and with perfect attention to each Kriya, I saw no reason to stop and told Yoganandaji that if he was up for more, so was I. Thus, another 108 ensued, and another, then another, and yet another, and still more until all-told, well over 550 Kriyas transpired. All were 8-9s with a few 10s, as well as some heretofore "undreamed of possibilities" occurring throughout the more than six-hour affair.

At times, just as with The Kiss but less extreme, there were moments where laughing and crying took place for no discernable reason. Possibly this is just the body's way of releasing energy. Additionally, the quality of the Kriyas themselves was the most powerful I've ever felt – each and every one – without exception. Imagine feeling ten physical orgasms at once and one might get the sense of how intense and exquisite it felt…**really**! Somewhere in the three to five-hundred range, my arms at times would spontaneously raise, palms up, level with my shoulders. When this happened, the kundalini expanded and encompassed my entire body from the waist up. During a few, with arms extended, the energy at the crown chakra would snap my entire body rigid and I knew beyond a doubt that this was the ecstatic rapture that is described in many religious texts, although the methods fomenting this are varied and always come down to Grace.

One other experience materialized on this remarkable morning, and despite the indescribable bliss pointed to above, reflecting back, it was actually the "main event" from what I've been able to discern. One of the primary goals and consequences of Kriya Yoga is burning karma and this, it now seems, was a colossal karmic purge. Somewhere in the 500+ Kriya range, my third eye (a.k.a. the Kutastha Chaitanya or the Christ Center) opened. My ability to keep track of time, along with exactly where I was in the

Kriya series when these peak events were occurring, was almost nonexistent. The ajna opening happens to me occasionally in meditation and sometimes even while not in formal meditation. Typically, in me it is large, about the size of a silver dollar, and rather than seeing the blue flame or the star [which Yogananda described in his teachings about the third eye], I typically see people, places, and events, most of which I don't recognize. The value of this is unknown and could be debated but it does what it does and as such, I simply don't care or wonder about it anymore. During this experience, however, the third eye was small; still circular but about one-half the size of a dime. Within it, I could very clearly see a face, and then another, and another, each lasting long enough to plainly see but not lasting so long that I could be distracted or get lost in them. In total, there were many hundreds of faces, of both men and women, of all races and ages, and of all shapes, sizes, and guises. I have no idea how long this took other than it just happened between one Kriya and the next. As with all true mystical experiences, this was outside the realm of time. At some point in the "slideshow," I was overwhelmed with the knowing that I was seeing my past incarnations flying by, and history points out that this sometimes is combined with a sudden, final Liberation or Awakening. Alas, while this was not the case with me, what did intensely permeate every fiber of my being and consciousness was that this massive Kriya-fueled happening was Grace-given and had burned the karmic ties to all the lifetimes that I had witnessed going by. At the end, I saw in my inner vision an immensely long train out in the desert with hundreds of boxcars slowly falling away, having been decoupled. All that was left was the engine and one boxcar, which intuitively represented the remaining karma for this incarnation.

In retrospect, I would add that while it may appear that we have many separate incarnations (for those who ascribe to the *concept* anyway), it is my knowing that there is actually only One Life. I love the poetic way that Wayne Dyer used to describe each incarnation: a parenthesis in eternity. Possibly, the metaphor of different life-chapters in the beginningless and endingless book of existence may convey the process as well. Nevertheless, in the end that all comes down to philosophy and semantics, and consequently is of no real interest to me. There is now only an ever-deepening embodiment of Awareness and Love. As this only happens in This Moment, the Direct Perception of Being is paramount.

Within a few days of this "karma-ectomy" [hmm…maybe I should trademark this term?!], Kriya stopped again and has not manifested since. The Grace of these two amazing events unfolded as it did and, as with The Kiss, I remain grateful and humbled beyond what words can convey. With all that's unfolded, *awakening has happened*. All that seems to remain now is to observe the residual karma burn and to dance The Dance with love and compassion for the benefit of all sentient beings.

With the culmination of these events, the rebirthing process was over. The ego-mind had been transcended, the Divine Hand on my shoulder had been lifted, and I was ready to re-enter the world and begin learning how to embody this fledgling awakening. There was awakened awareness in and as this mind-body but it had just come out of the womb.

While I had no idea where the awakening process was leading, as this portion of my "ride" was concluding, the core areas worked on now felt mostly addressed. Attachments had been cut, the illusion of being a separate self had been seen through and fallen away, and the kundalini-energetic issues and bliss had mostly subsided after grounding on Mount Shasta. Perhaps most importantly for my ability to work again, the loss of egoic-driven personal will had been integrated, giving way to the Love and Compassion of "Universal Will."

Dear friend, from the perspective of a "Monday morning quarterback" during football season, if I would have known when I started out on the spiritual path that all of this would have transpired, I might not have had the courage to begin. Fear not though, as not all awakenings unfold as mine did; some are much more gradual and easier! Then again, I wouldn't be doing my job here if I didn't say that some are even more cataclysmic than what I went through. One only has to read books by the late Bernadette Roberts or Suzanne Segal to see what a rough ride transcending the ego-mind can be. I suspect it all comes down to one's karma, or else awakenings would all be ecstatic and stress-free. Even with the easier ones, however, a complete, abiding transcendence and finally, the dropping away of the ego, is <u>never</u> a trivial thing. Nonetheless, it is the most blessed and wonderful evolutionary happening that we can strive for, so keep the faith my friend and keep on keeping on!

It is at this point that the next test of my mettle was about to commence, and it was imperative that I pass it. If I couldn't find a way to work again and make enough money to support myself…well, that was a road that I didn't want to go down. Whether there was some residual amount of optimism bias remaining or whether it was just unshakable faith stemming from everything I'd recently been through, I felt good about working again and more than a little interested to see what it would be like from this new place in/as consciousness. As bizarre as some of it turned out to be, my faith in this next phase of the Process was more than justified.

... It's also possible to live in a permanent, ongoing state of samadhi, called sahaja samadhi. In this state, samadhi becomes integrated into everyday life. You can live a completely normal human existence – working, eating, and interacting with other people, even thinking when necessary – and may appear to be a completely ordinary person. But inside, you have no sense of separateness, and are free of fear and desire. There's a continual sense of inner stillness, peace, and wholeness.

~ Steve Taylor

CHAPTER FOUR:
Entering The Marketplace

The next six months were a very unusual time for me. I was heading back into the business world that I remembered so well, and yet how I experienced it for all those years had changed. My training lasted for six weeks, four in Anaheim followed by two at the corporate office in Texas. From there, I spent twelve months on the road living in my company's hotels as an area GM, supporting thirteen properties in California along with three in Nevada. While most people settle down (or are already settled) when beginning a new job, due to the nature of my position, I found myself still on the road, living a nomadic existence. One monk at Hidden Valley aptly described me as a "wandering sadhu of the corporate world" and I feel that summed it up pretty well.

This chapter illustrates my feelings and observations as I did my best to return to my career but from a radically changed place in/as consciousness. Energies were still flowing to some extent, but nothing that was disorienting or debilitating. During this period, I learned that all my professional skills were still there, ready to be utilized when needed, but my goodness, everything else was very different! Before my Mt. Shasta trip, I was struggling with disorientation and being unable to clearly articulate the deepening insights that were arising. Here, I think you'll notice a clearer, more confident voice, as I was starting to get my sea legs, so to speak. This first email was written just two days before heading off to Anaheim.

August 8, 2018

"With the eyes of a child
You must come out and see
That your world's spinning 'round
And through life you will be
A small part
Of a hope
Of a love
That exists
In the eyes of a child, you will see"

~ Excerpt from Eyes of a Child by The Moody Blues

Icing on the cake, as it were, one of the sweetest things about the inner Stillness and unfiltered Directness of Perception that goes with Being Here Now (Sahaja) is that, unlike garden-variety looking, one sees with the wonder-filled eyes and heart of a child. I'm reminded of Marcel Proust's profound adage: "The real voyage of discovery consists not in seeking new landscapes, but in having new eyes." Aside from the obvious content of Manifestation, the context people *infer* and then *judge* is simply a reflection of their own individuated consciousness – the little wave in and as the Infinite Ocean of Conscious-Energy. The proverbial "We don't see things as they are, we see them as we are" aptly points to this. Most little waves, sadly, are typically laden with incessant thought, multi-sourced conditioning, and ego-attachments, coupled with the illusion of separateness that catalyzes loneliness and at the root…fear. In the "I Am," the "mirror" of our individuated wave of consciousness is clean, thereby allowing Pure Perception. Despite the ego-mind's bent for spiritual complexity, this is all actually quite simple!

It's been said that when a small child points to a cloud, or a tree, or a bird, *or whatever,* and asks "what's that?" after they're told "that's a bird" they never really see the bird again. I would attempt to mitigate this by responding "we call that a bird" but I digress. From then on, the mind labels and stores it conceptually in memory. However, as Sri H. W. L. Poonja (Papaji) noted in his classic tome *The Truth Is,* "**All concepts are borders**." Seemingly, there is no way around this as it is an eminently practical and necessarily developed evolutionary process that allows one to survive and function in the world. Despite this, through the God-given Grace that has befallen me over the last year, I have experientially realized that it is indeed possible for *anyone* to reestablish their innate, original, natural Awareness, just as Yoganandaji pointed to when he said Awakening was "the birthright" of everyone. When in the Beingness of Sahaja, one is blessed with options, so to speak, depending on what's needed; to look or to <u>see</u>.

I might have mentioned during one of our earlier jam sessions [spiritual dialogues] that Sahaja comes and goes, being my natural waking state 2/3 to 3/4 of the day, give or take. Obviously, there is no way to track or measure this, even if there were *anyone there* to do it! Nevertheless, it manifests more fully and deeply with each passing month and I have no doubt as to the *inevitability* of an abiding Sahaja, with the *when* and *how* of its unfolding irrelevant and not even remotely a question or concern in the mind. The Process has become totally natural, spontaneous, and easy, with no personal volition involved. With the integration and stabilization journey stemming from The Kiss now appearing mostly complete, the gradually flowing Process of "filling in the missing pieces" has actually become quite fun and adventurous!

Christ's pointer to "become like little children" never meant anything to me until after The Kiss. When I walk around the ashram or anywhere now, and take in the birds, clouds, trees, people, etc. I <u>see</u> them anew, *just as they are*, with no evaluations, classifications, or judgments, and it's so preciously magical and beautiful! Prosaic though things often appeared to my former eyes, in the Stillness and Clear Seeing of Sahaja, everything and everyone becomes miraculous, vibrant, wondrous, dynamic, holy. The illusion of separation completely falls away – Oneness IS – and my heart swells with love, compassion, and appreciation for All Things.

In my walk last night, this song from my youth [quoted above], included on their superlative *To Our Children's Children's Children* album, came to me in a flash, along with everything just written. And so, I thought I'd share it with you in today's installment of the *Still Kickin'* series, even though some of this has been discussed in our talks over the course of this last year.

Phil

When I talk about living fearlessly, it's worth pointing out that there are two kinds of fear. There is an instinctual fear (an escalated startle response, I suppose) that is built into the body-mind apparatus that still serves us and, to my knowledge, never goes away. This type of fear catalyzes the familiar fight-or-flight response, which was present, for instance, during my late-night visitor while camping on Mt. Shasta. The fear that is <u>transcended</u> by awakening is psychological fear, i.e. *living* from the place of fear. Fear of the unknown (which is every moment) is an obvious example. When radical acceptance and trust in This Moment are present, fear-based thoughts and living fall away.

While on my way back from Mammoth Lakes, California, where I was interviewed and hired for my new gig, I went on a hike to see the ancient bristlecone pine forest. The next day, a heart-related health scare put me in the emergency room of a hospital for part of a day. Although nothing came of it as far as diagnosis or treatment went, the doctors did advise me to eschew five-mile hikes at 10,000 feet. Yeah, I know, not the brightest idea I've ever had, but the mountains and the forest were calling, and as it was with John Muir, I had to go!

Due to my recent hospital visit, a monastic friend caringly asked me to email him each day. Given his busy schedule and my reclusiveness, this was an easy way for him to know that I was all right, hence my calling this email sequence *Still Kickin'*. Since I was going to be doing this, it seemed logical that rather than sending blank emails I might as well put something of value in them. Thus, each day I sent him a quote or book excerpt that meant something to me at the time. Given the extraordinary events of the last eleven months, it's fair to say that the few people who knew what had been happening with me were more than curious about how this next stage would unfold!

August 18, 2018

Thank you so much for checking in on me. Yep, I concur, I'll take HVA over Disneyland any day that ends with the letter y! [I wasn't working for Disney but training at a nearby hotel.] However, to each their own and for all the impossibly cute little people I see running around, adorned with mouse ears, fairy wings, and enormous smiles, I'm glad Mickey and his friends have this place.

The training is going very well. The way they have it designed, coupled with the large investment they make (six weeks total), it is a very comprehensive introduction to the company. It'd be too much to write about but working with/in/as this new non-dual awareness is, well...*fascinating!* It's not that it's either on or off. Its underlying Presence is always here as you know, but being almost permanently settled into it now I'm not sure how to explain it other than saying the Silent Mind is somehow "set aside" in order to use the thinking mind. Six months ago, this was not always possible. Late last year? F-o-r-g-e-t it! Due to worldly [financial] circumstances, I would have liked to have gotten going with work sooner, but given the big picture, it all unfolded as it was meant to, hence our need for trust and surrender.

The body seems to be holding up well from an energy standpoint. The heart, which still has its odd moments from time to time, will either make it until I have insurance or it won't but God willing, I have the sense that it will. Either way, there's no worry or thought about it.

PW

The next email was another dear friend checking in on me. This individual holds a very special place in my heart for many reasons; perhaps the greatest reason is that she and her partner at the time introduced me to Adyashanti before I left for Texas and Georgia. As a result, the entire course of my post-Kiss sadhana changed, and my gratitude for this cannot be expressed in words.

August 20, 2018

Hi there and thank you so much for your email! I can only speak from my experience, which is different and/or limited compared with Adya's. I would posit that the *goal* or *desire* of "merging" or achieving "union" with God/Spirit/Source is an illusion, as there is no real separation possible. We're not "achieving" union but rather, we're "losing" the feeling of separateness or, in other words, "realizing/remembering" that We Already Are One With Everything. For me, the mind-blowing thing is, in this everything-ness is also nothing-ness, along with nowhere-ness and everywhere-ness!

The surrender necessary for all this seems to come from the amazing realization that, when drilling down deeply into our sense of "self," we find that there's nothing there! There's simply nowhere to stand and nothing to hold on to, and this is when [the illusion of the separate] self appears to be most open, *vulnerable,* to transcendence. For me, this realization was made manifest through Grace. It was nothing I did or could have done! This isn't stated in humility but in fact, as the "I" that seemed to be there…wasn't! Ego simply doesn't have any inherent separate reality of its own, so how can it "do" *anything?* Unfortunately, reading and hearing this doesn't generally do the trick. The Ultimate Understanding just seems to unfold as It Will and while mostly there, this is still a Process that continues to deepen/unfold in me as well. While grounded (i.e. stabilized) into Sahaja for the most part, the stew continues to be seasoned and stirred, so to speak.

What really helped me post-Kiss was Adya talking about surrendering Self, as it seems to be common that people get stuck there after transcending the self. The high states of Self are amazing, what with siddhis sometimes manifesting and potent energies flowing in/out, often along with immense feelings of love, peace, bliss, and all the rest. Who wouldn't want to hang out in that?! And yet, Adya helped me to see and ultimately experience that these too must be surrendered in order for Sahaja to happen. I believe this speaks to his initial point about one's spiritual orientation. If we're oriented to make our sadhana about *giving* then we naturally will surrender the Self, which moves us beyond Oneness of Self and Spirit into the Oneness of Sahaja, which has actually been described as the natural state (also described as a no-state or non-experience). This surrender isn't done to *get something* though, as that's not authentic surrender. I can't tell you how to surrender authentically, as I don't know. It seems to simply come down to Grace, karma, and one's [spiritual evolutionary] ripeness.

I don't know if anything I have written here has even addressed your questions my friend; it's just what came up from and out of consciousness. Please believe me when I tell you that I really don't feel that I know much, if anything! All these books and talks serve us to a point but the danger in them is the ego-mind will try to latch onto it all. Then, whether we know it consciously or not, anticipation and pressure for Grace to unfold can build, which only serves to restrict Grace! My general advice to anyone, if asked, would be to tell them to relax into it and not concern oneself with the timing of it.

Phil

While I was using the term "sahaja" a lot during this period, here now I don't feel that it's the best pointer for where I was at this juncture. The "baby Buddha" stage has aspects of sahaja but it's not firmly there yet. The reason I used the word at the time, and why I chose the epigraph for this chapter, is that awakened beingness was integrating into the world without a sense of doership or separateness and in a constant state of stillness and peace. I don't think there is a single word to best describe the immediate aftermath of an awakening, especially if it's not abiding – which for me didn't transpire for another six months.

These next correspondences find me in the lone star state and my two-weeks there were fascinating!

September 10, 2018

Dear Friend: What a day! I'm not sure what to say. My participation in today's training events was like relying on muscle memory. The knowledge is all there, somewhere, and the correct stuff comes out of the mouth and yet…inwardly it feels as if *I am disappearing.* At one point in the training the emptiness/awareness inside the head felt so VAST that it was like there was *no head* and that the entire room WAS in my head. The "outside" had become my "inside" or, put another way, there was no inside/outside but rather, there was only empty-aware-space. I was all but gone. That doesn't really do it justice but words aren't going to cut it for this. This emptiness is not that full/complete/deep (not sure of the best word) all day (as it is in this moment) but as I have mentioned before it's intensifying, like waves climbing the shore as the tide waxes. This was happening in Anaheim too but not as…vast.

What more can be said? It's beautiful. It has <u>all</u> my attention. I remain grateful for What Is. But "what" <u>is</u> "it" that "is?" I just don't know. The wonderful thing about this is that I am OK with not knowing. I Trust. I Love. I Am.

Phil

September 14, 2018

The training continues to unfold very well and it's been both fun and interesting. My penchant for humor has been in top form this week. I have by far the most extensive experience of anyone here, and on the second day was given the name, "the professor." I'm not sure though, it might just be my gray hair and reading glasses!

There have been some interesting comments [during the company training] which I attribute to Presence. One young woman told me that even though I was participating a lot in the group (approx. 24 people), when I wasn't she told me, "You seem so quiet, I can't help but wonder what you are thinking and taking in." I just smiled and shrugged, as telling her there was *no thought* and *no one taking anything in* didn't seem like a good idea. Another time, they had an image on the screen that had no definite answer as to what it was, leaving it up to each person to interpret its meaning. When the trainer asked me what I "saw," out of the stillness came a quiet, matter-of-fact, "I see what is." You can imagine the looks I received! The trainer, looking up to the ceiling, repeated my answer and softly said, "He's blowing me away." Now, if she had asked me what I was "looking" at, well, I'm guessing there would probably have been a much different and more conventional answer!

Finally, we've been doing some role playing so they can practice coaching, counseling, and motivating employees. After watching me this morning [doing it without any practice or preparation – extemporaneously] the young man who was with me in Anaheim suddenly looked up at me and with a bit of wonder said, "You're like a Zen Master." Shrugging, I felt as if he was saying it to no one and nothing. So, it's been very interesting!

Phil

Around this period, the kundalini energy began manifesting differently. It was greatly diminished internally and had instead become more of a Transmitting

Presence that people around me couldn't help but notice on some level, or fail to comment on. As it <u>was</u> peculiar, thankfully this Presence subsided after the awakening became abiding. While I cannot say for sure, it appeared that the more normal non-dual awareness became for me, the less perceptible the Presence was, and therefore the more normal I came across to others. At this point, normal (whatever that is) was looking good! While all my skills and experience could be accessed, there was no thinking about it first.

October 13, 2018

Hello my friend and thank you so much for sharing your recent sadhana experiences! It seems that you have adopted a wise strategy in just letting It do what It Will. I've found The Process to be intelligent, and that includes the energies that flow within and without. From my experience, energies in and around the crown (and other) chakras are a natural part of The Process. I have no idea how or why It does what It does but then, I don't need to know! At times, Its [kundalini in the ajna and crown chakras] felt like ants crawling around, at times like some giant, pulsating frog jumping up and down in and outside the head, and at times like there's a triangle of energy flowing between the medulla, the ajna, and the crown. I've come to observe/regard all spiritual experiences and phenomena with a "grateful indifference." Gratitude for what Spirit is doing but indifferent to it, so as to not become sidetracked from the inner stillness and/or possibly become attached to whatever is happening. Comparing What Is Now to *what was then* robs us of Being Present. In regards to my sadhana, over the years inner <u>Stillness</u> became the main component of my unfoldment until this last year, when everything was turned upside down and inside out. Not out of choice or by design but rather, that's simply where God has taken me – and "I" am just along for the ride.

I strongly encourage you to go over all this with [one of the monks] when you meet with him, as he's much more knowledgeable about all things Kriya than I am. All I can share is the experiences that have unfolded within this mind-body organism, and it's different for everyone. I always encourage people to allow The Process to become unique within them, rather than try to duplicate or emulate what's happened to someone else…as if we could somehow limit what is essentially an infinite process to our preference or concept of *how we think it should look!* To allow as much time for talking as possible, you may want to forward your monastic counselor your message to me in advance of your meeting and if you like, my reply here as well. There's nothing confidential here on my part. Please remember that he's the professional in this area. I'm just an incredibly fortunate average guy who has been blessed with much Grace in this life.

Please keep me posted as things progress. As I mentioned to you last, I've had a strong feeling that given how our conversations came together (not something I typically do there, along with what you've been describing to me), your sadhana may be taking an interesting turn! When it happens, and in what direction it moves, I have no idea. In our Openness to Everything, while being attached to nothing, Spirit/Grace is freer to do as It Will and based in my experiences, it is a privilege to witness It unfold.

Phil

I didn't notice at first, but in the fall of 2018 I began to receive emails from friends who wanted to discuss and/or ask questions about their spiritual journey. I certainly never set out to adopt the role of some sort of spiritual teacher or counselor. Nor is it my intention to do this by publishing *Grace Happens*. Up until this was published, only a handful of people even knew about the awakening, which was how I wanted it. However, that didn't prevent emails from starting to be exchanged or discussions being held. I cannot say whether what was communicated through Phil was useful to those who sought his observations and counsel, but I can state that through their questions and through our dialogues, Phil not only became more proficient in talking about the awakening but it also seemed as if, cognitively, he understood it better. Saint Francis said in his famous prayer, "For it is in giving that we receive" and this is true due to one fundamental aspect of Reality – "there is only one of us in the room" (an expression from CWG that I really love).

December 26, 2018

I am very glad to hear that my email and the pointers I shared resonated with you to some degree. One never knows! Since September of last year it's been terra incognita for what's left of the mind-body known as Phil. Given this, having a few close friends who can, to one degree or another, relate and offer support has been immensely helpful. With the integration mostly over (I really liked Adyashanti's definition of integration [see epigraph of chapter five]) there now seems to simply be a "karmic runoff" of what's left [the inescapable elimination of remaining unspent energies and desires]. There's really nothing much left – to "do" <u>or</u> of "me." It's extremely odd to have lost the self-referentiality of an "inner life" and having it substituted with something that's essentially impersonal. That might sound, and I'm certain would be, somewhat hollow or even depressing, if it weren't for the co-arising deep, intimate interconnectedness with All Things, along with the increasing love and compassion that goes with it. I never could have foreseen such a thing but that's no surprise really, as *the ego-mind simply cannot see or imagine what is beyond itself.* While my spiritual practices did, in fact, leave me "Grace prone," as Adya puts it, it still all comes down to God's Grace Happening, which leaves one feeling immensely grateful and humbled beyond what mere words can convey.

PW

By early 2019 I was almost feeling "normal" again, as in how I felt pre-Kiss. Except now there was an *abiding* Directness of Perception and Non-Dual Aware Consciousness. Whereas there had been an ebb and flow of this for thirteen months – the "I got it, I lost it" that Adya often talks about – it suddenly dawned on me one day early in the New Year that it wasn't ebbing anymore. There was just Flow. There was now a visceral, self-authenticating (i.e. self-validating) awareness-experience of Being One with/as All Things. There was no doer, no separation, no "me." From this Beingness, a much deeper integration and acclimation was able to transpire. As this unfolded, I was no longer just on the mountaintop (chapters two and three) or in the marketplace (chapter four). Instead, throughout the first eight months of 2019, I gradually became accustomed to having one foot firmly entrenched in both, indicating that the awakening was becoming stabilized and more mature. I was really taken with the following passage and felt it perfectly summarized things to this point and moving forward (bold emphases mine):

> When you awaken to truth as it really is, you will have no occult vision, you will have no "astral" experience, no ravishing ecstasy. **You will awaken to it in a state of utter stillness, and you will realize that truth was always there within you and that reality was always there around you.** Truth is not something which has grown and developed through your efforts. It is not something

which has been achieved or attained by laboriously adding up those efforts. It is not something which has to be made more and more perfect each year. And **once your mental eyes are opened to truth they can never be closed again.**

~ *The Short Path to Enlightenment: Instructions for Immediate Awakening* by Paul Brunton

> *Sheila: Is this integration?*
>
> *Adyashanti: ... It's not my favorite word. It's just a concept. It's not inherently a rotten concept, but it tends to mean, "I've had some sort of spiritual experience and spiritual practice. I've meditated and feel peaceful and good, and I want to bring that feeling into my workspace, my relationships, or into me." As soon as we're trying to integrate on this level, we're actually missing the whole transformative element and the truth that you cannot take something that's infinite and stuff it into a small box called "my life."*
>
> *It's actually the reverse. We take "my life" and we release it into the infinite emptiness and space of true being. This is inherent, so we could say this is integrating, but it's integrating opposite, or upside down of the way it's usually done. Usually when we hear about integration, there's still a personal self that's controlling, that's integrating, that's trying desperately to bring their deepest experiences into their everyday lives. The impulse to do so is totally understandable. But this really, deeply misses the point. The point is actually something that is much more frightening to the personal self, where I'm releasing my life into something vast, into something unknown, into something unknowable, and I'm basically releasing my personal control. If you can pull that off, you've got integration. But you don't have integration that you have control of.*
>
> *~ John J. Prendergast, Peter Fenner, & Sheila Krystal (editors)*

CHAPTER FIVE:
Integration And Acclimation

Entering this pivotal phase, there are several salient themes to be cognizant of. First, the awakening had evolved past the "I had it, I lost it" phase into an abiding non-dual awareness-experience, and I was finally beginning to fire on all cylinders. My insights continued to deepen, and there was much more naturalness in my embodiment of them. Stemming from this, the emails moving forward largely speak for themselves, hence this chapter (and the next) being email-centric with less commentary. Some readers of the early drafts of this section commented that the energy of the emails shifted markedly, as if I was announcing, "I Am Awake, hear me roar." I never thought about it but in comparison to my earlier correspondences, I see why it might appear that way.

While there had been a contentment to simply "Be" in the aftermath of The Kiss, a subtle change and Impulse-Inclination towards "movement" occurred entering 2019. This is not the "outer" movement that was described in chapter four regarding my returning to the working world, but rather an "inner" movement: the rekindling of my sadhana. I no longer felt like a newborn baby. From here on out, I felt like a rapidly developing toddler moving straight into adolescence. The method my sadhana chose surprised me – I was reading again. The fascinating aspect of this was that the books I had were all reflecting my emerging insights! Much of what I was reading was helping to put a vocabulary to the Truth that I knew and was living from but couldn't yet explain very well on my own. There were a multitude of quotes and passages being shared in my emails (with only a few represented here due to space constraints) that went far beyond supplemental, sagely-sounding axioms, but rather were the pith of my deepening insights. With the re-emergence of reading as a part of my sadhana, I realized that this technology had changed for me. Pre-awakening, spiritual reading was mostly bolstering intellectual erudition, with little in the way of a lived experience of it. In other words, in the beginning of my spiritual journey, I was becoming more educated about spirituality and metaphysics, but it wasn't changing *where I was living from* a whole lot. In stark contrast to this, now non-dual awareness was present in every moment, while my intellect was the one playing catch-up.

The last significant theme of this chapter is the growing integration and harmonization of the Mind-Heart (i.e. Wisdom-Love) aspects that Nisargadatta pointed to in his classic quote mentioned in chapter three (email dated 11-6-17). Much of the wisdom aspect is seen in my early emails, while the heart aspect reveals itself in the latter ones. With all this came an intense desire to serve. Whereas early on post-Kiss, I couldn't find a reason to get out of bed due to the loss of personal will, that had been replaced with love and compassion for all sentient beings. I was now Realizing the fundamental purpose of the awakening that I had been blessed with – to unconditionally give without goal, agenda, or expectation – to just give!

January 10, 2019

An intimate, transforming Awakening in consciousness happened. Now it's been acclimated to, it has left me here, in the very place Llewellyn Vaughan-Lee speaks of – being the fulcrum between the Absolute and the Here Now physical plane, and why it is so important to our world, now more than ever. Intuitively there was/is an understanding of this already. However, Llewellyn's book [*For Love of the Real*] paints such a beautiful and articulate picture of this Beingness of the proverbial "one foot on the mountaintop and one foot in the marketplace" that I just had to share it with you. For me, to this point the most reassuring, hopeful, and beautiful thing about our unfoldment is that the depth of Awakening never ends: "… swimming in the infinite ocean, who is nearer the shore?"
~ Radha Mohan Lal

There's been an ever-deepening knowing that here now, it's not about "me" but rather where and how I may be of service. Whatever preferences "I" may have are irrelevant it would seem. And, there is no "personal I" that chooses…God chooses for us, once the personal self is gone. While there are still a few shreds of a personal Phil remaining, it's such a small amount, seemingly, that post-Kiss there's no turning back now and…no one that would want to. There's an impersonal quality to it, in that the sense of having a "self-referential inner life" is gone. But concurrent with this is an *ever-deepening experience* of Connectedness to All Things that *makes love, compassion and service the only reasons for bodily existence. Every day it feels as if I am being emptied of what's left. And in the emptiness, I am filled evermore with Love.* I cannot write or share this without tears of gratitude gently falling from my ever-opening eyes.

Phil

While I sent my friend a number of the passages from Llewellyn's book that deeply spoke to me, the one below is my favorite, as it speaks to where I was finding myself – having the ego annihilated and having learned to float in the formless. An abiding awakening had begun.

> Sufism is defined as "Truth without form," and in the words of the Sufi martyr al-Hallāj, "When Truth has taken hold of a heart, she empties it of all but Herself." This is the process of annihilation, fanā that leads

to baqā, abiding in God. You can only abide in God after you have been annihilated, after you are no longer there.

January 20, 2019

Here now, it appears from the non-dual Beingness in consciousness that is Phil, what de Chardin was pointing to is what is happening at this stage of the new, ascending Yuga – both individually and collectively. I am especially taken with the text I put a bold emphasis on:

"... It is as if the physical world comes into being so that consciousness can become aware of its own nature. This is reminiscent of the French Jesuit theologian Pierre Teilhard de Chardin's idea that the universe is directed towards a goal that he called the "Omega Point." He conceived of this as **an evolutionary impulse within humanity, as well as within the universe itself, that was ascending towards consciousness, resulting in an individuated consciousness directly (re)cognizing its own nature**. At de Chardin's Omega Point there is a direct, non-conceptual comprehension of the ground of "being" by the fundamental cognizant aspect of the ground of 'being itself,' with human beings as the instruments through which this realization occurs. At the Omega Point our true nature recognizes, comprehends, and illumines itself. **From the atemporal point of view, we are already at the Omega Point, and what is happening in our world is the footprint of this realization projected backwards in time**. This is to say that the events playing out in linear time are the very vehicle through which the Omega Point realizes itself through us – provided, of course, that we recognize that this is the case."

~ *Quantum Revelation: A Radical Synthesis of Science and Spirituality* by Paul Levy

Fascinating stuff to contemplate and a great new book too by the way!

Phil

While this strays more into philosophy that my actual experience (something I've tried not to indulge in much while writing this book), I feel this is a worthwhile concept to examine. Teilhard's "evolutionary impulse" has always rung true to me, as All Things are Absolutely Interconnected. Consciousness then is always evolving, both at the macro level and within the smallest subatomic particle. Moreover, but somewhat counterintuitively, this is not a necessarily linear progression, as that is a function of how our brains process data through the senses. To use a fitting word from the CWG material, everything is happening "sequentaneously." In other words, the knowing and the experiencing are happening sequentially *and* simultaneously! This paradox is an example of the non-dualistic "both-and" paradigm as opposed to the much more conventional "either-or" that logic prefers. Post-awakening, I saw that linear time is a mental construct within mind-projected duality, and that when duality ceases, the retro-causality that de Chardin was putting forth became self-evident. Before your brain has a meltdown, modern-day physics supports this, so it's not just a metaphysical theory, although it is interesting to note that metaphysics was positing this a couple thousand years before our current scientific models came up with it!

Even though this splits Oneness (non-duality) into twoness (duality), which can't be done, let's look at this from both perspectives: the relative and the absolute. In relativity, there is a "future pull," so to speak, from an Omega Point already actualized. From a place of egoic-consciousness, we think that we're the ones who start the search for God and Self-Realization, but it is God in and as this Omega Point that is pulling All Things toward It. The ego, not knowing any better, co-opts this Impulse and declares itself a "spiritual seeker" or some such thing, and *another identity is created*. But the ego (which is a fiction!) cannot <u>do</u> this or anything else. It is the Universal Impulse, both in and as us, that sparks evolutionary and involutionary movement within the relativity of Conscious Manifestation. Now, setting the dualistic framework aside for a moment, which de Chardin was operating from, The Absolute (The Godhead) has no viewpoint. Nevertheless, as a pointer one could say that if It did have one, it would be that *there is no movement*. Nothing evolves. Nothing has happened, or is happening, or ever will happen. As paradoxes go, this may be the ultimate one!

January 21, 2019

I have been cognizant of quantum theory, at least from a layman's perspective, for many years. What deeply grabs me about this subject *right now* is that it very simply and clearly points to my Direct Perception of Reality. In a sense, the Christian mystic "Cloud of Unknowing" is analogous to the "possibility field" of the wave function. There are times when this Beingness known as Phil is so deeply in the Unknowing of the Now, that *in each moment the knowing is found!* Language sometimes fails me and therefore, I continue to wish that I had the articulation abilities of the great spiritual and scientific communicators. This is no doubt one reason why I continue to share the books and teachings that keep finding me. It's been miraculous!

Conscious manifestation comes into Being in every moment but the only way to directly experience it (not truly an *experience* as there is no subject-object but again, words are clumsy) is to BE the Stillness of the Unknowing/Knowing. The **Interconnectedness** can be felt – it can be seen – it is what the Is-ness/Beingness IS…dependently co-arising. [The following are two excerpts that I sent to my friends with this email, bold emphases by me.]

"The Buddhist sage Nagarjuna expresses this same state of '(no)-things' when he says, 'Things derive their being and nature by mutual dependence and are nothing in themselves.' In Buddhism, this state of 'no-thingness' or emptiness is characterized by a process known as 'dependent co-arising,' which is considered to be the very condition of and process by which empirical reality is constituted. In dependent co-arising, **we are dreaming up the universe, but in a circular, nonlinear, and acausal process that exists outside of time, the universe is dreaming us up to dream it up**, ad infinitum and vice versa. In other words, **every part of the universe evokes and is concurrently evoked by every other part** in a seamless expression of undivided wholeness."

"**Dependent coarising is not a belief or a theory to which one assents, but an insight that one is invited to experience and encouraged to win through focused and disciplined inquiry.** This view is not a final affirmation about reality, as it doesn't seek to define a reality external to the observer, instead it is a way of seeing that focuses on how our experience of the world and ourselves arises."

~ *Quantum Revelation: A Radical Synthesis of Science and Spirituality* by Paul Levy

Phil

February 8, 2019

I would agree that The Ground of Being, or The Holy Spirit as you put it, can indeed be Self-Realized by *anyone,* as it is our essence. There isn't anything that It is not, hence the illusion of separateness being the fundamental root of all suffering. I wouldn't say that it has been, as you stated, "stepped on, mutated" etc. as It remains untouched and pure. Only in the ego's illusory attempt to prove its inherent reality do we, as you wrote, "detour" and "tangle up" our lives, thinking we're something we're not – usually the body and/or some type of skin-encapsulated ego confronting a universe "out there." It's all a projection of mind.

Consider this passage: "If we are asleep to the dreamlike nature of the universe, it is easy to fall into what [David] Bohm calls 'self-deception' (Buddha called this 'avidya,' i.e., 'not seeing,' 'ignorance') through which, by misunderstanding the nature of ourselves, the universe, and our place in it, we unwittingly and unnecessarily enslave ourselves. By failing to comprehend the nature of our situation we lacerate and cripple both the universe and ourselves, erroneously misidentifying with a false, separate self that is seemingly disconnected from the whole."

~ *Quantum Revelation: A Radical Synthesis of Science and Spirituality*
by Paul Levy

The Truth can and indeed does shine through as you say! However, I would not ascribe it to "luck." That's where the passage by Adyashanti I sent you about being "Grace prone" really hits the nail on the head. That's what spiritual practices are ultimately designed to do – they diminish the self enough to where Consciousness flowing from The Godhead *Wakes up to Itself.* If there is one vital message from what I have written about since The Kiss, it is this – if it can happen to me it can happen to anyone – and It does happen – and It will happen. Ultimately, *inevitably,* It <u>has</u> to happen because that is Who and What We Are – All That Is. Yogananda called it "Spirit and Nature Dancing Together." Or in other terms, The Absolute and The Relative or, The Godhead and Consciousness or, The Unmanifest and The Manifest or, The Field of Pure Potentiality and The Field of Actuality. There are lots of descriptive pointers. In the "optical illusion of consciousness" that Einstein famously spoke of, we think we're a noun when we're really a verb! We mistake ourselves as "the dancer" when in fact, we're The Dancing. [A metaphor that Adya sometimes uses and one that I have always found extremely appropriate.]

That's all that's coming through for now. After all, I'm the writing not the writer! The thing is, this isn't a concept…it's my reality now. Unfortunately, none of this can be Realized conceptually by the mind. In the same way, using the standard definition of the word, it's not even an "experience" as ultimately, when the realization is complete, there is no one there to split the subject from the assumed, inferred illusory object. Duality is mind-projected! Fortunately, Absolute Unicity is a Beingness that IS, when all else falls away. That's why sadhana is a Process of subtraction not addition. What could possibly be added to All There Is?!

Phil

February 13, 2019

Hey there:

"Niels Bohr (1885-1962), considered the father of quantum physics and a scientist whose reputation is only slightly less lofty than Einstein's (1879-1955), was among the first to conclude that physical objects do not have an independent, objective reality. He stated categorically that physical objects only appear when we observe them—and his assertion has never been disproven. Welcome to Wonderland."

~ *The Physics of God* by Joseph Selbie

Adi Shankara famously (and in the paradoxical style of quantum mechanics) said:

"The world is illusory;
Brahman alone is real;
Brahman is the world."

My favorite description of reality comes from Swami Muktananda. When asked, "What is real?" he replied, "**What is real is that which never changes.**" If this is true, *what never changes?!* Nothing known in all of manifestation never changes. This then, does point to consciousness (and therefore everything in it) being a *projection* and not a separate, independent, objectively real "thing." The physical universe, including the higher planes of consciousness such as the astral and causal realms, may be "relatively" real but they are not "absolutely" real. What then, is projecting consciousness? The Christian mystic Meister Eckhart called it "The Godhead." It's called "The Void" in Zen, and "The Absolute" in other eastern spiritual traditions. In science, one hears terms such as "The Field of Pure Potentiality" and "The Quantum Plenum of Pure Infinite Potential," all of which seem to point to the same thing – God as the unmoved mover. As you say, quantum physics has indeed taken the world into the realm of metaphysics, much to the head-in-hands consternation of some physicists!

It's all interesting, fascinating really. However, unless one uses the revelations coming from quantum mechanics and/or the age-old pointers of (primarily) eastern spirituality, then it's just mind-play. Intellectually interesting certainly, but of limited value, assuming awakening is one's goal. I've found that after the fact, all this does fill in some of the missing pieces but none of it will get one there by itself. Both the search for and the ultimate Truth of Reality are always and only, it seems, found within.

PW

May 1, 2019

Hello! As far as you kindly stating I was "releasing the ego" and "putting aside my ego" *well*...I know it doesn't make much sense to the mind but truly, "I" did neither of these things and no one else can either. It just "happens" when the time is ripe. The illusion of separateness, of an individual self, cannot be set aside because *there is no one there to do the setting aside and there is no individual self to be set aside*. It's the damnedest thing! Prior to The Kiss, I understood this concept intellectually but it didn't affect how I lived. Once Awakening to a sufficient degree happens, there's simply no one left to receive the applause. No sense of achievement and no inner life. Any idea of attainment or doership becomes a palliative for self-referentiality. It doesn't sound like a sales pitch for beginning and slogging through the spiritual path but it turns out, that's how it is. Ultimately, like so many others, I have found that the depth of Awakening is measured by *where we live our life from* in the ordinary, everyday contextual field that Consciousness Is. We Already Are That Which We Seek. The spiritual path isn't moving from a place where we are to a place where we're not. It just seems to be a process of letting go of *everything* and ultimately Realizing we are both no-thing and therefore everything! Life becomes miraculous and wondrous, along with being quite ordinary and, at times, still challenging and not so fun. All in all, where I find myself now is so very odd and yet, it also seems as if it couldn't have unfolded any other way. For me, the most beautiful realization, other than our Oneness with All Things, is that the deepening of Awakening never ends. Everything in physical form is "awake" to the degree it is, and everything just keeps on waking up... forever. It is Awareness, in and as the medium of Consciousness, waking up to Itself! [Of course, It's already fully awake but what I was referring to here was the infinite localized expressions of It becoming more awake.] Awareness dreams up everything in and as Consciousness, which then dreams up Awareness. It appears to be a recursive, never-ending process of Being and Non-Being.

The following passage from *The Impact of Awakening* by Adyashanti points to this [and it's one of the most influential things from Adya that I've ever read]:

"This is not the liberation that most people envision when they start out. Consciously or unconsciously, most people envision a freedom that they can attain and possess. Many who glimpse the enlightened condition tell me that it is so much bigger than they ever could have imagined. To realize that freedom is not something that you possess, but something that possesses you, is often experienced as shocking, frightening, and unbelievably liberating. It is a revelation that swallows up the dream of a separate you and reveals Self to be a limitless expanse. What I am describing is the experience of Self void of any sense of selfhood, a timeless and uncaused condition which is constantly birthing manifest existence into form.

To have a glimpse of this profound freedom requires very little, but to live it requires the destruction of every concept of self you have ever held or will ever hold. This freedom is a flame that burns the need to struggle to ash and reveals one's Self to be all that is."

Phil

Now roughly twenty months into the awakening process, Adya's books (as opposed to his audios that I'd been relying on to this point) became incredibly helpful as I started reading again. They put words around the intimate and visceral awareness-experience of the Beingness that I Was. Until this point, there wasn't a clear conceptual understanding of this, or a serviceable vocabulary to express it.

While this wasn't intentional on my part (nor was I cognizant of it) from here on, the tone of my writings in this chapter shifted from the wisdom aspect of awakened (non-dual) consciousness to the heart aspect of it. As these polarities are fundamental to our true nature, the post-awakening path becomes *Being* an ever-clearer expression of these two and, as far as I can see, this never ends.

June 1, 2019

Based on my experience in the desert in late 2017 and early 2018, I'd suggest that you keep as inwardly still as possible and with that, as deeply as possible, holding back nothing, FEEL whatever comes up, even if you think it'll kill you. Don't worry, it won't! Don't evaluate it, censor it, or moderate it – just feel.

But with that, try to remain as the Awareness that is giving space to that which is being felt, or at least be the Witness, which is about half way there. We can't deny the feelings that go with being human, nor should we, as it's not healthy. However, from a different perspective, we're not what we're feeling (or thinking!) either, even though it often seems that way at the time.

To me, *processing* means feeling what is felt fully and completely. But if we maintain the sense of Awareness that We Are, in and as our true essence, then what is felt doesn't take us over. In other words, we don't identify with it. If you do identify with it for a while, that's perfectly OK too, as that happens. There is no right or wrong here. But the more we're consciously aware and present, the less the identification with that which is being felt or thought, and the quicker the processing "process" unfolds, or so I've discovered anyway. If what is being processed doesn't completely flow through, there will be some amount of energy that gets stuck and eventually it has to be processed again, somewhere down the road. Why chew your karmic cabbage twice?!

Above all, please don't try to be more or different or better than you are right now. Only the ego-mind does that. Realization, Awakening, these happen in the perfect time and place. Just fully Be This Moment Now, which includes you and everything else in The Universe. That's enough! And, when one is fully This Moment in all moments, one finds oneself Awake!

Phil

As one of my monastic pals is wont to say, it's a fascinating "privilege" to watch Spirit as She works through us when there is no one to get in the way. Occasionally (as was the case with the above email), an impulse comes to write and it's so strong that it literally makes me jump up, grab my iPad and… writing happens! It often flies out with *no idea* of what's being written, as "I" have no intention of writing to begin with! Many times after it is written, I read it and ask, "I wonder if this will make sense or resonate at all." The answer is usually, "I have no idea, let's find out" and then I hit the send button. Fortunately, with Divine Intelligence leading, what's written almost invariably finds the bulls-eye, which is continually evidenced by my friends' heartfelt replies to me.

During the first week of June, a close friend wrote to me about an intense experience of Oneness. Overcome by the feeling of seeing a mother hawk as she was trying to help her dead baby on the ground, my friend reported *becoming* the mother hawk. In moments like this, when illusory separation falls away, we experience Unity Consciousness as well as the pain, love, and any other feelings that often go with it. In the ensuing email, I shared a similar experience of Oneness that I had with a homeless woman.

June 5, 2019

Dear Friend: It's been my experience that as compassion deepens in us, our hearts open more and more. It seems *sympathy* comes first and then as evolution happens, the ability to *empathize* manifests. I cannot speak precisely to your experience today but it has been my experience that as we unreservedly allow the spiritual heart to Feel what It will, the Universe provides us happenings in the contextual field of Life to feel even deeper, as this is what develops greater compassion for <u>all</u> sentient beings. It's almost like muscles that become stronger as we work them out. As we experience a greater sense of expansion and with it, the feeling of Unity with and as All Things, a third level is reached: Oneness. This is what Master [Paramahansa Yogananda] pointed to when he recounted his experience as the dying soldier being killed by the bullets. My experience wasn't to the level that his was, but it was far more than mere empathy.

While in Tulare, California late last year, I came across a huddled person in a stairwell. This was not uncommon there and so I walked up prepared to ask the person to leave. When I announced myself and asked what was going on, an old woman looked up at me. She had a tattered plastic bag filled with bits of old food and junk, she had one shoe with no laces, the other foot just had heavy socks, and it was obvious that she had mental health issues. When I began to question her and tell her she couldn't be on property, her hands curled up around her head, she tucked her head down, and in that instant I could feel all the pain, suffering, abuse, neglect, and indifference that she had experienced in her life. Even now it's hard to write about this, which I've never done. To this day it is still raw in my consciousness.

The next hour was spent talking with her, offering what assistance I could, and finally getting her an ambulance so that she could spend the night in a warm hospital bed, get some food, hopefully some shoes or other survival/comfort items and then, as these things almost always end, she'd be back on the streets but maybe just a little better off. The young paramedics seemed put out, and obviously felt like it was a waste of their time. There wasn't one bit of compassion for her at all, which I sadly remarked on. They wouldn't even look at me as they left.

What came next may have been what happened with you. Again, I cannot speak to another's experience, nor is it usually helpful to compare these things. In any case, I went to my room and the gravity of it began to sink in. But it went far beyond sympathy or even empathy. *I was her.*

I witnessed my body curled up on the bed in the fetal position, sobbing uncontrollably. I kept seeing her pulling her hands back to guard herself, her head dropping, anticipating me treating her like everyone else probably does, and her feeling that *she just couldn't take any more*. I <u>was</u> the pain, suffering, abuse, neglect, and indifference that she had experienced in her life. There was no separation and in the Unicity of Being there is none. There is only one of us in the room. This had never happened to me in this way and I was internally reminded of Master's experience with the dying WWII soldier. It went on for a long time and all I could do was FEEL IT – and it was possibly the most intimate and intense pain I have ever felt as obviously, I've not lived a life like hers in this incarnation.

What was also present was *the knowing that I was not her, nor was I what I was feeling*. I was *the Awareness* that gives space to what was being felt. Metaphorically, I was learning how to keep one foot anchored on the mountaintop (Awareness) and one in the marketplace (the day-to-day contextual field of Life As It Is). I'm much more acclimated to this now but it has only come through experiences like this one. My dear friend, it takes courage to feel and embrace our humanity. **It takes courage to Awaken.** This is where the awakening that we are is revealed. Anyone can have amazing spiritual experiences, but as Adya puts it, the true measure of our awakening is revealed by *where we are living from*. Peak experiences are wonderful but it's the Sturm und Drang of everyday life that shows us the true depth of our Realization. All the rest is simply "experience" and as those are ephemeral, they really don't mean much at the end of the day, wonderful and transformative though they may be.

I don't know if any of this helps but it is what happened with me. Just because it wasn't a person you were feeling doesn't mean you can't feel what its feeling! It doesn't mean you can't Be It in that moment. It appears that you are manifesting lessons and opportunities to feel, possibly for the purpose of developing the ability to not be taken over by it. To this, I just don't know. It is up to each of us to intuit what we can from these moments and even then these understandings can and sometimes do change over time, in our ever-greater sense of Awakening and Being.

Phil

Paradoxically, post-awakening I've found that while *I feel more intensely than ever before*, there is no-thing here – a personal self within – that can be hurt by what is felt. Awareness forever remains untouched. Nevertheless, there is great compassion present for suffering when it's encountered, and a resolve to be of assistance if at all possible. As we're human, it can hurt like hell, but with this is an acceptance of What Is, As It Is, in This Moment. This is Love and Wisdom working together.

June 5, 2019 – Follow up reply to the email above

Well thank you too! If it hasn't occurred, you are a teacher of mine as well. Allowing me to share and articulate my experiences and awakening deepens my understanding of them. Being of service to you and all others is one's primary purpose in life after awakening. Since deep spiritual dialogue never happens in my day-to-day reality (at least not right now in my daily business environment) being able to spiritually "jam" with souls like you has been and is, both helpful and important. As Ram Dass stated, "We're walking each other home." My only proviso to this is that… we are already home, so we're really just waking each other up to the fact.

On another note, please…don't try to cognitively figure everything out. First of all, we can't and secondly, I think it slows The Process down, as the illusory "I" is just getting in the way of our Direct Perception of Reality. If we're thinking about it all, we're not in the present moment. What is needed to be understood will be understood in its own perfect time. *Be Still and surrender to This Moment.* Feel into and as the eternal Process flowing as It Will, and try to enjoy the ride! Your path home is and will be singularly unique in all of eternity!

In closing, I am once again sharing the spot-on quote from A.H. Almaas that I sent you last week, as I feel it deserves repeating:

"Usually, we believe that our mind has to organize our experience, giving it an order that is stable so that we can feel oriented and secure in the next moment. We don't trust that reality has its own self-organizing force. But it does – it has been organizing and reorganizing all the time. We think that we have been understanding reality, but it is reality itself that organizes and reorganizes our understanding."

PW

June 9, 2019

… Regarding the integration of Awareness and the Beingness in/as day-to-day Life (mountaintop and marketplace) these profound moments of connectedness happen a lot and are often happy and joyous…not just painful! They typically are much briefer and are really quite beautiful. Just the other day I had one in the supermarket! There was a beautiful little girl about one year of age sitting in her mom's shopping cart, and while her mom was picking something out, I caught the little girl's eye and we just *connected*, soul-to-soul. Her face got all scrunched up with a huge smile and for less than a minute it wasn't an old man and a toddler but rather, two souls connecting. She could tell I was "seeing her in there" (the body) and she was recognizing me that way too. It was *incredibly* sweet and beautiful and it's just as indelibly etched in my consciousness as the old homeless woman is. These types of things happen a lot more post-Kiss, probably because there is not much, if anything, getting in the way of Direct Awareness-Experience.

I have also been reading a little again. Of late, A.H. Almaas and Ibn 'Arabi have found me. Both are exceptionally deep and profound. I will close by leaving you with quotes I like from each.

"I see that my function from now on is to be a mouthpiece for the absolute. I am an expression of the absolute, an expression that reveals its truth, its majesty, that speaks from this mystery. I begin to understand that all the knowledge I have encountered about the soul and its development is secondary to living in the absolute."

~ Luminous Night's Journey: An Autobiographical Fragment
by A.H. Almaas

"The wise man is not he who speaks of wisdom or makes use of it, but he whom wisdom makes act, even if he is not aware of it."

~ The Unlimited Mercifier: The Spiritual Life and Thought of Ibn 'Arabi by Stephen Hirtenstein

Phil

June 26, 2019

Dear Friend: Try to remember the mantra Michael Singer [the bestselling author of *The Untethered Soul* and *The Surrender Experiment*] used during his trials – "No matter what happens, I will be just fine."

Anyone can confidently proclaim they trust the process when things are going along the way they want! My Authentic Trust in God's plan for my unfoldment only *truly meant something* when things, seemingly, were at their worst during the uncertain, upheaval-filled nine months of my rebirthing journey. Looking back now with the clarity that comes from a much deeper, experientially-based understanding, the "worst" moments were actually the "best" moments for spiritual opening-opportunity to happen! The "worst" moments are God offering us Her (fierce) Grace! We have to be made authentically *vulnerable* enough for a Real, transcendental breakthrough, as that is when the ego-mind is in its weakest, most desperate state. It's <u>OK</u> to feel scared; now is not the time for false strength. The illusion that we are a separate self in control has to be, and make no mistake eventually will be, GROUND INTO THE DUST and it usually ain't any fun. These are the critical moments in our spiritual awakening when <u>all</u> we may have is courage, trust, and surrender. [And, hopefully, the support of family and friends too.]

<u>This</u> is the script that You and Life are co-creating for your *mutual evolution!* Dive headfirst into The Deep with no fear of drowning and *this too shall pass!* Everything runs in cycles. As Wu Hsin said, we "learn to float." Talk to Yoganandaji. Give it all up to Him! We are blessed beyond words to have a Guru walking the road beside us. Utilize the incalculable resource that He Is! We do not walk "the path" alone...ever! As we Awaken we unmistakably and intimately...directly see and feel and know our Absolute Interconnectedness with/in/as All Things. In that Unicity of Being, we find a peaceful acceptance with What Is in This Moment. This doesn't mean we necessarily like it, and it doesn't preclude wanting to make the circumstances of our lives better (a safe place to live, a steady income,

good health, a meaningful way to be of service to others, etc.), but we nonetheless are OK with Life...As It Is, here and now.

"Let it all go – surrender to the present moment, and know that the universe has a plan for you and everything will work out just fine." ~ Anonymous

Phil

June 26, 2019 – Follow up to the email above

Writing that message to you this morning brought tears to these eyes as well on several occasions, as I kept flashing back to my 2017-18 desert sojourn, living out of my car, gradually going broke, and feeling more <u>alone</u> than I ever had before or thought possible. Not knowing what was happening, (awakening or going crazy?!) and without a clue as to what, if anything, the future had in store for me, all I could do when not in the bliss of undifferentiated unitive Beingness was to tell myself just what I told you in my earlier email. It will all work out the way it's supposed to… just trust! There are a few billion people in the world who are far worse off materially than you, not to mention approximately 99% of the planet operating with a far, far less awakened consciousness than yours. The Universe is always conspiring for our (and Its) long term highest good, so with that in mind, how can anything go "wrong?" Keep on keeping on! [A favorite saying of SRF VP Brother Achalananda that I often use during tough times like these.]

PW

July 21, 2019

"Ascending, the forest becomes darker. Knowing becomes unknowing. Knowing by unknowing reaches the Light while reason crumbles in the darkness. Scholars argue about such things, but they never leave the ground. The highest science is one that leads to ecstasy in the unknowing."

~ St. John of the Cross

Paradoxically, it is in the "unknowing" that we "know." It is also an immensely free and liberating place to Be. *What do we really know* other than I, as this moment, AM? We may certainly know a lot *about* many things but what few come to *experientially know* is that while the ego-mind *thinks* it knows a lot, it actually knows almost nothing, with only mind-created belief systems to vainly hang on to, most of which are given to us by people who were given their beliefs. This is the trap and limitation of the intellect and why it must be transcended, crossing over the 500-level on Hawkin's scale of consciousness, before Divine Intelligence becomes the Impetus for action. As Sri Ramakrishna used to say, (I'm paraphrasing) the thinking-mind and intellect are wonderful servants, but they also are terrible masters.

The concept of retro-causality is fascinating, and seems to have a basis in our understanding of physics to this point. From my living perspective in and as an individuated, non-dual aware consciousness, the *concept of time* is like other mental abstractions such as *causality* and *duality*. They are relatively real stemming from observation in-form, but from unitive Beingness, they are all purely mind-projected. While "mind" has a lot of connotations, for our purposes today I am applying this very simple definition/equation to "mind" that recently occurred to me. Mind = Awareness + Experience. "Awareness" is our true essence, intimately and dependently co-arising with Experience, in and as the contextual field (i.e. Ground of Being) that Consciousness Is. Furthermore, for the sake of clarity, I define "Experience" (again, for the purpose of this discussion) as the sum total of our three bodies' (physical, astral, and causal) thoughts, feelings, sensations, and perceptions.

Phil

The advice given in the next email is outside my expertise and was only offered due to the loving nature of my friendship with these two wonderful people. Having relationship challenges, one of them sought my advice. I feel this is a practical example of love-wisdom being brought into very human terms.

August 9, 2019

Thank you for the update on things there. The self-destructive behaviors and reactive patterns you described that [this person] is battling do not seem likely to permanently dissolve just because you are there more, but hopefully it will help. If the relationship ultimately does go south, at least you will know that you did all you possibly could. Does [this person] receive professional counseling? If not, I would not be very optimistic that these issues will be transcended. Hopefully, if [this person] is not already undergoing counseling, there is an openness to it, and [they] can find someone there who [they] will like and trust. Unfortunately, deeply-seated psychological issues such as the ones you described almost never fall away on their own. Additionally, I am betting they foment a profound and deleterious impact on [your partner's] physical wellbeing too.

As for you, it sounds as if you have logically analyzed all the ramifications of your plans, which is where I'd start too. When asked, I always encourage people faced with major, life-changing decisions to apply as much logic and common sense to the issue as possible but having done that, let it all go and inwardly listen to one's intuitive heart. If both logic and intuition are saying the same thing, then it's an easy call. If not, well, I usually suggest listening to the heart rather than the head but the latter shouldn't be completely dismissed either, as often one's fears, uncertainties, and/or doubts can occlude the intuitive-feeling impulses that we receive from God.

I'm always hesitant to use the following axiom as it has become rather trite over the years but: those whom you come in contact with, especially those who are closest to you, are a mirror for you, my friend. If what's happening pushes your buttons so effectively, then that is where you have evolution happening. Nothing fun or easy about it, but there it is nonetheless. I completely agree with you that being faced with [these sorts of things] is challenging. Except, of course, when they aren't. Be that as it may, try to inwardly look at <u>who</u> or <u>what</u> is being hurt/offended. This is critical! You are <u>not</u> what is being blamed, or hurt, or offended but in its place, *You are the awareness* that gives space to that which is being hurt or offended. Only the ego-mind takes these slights personally and then, it does so only because *we identify with it as being us.* In other words, *who/what we are.* As best you can, try to be The Witness of who/what is being hurt. This creates a *gap* that allows one to, sometimes, *not be taken over by the moment* and therefore we can be <u>responsive</u> and not <u>reactive</u> to What Is. This doesn't in any way mean we don't feel, or that we should try to deny our humanness. Rather, it simply helps us to know, experientially, that we are in our *essence,* beyond the domain of the material world. Developing a witnessing consciousness is spiritual work-in-progress and not necessarily easy, but like anything, we get better at it with time and effort, and we are always aided in our sincere efforts by God's Grace. The witnessing state is not the Unitive Being that comes with the dissolution of ego and dropping away of the illusion of a separate self, but the two do share a cab ride about half way to the destination. If [your friend] consciously or not, isn't pointing to the area(s) that you are evolving in, rest assured that The Universe will manifest something or someone that does! As I See Life Now, All of Manifestation is awakening and therefore everything comes together perfectly to create the contextual field and "grist for the mill" for awakening to happen and Life to evolve. That being said, *we surely do not have to be a spiritual doormat* and accept abusive relationships and/or life circumstances. That can also be (yet another!) illusory ego-mind trap. If you haven't already done so, I encourage you both to have loving, authentic communication with each other before making any big decisions. If there aren't respectful boundaries that are agreed upon, goals to be worked towards, and deal-breakers that are understood, then the likelihood of an outcome that works in the long term seems slim.

Please remember that *I am always available to and for you both*. However, in all honesty I cannot say that this modulation of consciousness known as Phil has brought with it any definite answers to the infinite challenges that Life presents us. In fact, the only knowing I have is that I don't know.

Phil

My recommendation for professional therapy might surprise some reading this, but even though I've never had the impulse to avail myself of it, I strongly feel that psychological counseling can be tremendously useful, whether one is spiritually oriented or not. I've met a lot of people in my life (secular and religious) who just needed someone to talk out their issues with, and in more than a few instances, they were so in need that they utilized me in the role, even with my caveat up front that I'm not professionally trained. Furthermore, my experience has shown me that being tied to a spiritual organization, as monks and nuns necessarily are, can make seeing a therapist more difficult than it is for householders in the world, as there is often a stigma about going outside the organization for help. "Spiritual bypassing" is a well-known term and tendency to use spiritual concepts and methods to get around facing unsolved psychological wounds, emotional hang-ups, and unfinished developmental work. I've gotta say that in my time, I have met some individuals who clearly had issues of some sort, and even stated this openly to me. But when I'd ask how they were dealing with them, they'd say, "Well, I'm doing a zillion Kriyas every day" or, "I've quit school and I'm meditating all day long." Hearing this I think, "Good God, that sounds like a recipe for disaster." I'm not saying that one *couldn't* or *shouldn't* do either of these, but there is nothing I've seen that would lead me to think that these types of techniques will help someone overcome a feeling of unworthiness (psychological), relationship issues (emotional), or childhood trauma (developmental), for example. What's more, I have seen where intense spiritual practices have made these types of issues worse.

Listen, I get it. Many in spiritual circles see psychology as somehow inferior to spirituality and that the wrong therapist (however well-meaning) can do more harm than good, especially when attempting to diagnose a spiritual awakening. I experienced this myself with one well-intentioned friend. One only has to read Suzanne Segal's story in *Collision with the Infinite* to see how this happens. That said, few people are actually dealing with the annihilation of their ego! They are trying to transcend their ego while dealing with the plethora of issues that are ubiquitous today, and as the old saying goes, "One needs the right tool for the job." I view the psychological framework as I do the foundation of a house: for the structure to weather life's storms, the foundation needs to be firm. For non-spiritual folks, this foundation will set them up for a well-adjusted life. For anyone reading this book it's even more important, because the goal is awakening! As one can surely appreciate from my story, the awakening process can be intense, and without our psychological foundation in order, something like an ego transcendence (abiding or not) can be challenging beyond description.

Unhealthy-to-ignore psychological characteristics of our humanness (e.g. personality traits and preferences, communication skills, interpersonal dynamics, sexuality, and the capacity to function productively and peacefully at home, at work, and/or in society) may have the same need for growth as they had before an awakening. *Perhaps,* they'll even be <u>more</u> in need of growth, so please don't claim that you haven't been advised! With this in mind… for anyone out there whose goal is Self-Realization, if you feel that there is unresolved trauma of some type within you, then by all means avail yourself of the technologies that are designed to deal with these. Your sadhana and life in general will be better off for it!

To the skeptics I say, *be open*. Psychology is a rapidly developing science and many leading-edge practitioners today are blending spirituality with it, just as many are blending spirituality with science. I foresee all three being merged together in the future. Moreover, there are well-known spiritual teachers today who adroitly mix psychology into their teachings. Adyashanti, Llewellyn Vaughan-Lee, and A.H. Almaas are excellent (albeit very different) examples of this, while James Finley is a first-rate instance of a spiritual teacher who is also a licensed therapist specializing in trauma.

My last point here is directed to those in leadership roles within spiritual organizations. For the highest good of all, encourage those who come to you with psychology-related issues to find help. Even better, for a large organization that not only counsels members but has a monastic order as well, interview some therapists and put one or more on retainer. This way, there will be a comfort level for all involved, and it will preclude the daunting prospect of having to search for someone when the need arises. This will also be useful for the therapist, as going in they will have a better understanding of the organization and the particular issues that may arise from it. Please! Come out of the dark ages on this – the stigma around mental health issues has to end.

As I wrote this next email, there were winds-of-change on the horizon, as it appeared that I was about to be downsized in the near future due to the company's plans to sell the majority of the hotels I was supporting. Despite this, I was not affected inwardly. We are always living in the unknown of each moment, whether we realize it or not. At this point, my awareness-experience was stabilized and integrated enough to where this was effortless...even faced with the possibility of losing my job.

I was still reading, however. Much of the reading I'd been doing for the previous eight months was, in the Christian tradition, known as Lectio Divina, an extremely effective methodology for a book like Nisargadatta's spiritual classic, *I Am That*, which I quote below. In this method, one reads a small amount at a time, letting it enter into and steep in one's consciousness. If you haven't tried this technique, I highly recommend it.

While on this topic, *I Am That* was a book that, upon first reading way back in 2001, didn't make sense to me at all. Now, after reading it from cover-to-cover, I began to share with friends the passages that had immediately grabbed me on a (pre)conceptual and/or experiential level, and I feel the following excerpt is not only one of the deepest, but one that describes Self-Realization with great precision and beauty. As such, this email seemed like the perfect way to end this chapter and the amazing time in my post-awakening sadhana that it covers.

August 24, 2019

… aside from describing the rapidly changing/crumbling professional framework in which I earn money and serve What Is, I thought you might appreciate something that Nisargadatta said about the "unknowing" I mentioned above. It struck me as both deeply profound and laughably obvious. That said, while I have been living in "The Cloud of Unknowing," there was never a mind-generated question about **what** this unknowing is or **why** this is so. These types of questions just don't arise anymore in the nearly ever-present Stillness of the mind. For some reason, I am beginning to prefer the pointer <u>Motionless</u> rather than Stillness. However, occasionally I will run across something that elucidates a question that doesn't exist…until the answer is found…if that makes any sense.

Nisargadatta was asked: "Is 'I am' itself the witness, or are they separate?" His answer was as follows and the bold emphasis is mine.

M: "Without one the other cannot be. Yet they are not one. It is like the flower and its color. Without flower – no colors; without color – the flower remains unseen. Beyond is the light which on contact with the flower creates the color. Realize that your true nature is that of pure light only, and both the perceived and the perceiver come and go together. That which makes both possible, and yet is neither, is your real being, which means not being a 'this' or 'that', but pure awareness of being and not-being. **When awareness is turned on itself, the feeling is of not knowing**. When it is turned outward, the knowables come into being. To say: 'I know myself' is a contradiction in terms for what is 'known' cannot be 'myself'."

The profound dialogue continued:

Q: "If the self is forever the unknown, what then is realized in self-realization?"

M: "To know that the known cannot be me nor mine, is liberation enough. Freedom from self-identification with a set of memories and habits, the state of wonder at the infinite reaches of the being, its inexhaustible creativity and total transcendence, the absolute fearlessness born from the realization of the illusoriness and transiency of every mode of consciousness – flow from a deep and inexhaustible source. To know the source as source and appearance as appearance, and oneself as the source only is self-realization."

~ *I Am That: Talks with Sri Nisargadatta Maharaj*

What absolutely rocked me satori-like was the statement I put in bold: "When awareness is turned on itself, the feeling is of not knowing." It is so obvious and makes complete sense! Post-Kiss, I find the intellect playing catch-up with awakened, living experience or, to put it another way, with the *Absolute Intimacy of What Is*. In the formative years of my sadhana, it was completely the other way around and I suspect this is true for most "spiritual seekers" until the "seeker" finally dissolves.

I guess that is all for now, my friend. As things are up in the air with my work situation right now, I will keep you posted. **One never knows**…which is always where the mystery and fun lie!

"If a man wishes to be sure of the road he treads on, he must close his eyes and walk in the dark."

~ St. John of the Cross

Phil

Now that you've crossed the river, my friend, where will you go? No water, no boat, no road ahead, no traveler. With Self forgotten, there is no within, not even a void to seek.

~ Kabir

CHAPTER SIX:
The Real Voyage Of Discovery

As I was suspecting in the final email of chapter five, I found myself without gainful employment, and as a result, unexpectedly back at Hidden Valley for my two-year anniversary of The Kiss. There, I formulated a plan for the next six months: spend time alone at Hidden Valley and in the desert, drive to Texas for the holidays to see my sister one more time, and then come back through Arizona for a forty-day retreat. Since management openings in the hospitality industry tend to evaporate in the winter months and reappear in the spring season, I sensed this was a time to reflect on everything that had transpired over the last two years. What's more, given the now palpable inner movement I previously mentioned, I decided that this was The Universe providing me with a much-deserved break, as well as an opportunity to deepen my awareness-experience even more. What I obviously didn't foresee was the emergence of COVID, so instead of six months, this chapter covers a fourteen-month period, and the interruption between jobs has continued up until the time of this writing. While ideal for sadhana, this time-out was not ideal for my finances and this turned out to be a theme of my awakening: the finite/transitory aspects of my life were negatively impacted while the infinite/lasting evolution of consciousness accelerated and deepened.

Given what I was writing, there is even less commentary here and more bracketed comments in the emails, especially within quotes and passages, as I was beginning to collaborate with the authors. Please note that within the excerpts all bolded emphases, bracketed inclusions, and/or italics are mine. Additionally, for the sake of brevity and clarity, I have removed the Tibetan equivalents to the key English terms when referencing Dzogchen, which I surprisingly became immersed in during the summer of 2020.

This period reflects a new beginning, as I embarked on what I felt was the real voyage of discovery. The river had been crossed and now there was no road and no traveler and nothing to seek. I had been reborn, struggled through the toddler phase, grown in my adolescence, and now I was entering spiritual adulthood. My writings during this phase also reveal the pendulum swinging again, this time deeply towards the Wisdom aspect of my Beingness.

The following email was personally important to me, as it recapitulated the most challenging aspects of the first nine months of my awakening, and also provided me with an opportunity to formally thank the abbot of the ashram for assisting me with the awakening in the wise and beautiful way that he did. While this wasn't something he was looking for or felt was necessary, I did feel it necessary and as a result, we have a heartfelt opening to this chapter.

September 30, 2019

Dear Friend: Amazingly, today marks the second anniversary of the death of "Phil" as a separate self, and the beginning of his subsequent (re)birth into/as non-dual Awareness. During a meditation-walk last night, an impulse arose that left me knowing that I could not let this occasion pass without thanking you, and explaining why your counsel made such a difference in the post-Kiss process. Please – forgive me for its length! As I have already written you some since my arrival here, moving forward I will do my best to give you a break from my well established predilection for long-winded (but sincere!) spiritual correspondence…at least for a while! [This very kind, patient, and wise soul had been the recipient of many of my emails over the years and God Bless him for it!]

Two years ago today, I got up out of bed like every other day throughout the course of this incarnation. However, I had no idea that it would be my last… and first. While the events that followed were unfathomably synchronistic – books/teachers/teachings, time alone, time here at Hidden Valley, time with friends and family, etc., I do not feel that I ever formally expressed my gratitude for the vital role you played, in a way that you deserve. It is my sincere hope that this letter will rectify that unfortunate oversight.

My friend, there were so very many awe-inspiring and heretofore unprecedented "happenings" in the nine months that followed The Kiss. With hindsight, I now can say they constituted a "(re)birthing." While the process continues to this day and *will continue to deepen forever,* the culmination of those nine months came with the pilgrimage to Mt. Shasta and the subsequent Kriya-fueled "karmic purge" which transpired here at the ashram. From there, it felt as if God deemed that I was ready to rejoin the proverbial "marketplace" again and begin to learn to function in it; this time, however, from a non-dual unitive Beingness in and as Consciousness – our Natural State.

With all the key events that unfolded, please indulge me here, as it is important that I share what I now look back on as the two most important tipping points. I am relaying these, on this most blessed and unexpected anniversary, as you were integral to both.

The Loss of Personal Will: Blissed-out and bewildered, I couldn't find a reason to get out of bed every day [or "do" much of anything] and you were the only one astute enough to recognize this and ask me if the loss of personal will was the problem. I so clearly remember sitting in your office and thanking you for asking the question, as it actually helped me to identify the issue. At that point, I was *cognitively* unable to see it; it was an answer that filled-in an unrecognized question for the then-fledgling, non-dual awareness-experience of What Is. I have often thanked God that I was going broke, as the survival impulse was the only thing that was able to get me moving! If I would have had financial resources, I could have very easily headed off into seclusion for months or possibly even years, basking in the intoxicating bliss but potentially not evolving through and past that initial stage. As it was *thankfully* transcended, I discovered the only other reason to start each new day – LOVE. Love for God, love for those I would meet each day and the immense privilege of Being of service to them through this newly awakened mind-body apparatus, and love for the sheer wonder in/of/as each moment witnessed and lived.

Sanity and Surrender: Throughout this life, I have been (mostly!), as psychologists would characterize it, a "high-functioning" or "self-actualizing" individual: reasonably intelligent and successful enough in the world, with excellent interpersonal skills and meaningful, lasting relationships with family and friends. **Never** in this life had I ever questioned my sanity, nor did I ever think that I would. And then I found myself on a desert sojourn I never imagined – unemployed, going broke, living out of my car, [some of my closest friends] looking at me with pity and speaking to me as if I had thrown away what was, to them, a respectable and sensible life and above all, experiencing an ego-mind annihilating **aloneness** and **silence** that was immeasurably beyond anything that I had ever felt, or imagined. It was during the inevitable times when the Unitive Bliss would ebb that I could not help but to question whether the proverbial cheese might actually be slipping off my cracker. You were the only one I implicitly trusted enough to ask, as I intuitively knew that only you had the spiritual understanding to see what was happening and answer me in a way that I could absolutely rely on. In that critical moment you related the story of Rumi, when everything was (seemingly!) being ripped away from him, asking God if He even wanted his sanity too, along with everything else He was (seemingly!) taking. Rumi's decision to even relinquish his sanity if need be was *exactly* what I needed to hear! Only then was I able to see that in the final, agonizing death throes of the ego-mind, that was how deep, all-encompassing, and uncompromisingly authentic the surrender of identity had to be. It was the last leg, so to speak, that was holding up the crumbling ego-mind structure of the personal, separate self. Without you sharing exactly that in that critical moment of doubt, I may not have found the faith and courage necessary to lay EVERYTHING at God's Lotus Feet, and I may have turned away from The Abyss of The Absolute that Grace had finally and miraculously brought me to. Here now, I find the possible consequences of such a tragic misstep in that most critical of junctures incalculable.

When it was stated by the Masters of all spiritual traditions that one must surrender *everything* to pass the Gateless Gate, they really did mean *everything*. The joke, and cosmic irony as you surely know, is that once we do pass and finally look back, we see that nothing was given up and that no one died, because there never was anyone Real there to die, and that we never had anything that was ours to relinquish to begin with! *It was all, quite simply, an illusion* – an erroneous inference of the mind and senses, and the mistaken belief systems of our collective cultural story. *Nothing at all was lost, as there never was* **anything to lose**, *or anyone to lose it.* Amazing! However, until we finally wash up on the far shore we cannot see this, hence the utter and indescribable existential terror of the ego's death process...at least how I experienced it. Other's mileage may vary!

I haven't the words to describe how profoundly grateful I am for you Being just what I needed, just when I needed it, during the two key moments described above, so all I can say here is Thank You! In those crucial, fragile times, I truly feel that Spirit was working through you. I realize that there isn't anyone really there in "you" to accept the applause (a good thing!) but on today of all days, the impulse to express my deepest appreciation made this heartfelt email mandatory.

Spiritually and materially, what's to come now, two years on? In this moment, I simply have no idea! As I mentioned to you in our last jam session, I am most grateful that I didn't fall into the potential ego-rebuilding trap of excitedly running out to share this new-found Realization of nothing-ness and everything-ness with the world. It's certainly very easy to see that, historically, the role of a spiritual teacher is fraught with pitfalls and temptations, so for now, no thank you to that. I am not ready, if indeed I ever will be in this lifetime. Besides, I can't help but find that there are more than enough spiritual teachers in the world as it is! That said, within "me" there is the presence of a prayer that there will be a way that the God-given Grace of The Kiss and all that unfolded after can somehow be shared. Assisting others in their journey would make the blessings I have received that much greater – not to in any way point to "me," as we both have Realized that awakening is not something we can do. It simply and impersonally happens when our individuated consciousness is ripe. Obviously, we also cannot forget the fact that We Are Already One with/as All Things, hence the term "attainless attainment." Consider this fitting passage from the book you recommended to me a few years ago:

"When the Heart Sutra, for example, declares, 'There is no attainment, with nothing to attain,' it challenges some very fundamental assumptions we have about ourselves and our 'spiritual' practice because we want to be able to show something for our effort. Any idea of attainment or effort becomes a palliative for self-referentiality." [And may lead to spiritual materialism.]

~ *Trust in Mind: The Rebellion of Chinese Zen* by Mu Soeng

As I look around the world now, seeing my spiritual Brothers and Sisters striving so diligently, I do wish that all this could somehow be a beacon of hopeful promise. If awakening can happen to someone with my checkered past (I was never an exemplary devotee by most anyone's standards either) then it <u>can</u> and inevitably <u>will</u> happen to them! Through what's transpired over the last two years, I pray that I am able to give even more hope to so many who, under the ego's spell, see themselves as unready for awakening or worse…unworthy. Or even if they feel they are deserving, they think it'll be umpteen lifetimes before awakening happens. *It just breaks my heart.* I pray that somehow what's happened with me may one day help with this.

With my deepest gratitude for having you with me on my journey throughout the years, I remain your brother in God's Infinite Love.

Phil

As I wrote above, there was an impulse to assist others in their awakening journey, and as events transpired, this wonderfully came to be (see Epilogue for more on this). The rest of the emails in this chapter were written to close friends, two of whom I saw as being in the awakening stage of "circling the drain."

November 10, 2019

To your incredibly important and existentially fundamental question about suffering continuing even when we *intellectually* understand why: Adi Shankara explained that while the foremost source of suffering is our identification as an egoic separate self, the **mechanism that perpetuates the suffering is superimposition**. In other words, when one mistakenly identifies as a separate ego-mind-body, one is unknowingly attempting to *limit infinite consciousness* by *superimposing finiteness on it.* That finiteness could be **any** concept or identity the ego-mind creates/adopts for itself, not to mention the ignorance-based labels we are handed from birth by society-at-large, coupled with an erroneous cultural story that is mostly rooted in scientific and philosophical materialism [as well as physicalism and panpsychism].

While I have not seen this anywhere else, after reading Shankara I came up with the following analogy or metaphor for this: It's a bit like being fitted with a pair of shoes at birth that we have to wear our entire lives.

There *may be* a few precious opportunities to take them off (for example, during brief periods of peace when a desire has been fulfilled, during meditation, viewing an amazing sunset, or gazing into a loved-one's eyes), but other than these types of peak moments, we are stuck wearing shoes and can never go barefoot – our Natural State. Unfortunately, as infinite consciousness essentially and, it appears, necessarily (at least in the beginning) *limits itself to assume form* (human or otherwise) for the purpose of (re)cognizing itself experientially, a sense of finiteness and separateness occurs. OK, now back to the shoes. The pair we are given at birth are two sizes too small! Over the course of many incarnations and not knowing any better, we become accustomed to the poor fit and sadly assume this is "normal." Eventually, when enough suffering has occurred coupled with Grace, we adopt various spiritual methods and break them in some for a better fit. Nevertheless, while they may hurt our feet less, they still hurt! So, back to your question and the root issue at hand. We still experience separateness and still suffer as a result, even though now, through spiritual teachings and the peak experiences our efforts sometimes produce, we cognitively understand that it is happening and why.

Unfortunately, the illusion of being a separate self is so powerfully hardwired into the mind-body apparatus [which, from a non-dual perspective, is consciousness itself] that this "superimposition" still goes on, unnoticed or noticed. As stated above, eventually there's enough suffering to get us to begin questioning the entire set-up and from there we start down a spiritual path. Even then, from the viewpoint of the separate self, it can take a "long time" before we Realize (i.e. Remember) the true nature of reality and our natural state of Beingness. The illusion is anything but trivial. However, once it's seen through, at least in my experience, it is hard to fathom why it was so difficult! Awakening was my cosmic-slap-on-the-forehead-yelling-"doh" moment! I would actually find it all incredibly amusing if it weren't for the fact that this is the cause of our planet being in the condition that it's in. That being said, and somewhat paradoxically, if it weren't for the mechanism of superimposition and the suffering it perpetuates, we would probably never awaken! [Therefore, from a place of Wisdom, *everything* is Grace.] Without suffering, what would be the impetus to look deeply into the nature of all manifestation (i.e. Self) and Realize that we are not an actor in the movie but rather, we are The Screen – Consciousness Itself?! [This representation is often used by Rupert Spira and, being one of my favorites, I am relatively sure that I picked it up from him. I think it does an excellent job expressing the concept of being "The Dance" and not the dancer.]

Only through an abiding Realization of Oneness are we finally able to take the ill-fitting and now unnecessary "shoes of separateness and suffering" off once and for all. Suffering ends, as there is no fictitious "I" cramming infinite consciousness into a finite, erroneous, and illusory mental construct. Self-Aware Consciousness turns back in on Its Source – The Absolute – and Knows Itself once again.

Phil

November 12, 2019 – Follow up to the email above

Hello again: As I wrote in the other email, the illusion isn't trivial! It is both the *mechanism* and the *byproduct* of how infinite and intelligent formless consciousness converts Itself into a modulation of finite, in-form consciousness [space-time and matter, which then creates the contextual field for Life to arise]. As a result, it is built into the very fabric of All That Is – Existence Itself. Transcending the illusion is the single most difficult thing known to humanity, so you might want to cut yourself some slack. Please know that I truly and deeply feel your frustration, impatience, and suffering!

As unsatisfying as it most likely is to hear again, I have nothing else to ask except this:

1) Who or what is the "me" that is [as you said] being drawn into the illusion?

2) Who or what is the "I" that [as you said] feels addicted and doesn't want it?

Even though you already know this conceptually, I will point it out yet again: The "me" and "I" that you refer to will never–ever get rid of the illusion. I mean NEVER.

The "me" and "I" that is trying so hard is a manifestation of the illusion. It simply cannot be done and as it appears from here now, what is making the consternation worse (not for the "Real" You as Awareness but "you" as a psychological construct…the ego) is that there is an *attachment* to becoming Self-Realized. Arguably the most important verse from *The Hsin Hsin Ming* [Generally translated as "Trust in Mind" and attributed to Third Chan (Zen) Patriarch Jianzhi Sengcan] is: "Even to be attached to the idea of enlightenment is to go astray."

The "me" or "I" that feels addicted, frustrated, and trapped can't become Realized because, and you know this, *it isn't real.* It's as phony as a campaigning politician's smile. Adya tells us that Self-Realization happens "up from and out of" the ego's illusory, personal, separate-self-identification, and more importantly, my awareness-experience confirms it. Your spiritual "earnestness," as Nisargadatta called it, does you great credit! But as I said at dinner on Saturday, since the "I" cannot "make it happen," our best course of action is to *adopt an inner attitudinal stance of least resistance* and that comes from total surrender. Put another way, while it is our spiritual efforts that set the table, it is *God's Grace* that delivers the feast.

"Do" your spiritual practice, which might become no practice at all for a time, for no reason other than as an expression of Who/What You Are. If you can't quit comparing This Moment to your past spiritual experiences, wonderful though they might have been, then you will never Be Here Now. You'll always be a thought away from What Is, which is an infinite distance. [And when the mind is completely Still, reality is so close there is no distance at all.]

As Papaji said, "Once you stop your pushing, you'll feel the power of the pull." When awakening happened to Phil, not only was he not trying to make anything happen spiritually, *he wasn't even aware that he was not trying to make anything happen.* To become as "Grace prone" as possible in This Moment, we have to just be ourselves without trying to be ourselves! Sadly, in our culture, being totally natural is damn difficult after the age of five or so. Wu Hsin succinctly said, "The final step is the giving up of all steps" and "Being is Reality. Being *this* or *that* is not."

My friend, your suffering is my suffering. I feel your desire and despair more deeply than you may think. I am in your corner. *Relax into it.* Not for any reason or goal – that's not authentic relaxing! Sadhana is like dancing or listening to music. One doesn't do one's practice for any reason other than the enjoyment of doing it. Awakening will Happen, but only on God's terms and Her timetable – not the ego's. I'll close with my ever-present companion Wu Hsin and with my sincere prayer that you are able to hear what's being said, and understand why it is being said so directly: "When there are no longer any goals, then the goal is attained."

Phil

Having recently returned from my forty-day retreat, I was back at Hidden Valley for a short time, preparing to look for work and dealing with the jarring energy and noise of the world again.

February 25, 2020

It appears you are confusing how consciousness "individuates" itself as it expresses itself in and as <u>form</u> with "being" a separate "individual." As you're discovering Ramana and his teachings, I've copied the first paragraph of the first page of the first chapter of *Be As You Are,* as it starts with the essential principle of his deep understanding of Advaita Vedanta:

"The Self. This is the term that he used the most frequently. He defined it by saying that the real Self or real 'I' is, contrary to perceptible experience, not an experience of individuality but a non-personal, all-inclusive awareness. It is not to be confused with the individual self which he said was essentially non-existent, being a fabrication of the mind which obscures the true experience of the real Self. He maintained that the real Self is always present and always experienced but he emphasized that one is only consciously aware of it as it really is when the self-limiting tendencies of the mind have ceased. Permanent and continuous Self-awareness is known as Self-realization."

Only when the mind is Absolutely Still do we actually perceive Reality As It Is. The only thing "sacred" and filled with "dignity," as you described the individual self, is the ego-mind and this is to be expected, as all it wants to do is perpetuate itself. I shit you not my friend, beware of the spiritual journey! As Nisargadatta advised us, and I can attest to experientially: "The search for Reality is the most dangerous of all undertakings, for it will destroy the world in which you live."

The sense of being an individual is what one awakens from! If this isn't what your driving, inner desire is, then for God's sake quit reading Ramana now and just enjoy the dream state as best you can. From my viewpoint however, *I'm very glad that you are* reading Ramana!

Keep me posted and as always, questions, comments, and/or accusations are always welcome and I'll leave you with this epigrammatic quote from *I As* by Roy Melvyn:

"Conscious Life Energy is the substance of the world and the Absolute is the source of the substance. The unity prior to duality, yet immanent in it, is the shapeless root. It is That which does not depend on Consciousness, yet makes Consciousness possible. It is That wherein and whereof every 'I' appears and disappears. It is inconceivable for whoever attempts to conceive it. It is so clear that it is hard to see. Everything is this One displaying Itself in the multiplicity, this dance of interdependent counterparts, of presumed separate subjective self, presumed separate world, and presumed separate God. Phenomenal absence is 'I'. Everything is 'I-as.'"

PW

This next email is a summation of the three months in Sedona where I was consumed by/in Dzogchen. I'd been carrying around some Dzogchen books in my e-book library since late 2019 when I intuitively bought some, even though I knew that I didn't intend to read them anytime soon. Somehow, I just knew they were important and wanted them on deck until The Universe called them up to the batter's box. Considered the highest vehicle in Buddhism, Dzogchen (a.k.a. atiyoga) was brought into this world by Enlightened luminaries such as The Buddha, Garab Dorje, and Longchenpa (a.k.a. Longchen Rabjam). I feel Dzogchen best translates as "Great Completion" but it is often translated as "Great Perfection" as well.

With my admittedly limited understanding of Dzogchen being indicated upfront here, one can't leap directly into its meditation techniques. A qualified Rinpoche needs to be involved to some degree, along with a solid foundation in Buddhist theory and practice. Nevertheless, I am including this splendid quote, courtesy of the Seventh Dzogchen Ponlop (Karma Sungrap Ngedön Tenpa Gyaltsen), as I feel it sums up the Dzogchen view of what real meditation is:

"Meditation
There is nothing to do
It is about undoing."

June 18, 2020

I just ran across this and found it very interesting (and kind of odd), especially given the times we're now living in, plus how Dzogchen has recently found me and completely blown me away.

"At the end of the kali yuga, Dzogchen will burgeon and flourish while the lower vehicles will wane."

~ Guru Rinpoche Prophecy

Padmasambhava (Guru Rinpoche) was an eighth century Tibetan Master, and many hold him as the greatest to have come out of the Buddhist tradition, save Shakyamuni Buddha himself. It seems to me that given his divine stature, he would have been able to say this, although the "lower vehicles" almost certainly meant other forms of Buddhist teachings and practice, as opposed to non-Buddhist methods. Who knows though? Maybe only the most effective routes to Self-Realization will be the ones to survive into the higher age that we are now seeing born. I'm certain that the teachings of Yogananda and Meher Baba [among many others of course] were with this emerging Dwapara yuga in mind.

I cannot explain the near-total, one-pointed Impulse that's taken hold of me! If anyone can understand, it would be you, as you witnessed a small part of this while here. I sit here reading this stuff night and day and I often feel as if it's close to manifesting Nirvikalpa Samadhi — Phil is *aware* of Being, but on occasion just barely. The Ajna Chakra opens as I begin to read these ancient texts, and the delicious cool currents flowing in and out of it are the norm now, rather than the exception. It's amazing to watch and…it's accelerating.

This can't be anything else but Divine Intelligence using this mind-body for *something*…but *for what* is as yet unknown to me. And here now, it really doesn't matter. Knowing this is the case in the core of my Being only fuels greater determination to utilize my time here maximally. It feels immensely important <u>and</u> absolutely dharmic. It appears that my recent inability to delve into *any* spiritual teachings this year was simply "clearing the deck" for this all-out flood of truth and its accompanying energy. [The singular exception to this was Bernadette Roberts' remarkable book, *The Path to No-Self: Life at the Center.*]

Thank you for letting me share some of what's happening! It's truly impossible to express the full nature of "being done" like this. It sometimes feels as if infinity itself is opening up in and around me throughout much of my waking hours. I'm falling fast and hard but now, in and as Awakened Awareness-Experience, there's no resistance. Only complete trust, humble wonder...and immense awe!

Phil

Just as with my feeling that one needs a teacher to employ its meditation techniques properly, I also don't think there is any way one can just read a stack of books on Dzogchen and grasp its intricacies, let alone *teach* it. While absorbed in the Dzogchen tomes I had collected, I could easily see that some of the material was meant for seasoned practitioners, so consequently there was a chapter here and there that was simply beyond and/or not applicable to me. And yet, I still read these complex and illuminating books fifty or more hours a week for three months!

With nothing but an intuitive impulse generating my immersion into Dzogchen, you are excused if you're wondering why I did all this. In all candor, I simply don't know for sure! The descriptions used for the place I was in and as consciousness (and the insights that came with it), were the most pure and precise I'd ever come across, and *that is saying a lot!* I found that Dzogchen in general (and Longchenpa in particular) impeccably articulated the highest metaphysical truths. There are, of course, other texts that do the same in their own way, but for me during this period, what I was immersed in here was the pinnacle.

It's impossible to detail everything that transpired under Dzogchen's spell, but at some point, I realized that I wasn't consuming it but rather, it was consuming me. I even had lucid dreams where I was holding my iPad and merging with pure white light and loving energy stemming from the books... even though no words could be seen. Now, as wild as it might sound, if you quizzed me about the basic points of Dzogchen, let alone its finer points, I really couldn't tell you very much! More than this, however, was the *feeling* that there was a Transmission taking place. I don't know what level this was happening on, but it did bring about a deeper place in/as Unity and with this, *a motionless mind*. To describe this as best I can, I'll use another pithy quote from Padmasambhava: "When exhaustively contemplated, these teachings merge in at-one-ment with the seeker who has sought them, although the seeker himself, when sought, cannot be found."

Regarding the "motionless mind" that I was falling into and Being, these two quotes speak directly to my experiences. First, Ramana Maharshi stated, "Those who are devoid of mental attachment will perish in that which is motionless." Second, from *The Zen Teaching of Huang Po*:

> ... A sudden comprehension comes when the mind has been purged of all the clutter of conceptual and discriminatory thought-activity. Those who seek the truth by means of intellect and learning only get further and further away from it. **Not till your thoughts cease** all their branching here and there, **not till you abandon all thoughts of seeking** for something, **not till your mind is motionless** as wood or stone, will you be on the right road to the [gateless] Gate.

June 27, 2020

Dear Friend: As you are finding The Natural State [Awakened Awareness-Experience, or put another way, Nirvana] more and more, I thought the following breakdown of this rare and precious place in/as consciousness might be beneficial or, at the very least, interesting. One of the unique and remarkable characteristics of Dzogchen is its clear, concise, and exquisitely simple way of disseminating the most advanced of metaphysical Truths. The excerpt below elucidates three distinct (albeit not necessarily separate) aspects of Awakened Beingness:

"The natural state is divided into three aspects...

The first aspect is referred to by the phrase '**the fact of pure awareness**,' which means *the pure beingness of the natural state, its essence*. It is explained by the word 'pure,' because, like the reflective capacity of a mirror, it has never been nor can it ever be tainted by the reflections which appear on it. This is also referred to by the terms 'primordial purity,' 'void,' 'empty,' 'open,' [and] 'no-thing.' Thus, from this standpoint, 'samsara has never been experienced as something that exists,' just like a reflection in a mirror is not something real in itself.

The second [aspect] means **to realize or understand**. It explains how the primordial basis presents itself in actuality, its nature. That is, although the basis (natural state) is no-thing, like the capacity of a mirror to reflect, it is not a mere nothing. Reflections are always present and anything can be reflected. Longchenpa says that 'capabilities are spontaneously present.' 'Capabilities' refers to how our nature manifests itself out of our primordial basis. These are usually referred to as 'buddha qualities.' *The term 'buddha' was translated [as] one who has woken up to his or her capacities, whose capacities can manifest, radiate, and expand because he or she is no longer ignorant of the natural state.* As we have explained, other paths, based on the principle of cause and effect, gradually remove this ignorance to reveal these capacities. But here in dzogchen it is said that the capabilities are spontaneously present. *The mirror is not just a pure, open possibility to reflect; it also clearly, effortlessly, naturally reflects whatever is present.* Thus, this second facet is characterized by the terms 'radiant' and 'spontaneously present.'

One might ask, 'Isn't there a difference between the spontaneous presence of buddha capacities and the presence of the impure samsaric phenomena that I experience right now?' It depends on our perspective. The third aspect helps us understand why.

The third aspect, the responsiveness of our primordial state to whatever presents itself, is indicated by the term 'energy,' which corresponds to 'mind.' That is, *we are the locus of being, which is a pure, open possibility, presenting itself in radiant clarity.* The process of experiencing, of being open and responsive to what presents itself has energy, momentum. We can experience this energy openly without judgment, or we can become confused and distracted by it and regard it judgmentally. In either case, the energy remains that of the natural state, the primordial basis of our being. The mirror analogy can illuminate this: *If we know that we are the mirror itself, we do not experience the reflections* *judgmentally; however, if we feel that we are looking at the mirror's reflections from a standpoint outside it, then we make dualistic judgments about what we see.* This is what is meant by the ordinary mind appearing 'out of the creativity of playful energy in impure forms.'"

~ *You Are the Eyes of the World: Longchenpa*
by Kennard Lipman and Merrill Peterson

Phil

After reading a concise quotation that deeply impressed me, for extra clarity I added slightly to it [in brackets] for a first-ever collaboration between Dudjom Lingpa and yours truly. I do hope that Dudjom's not throwing a fit in his astral cave right now at the thought of my act of hubris!

"The essential nature of **appearances** [Consciousness] is the [luminous] mind, the essential nature of the **mind** is [unmoving, unconditioned, and uncaused] awareness, and the essential nature of **awareness** is ultimate reality [The Pristine-Primordial, Absolute Substrate and Source of All That Is]."

July 19, 2020

Since you have been appreciating my ongoing emails about Dzogchen, I thought you might enjoy these beautiful passages about the State (Beingness) of Realization from *Heart of the Great Perfection: Dudjom Lingpa's Visions of the Great Perfection: Buddhahood Without Meditation, and The Vajra Essence,* translated by B. Alan Wallace:

"There is no difference between all buddhas and all sentient beings except that the former are aware [of their Real Nature] and the latter are not."

"Realization is like this: Once you have determined the nature of all external appearances as unreal – and after you deeply ascertain that identitylessness is like a hallucination, the lack of true existence is like a dream, and nonobjectivity is like the outer limits of space – you naturally, without contrivance, dwell at all times and on all occasions without grasping at true existence."

"Experiencing this reality, dwelling in it, entering the womb of the nature of existence, coming to the nature of being within yourself, and ascertaining this to be free of good and bad and of benefit and harm is the experience of realization by which you acquire confidence. And this is enlightenment."

Phil

July 27, 2020

I received the following question from a close friend: "What is the root of the mind?"

The root of the mind – in samsaric delusion – [in some Dzogchen texts this is called the "conditioned mind"] is *hanging on* to the sense of "I." One's identification as a separate self has to be cut. The issue, of course, is that the self cannot <u>make</u> this happen, as it has no intrinsic reality. In the same way, neither does anything else. Phenomena (all of manifestation that we take in via the senses) "appear" even though they are without intrinsic being. To take them as truly existent is what constitutes delusion, and again, this includes "I as the self." To make it weirder, it's not that phenomena don't exist either! After all, if we can perceive something, there has to be something there. On this (and most everything else too) Shankara and Longchenpa agree – **appearances are not "real," they aren't "not real," and…they're not "something in between**.**"** Therefore, they cannot be conceptualized or communicated, but only pointed to. In Dzogchen, they *extensively* use very specific similes and metaphors for this. Ultimately, as Shankara stated, appearances are something *other than real* and *other than not real*. Seeing appearances (and the self) in this way is an important component to Awakening. With "Clear Seeing" sister maya remains but…*she is seen through*. In Dzogchen, this is called Nirvana. However, they (samsara and nirvana) are both the same as well. Ultimately, of course, there is only The Godhead; everything else is just an emanation of/from THAT.

Consider these three passages from *Finding Rest in Illusion: A Teaching of the Great Perfection, Volume Three* by Longchenpa, translated by The Padmakara Translation Group:

"When the primordial nature of the mind – a sky-like expanse, in which the jewel-like qualities of enlightenment are spontaneously present – is conditioned by coemergent and conceptual ignorance, the habitual tendency to the mistaken duality of apprehended object and apprehending subject takes form, and beings wander in Samsāra, which is just like an echo."

"[I]t is not possible simply to remove the hallucinatory appearances of Samsāra for the simple reason that they are not actually existent things. On the other hand, it is through halting one's apprehension and clinging to such appearances that the latter will disappear. When all apprehension or clinging is left to settle in its own nature, all this will be brought to an end. As it is said in one of the sūtras, 'How can the duality of apprehender and apprehended remain when all conceptuality collapses?'"

"Though all phenomena are unborn, until one's mind stream, inseparable from a limpid state of concentration, is free of thoughts, it is important to sever the root of delusion and to keep from straying into the ordinary state. As the sūtra tells us, 'Samsāra comes from thought, not from the absence of thoughts.'"

So, as the Christian scriptures suggest – Be Still. Ramana Maharshi stated that "Be Still" is the highest teaching. Nisargadatta encouraged people to "Rest in the I Am," which is stillness. Here now, I might say: relax into and remain in the stillness of your essential nature. This is, for me, *the essence of all teachings.*

PW

This may be obvious to some, but its importance requires me to be very clear. "Be Still" in this context doesn't mean abstaining from worldly action, but instead refers to the mind. As I'm often asked, "What's the best way to still the mind?" I have a simple one-word answer: meditation.

August 1, 2020

Today I'm sharing two passages from *The Golden Letters: The Three Statements of Garab Dorje, First Dzogchen Master* by Chögyal Namkhai Norbu and John Myrdhin Reynolds. I want to preface these with this: I feel the well-known and oft-used metaphor of a "mirror" these excerpts refer to is probably best visualized not as a two-dimensional surface, as the Primordial Awareness of The Godhead is the Source and Matrix of all

Manifestation throughout infinite dimensions. Instead, I feel a much more accurate conceptualization of the "mirror" would be an eternally unstained, crystalline holographic mirror, possessing an infinite number of reflective surfaces. This type of mirror is, as I am certain you know, reminiscent of "Indra's Net" from Hindu mythology.

"One's own [true, primordial] nature or face encounters or meets itself [Awareness turning back on itself]. *When one comes face to face with oneself, it is like looking at oneself in a mirror and then discovering that one is the mirror itself.* This is one's essence, which is the state of emptiness, corresponding to the nature of the mirror, and this essence transcends all expression in words. This [direct, self-evident] experience of integration is like space dissolving into space. The internal space of interior Awareness and external space, which is the dimension in which appearances [phenomena] manifest, integrate, and are realized [in pure perception] to be identical [non-dual]."

"The essence [of all manifestation] is Śūnyatā, or emptiness, the condition of the nature of the mirror. *If one knows or recognizes one's essence, that is to say, if one knows that one is the mirror, then everything comes together simultaneously at one single moment.* In this condition, one transcends time, for time is something created by the mind and exists only in terms of the reflections, not in the condition of the mirror itself. This timeless condition is a fourth time beyond the three times of past, present, and future. It is the 'great time' [The Eternal Now] that is the context or dimension containing these three times simultaneously. In this condition of being the mirror and not the reflections, there is continuously present a cognition or primal awareness that does not go beyond knowing just that unique and singular essence. *By discovering just this one single experience of the state of immediate Awareness* [Rigpa] *one discovers the entire universe. By knowing just one single phenomenon, or dharma, where Rigpa is present, then one knows all dharmas. To know this one thing is to know all things.*"

Phil

In early August, Dzogchen had run its course with the feeling that this had been part one and, at some point, the remaining Dzogchen books in my collection would become part two. So, let's set the deep Wisdom of Dzogchen aside. In closing, I am including one final email with a beautiful excerpt from Llewellyn's book, which swings the pendulum back to the Heart aspect of Beingness.

November 8, 2020

An *Impulse* emphatically suggested that this particular passage from *For Love of the Real* by Llewellyn Vaughan-Lee should be sent to you now… and so it is!

"The work of the mystic is to reconnect life with the Source. There are individuals who have been born to do this work, to reconnect the world with what is real, to align the world with the poles of love. If one has come into this world to be of service in this way, the substance of the soul has a special light. There is a different vibration in such a human being, because this substance carries a very particular imprint. It belongs to both the Creator and the creation, and is in itself a link of love between the worlds.

This substance is the most precious thing in one's life. It is like liquid gold. It is part of the core of our being and it connects us to a certain fabric of life. From a spiritual perspective, it is really why we are here. It is the deepest purpose of our incarnation – the very meaning of life … If the mystic lives her light, if she remembers what is Real in herself and in life, this substance of the soul permeates the cells of her body – every cell rotates around the axis of love with joy and remembrance. And this body alive with remembrance is not separate from the body of life, the Earth, just as the individual soul is not separate from the world soul. The substance, the light, moves through all levels of reality; it flows through the worlds. Everything in the life of the mystic becomes a pulsating remembrance that nourishes the whole."

Phil

We Are Already One

I stand among you as one who offers a small message of hope that, first, there are always people who dare to seek on the margin of society, who are not dependent on social acceptance, not dependent on social routine, and prefer a kind of free-floating existence under a state of risk.

And among these people, if they are faithful to their own calling, to their own vocation and to their own message from God, communication on the deepest level is possible. And the deepest level of communication is not communication, but communion. It is wordless. It is beyond words, and it is beyond speech, and it is beyond concept.

Not that we discover a new unity. We discover an older unity. My dear brothers and sisters, we are already one. But we imagine that we are not. So what we have to recover is our original unity. What we have to be is what we are.

~ *The Asian Journal of Thomas Merton*

I'll sing this song the rest of my life until I drop dead; whether anybody listens to it or not is of no importance to me.

~ U.G. Krishnamurti

CHAPTER SEVEN:
Q&A Interview

Interviewer (I): Welcome, Phil! We've started recording now, so first I want to thank you for agreeing to join us today and letting people know more about you.

Phil (P): Thank you for inviting me; I'm looking forward to our conversation today.

I: Just to get started, can you tell us about where you're originally from, what your interests are, what you do for work, and those kinds of things?

P: OK. Well, all this obligatory stuff isn't terribly interesting but I'll give you a brief rundown. I grew up in Portland, Oregon and lived there for basically half my life. At the age of 23, I got started in the hospitality industry and that was the beginning of what's been a 35-year career managing hotels, food and beverage operations, both free-standing and within hotels, and resorts. For 30 of the 35 years, I was in GM, Director, or multi-unit executive leadership roles. I suppose the apex of my corporate climbing years was at the VP level for a U.S.-owned and based international resort company, with assets throughout the Caribbean. Since leaving Portland for my first gig away from home, I've been living the life of a nomad, so to speak. As a turnaround specialist for much of my career, I seldom lived in one area for more than a couple of years, so I've been fortunate to have seen a lot in my travels. I did very much enjoy residing in Atlanta for 8 years, which was the longest I've been in one place outside of Portland, until moving to Southern California in early 2012.

As far as my interests go, I've always enjoyed reading since I was a child. I love books; hard copy and digital. For the last 20 years or so I've had no real interest in TV, but I do enjoy a movie now and then. One of my current favorite actors is Godzilla! He's been awesome in his last few outings. I especially like science fiction; the Star Wars kind is always fun, but what I enjoy most is intelligent Sci-Fi that makes one think. Hands down in the last few years, *Arrival* was the best thing to come out. I also thought *Blade Runner 2049* was killer. Denis Villeneuve is, for my box-office money, one of the best directors in today's movie industry. I can't wait to see what he does with *Dune*. I was very impressed with Alex Garland's *Ex Machina* too. While what it portrayed was science fiction, it isn't by much. It appears that type of thing will actually be here in the next 10-30 years. I've always had an interest in science, especially quantum mechanics, artificial intelligence, and what's happening on the leading edge of nanotech and biotech. With the latter, I think the implications of CRISPR [clustered regularly interspaced short palindromic repeats] are simultaneously both immensely exciting and alarming in the extreme. I suppose the same can be said for AI and its physical delivery system: robotics. Moreover, I am a proponent of worldwide dialogue on scientific ethics, especially as it relates to autonomous weaponry. If you've never seen *Slaughterbots* by Stuart Russell [a leading-edge computer science professor at UC Berkeley] about the potential of AI weaponry, I strongly suggest that you do. It's only 8 minutes long but it chillingly demonstrates the *very real possibilities* of our near-future AI-based military systems. While not a pleasant topic, our civilization's emerging technologies, especially this one, are in desperate need of analysis and conversation at all levels of society. Since it was published, I think the 2017 *Slaughterbots* video has probably had a few million YouTube views. That being said, I'd prefer to see it have a few billion views. Over the last few years, prominent scientists worldwide have been sharing their concerns about AI in general and AI weaponry specifically. Since you asked about my interests, I wanted to take advantage of my platform here to mention this.

What else? I'm a lifelong fan of the Portland Trailblazers, the Boston Red Sox, and the Pittsburgh Steelers. In my teenage years, I was heavily involved in the martial arts and chess. I still follow the latter fairly closely. In my early 20s, I spent three years playing rugby for the Portland Rugby Club, primarily as a wing, until I got into hotel management. My GM quickly put the kibosh on rugby when I came into work after a game looking like I'd been in a bar fight (laughs) and I couldn't blame him! I've always loved music, mainly rock, jazz, folk, and a smattering of classical, along with lots of strange, sometimes obscure…I guess "world music" is how it's typically labeled. I enjoy most of the modern-day kirtan fusion as well and pretty much have everything by all the well-known western artists in the genre. I have always had an embarrassingly large collection of music and likely always will, although digital formats and playback devices have made this more manageable. That said, it has to be lossless. I don't do the dreaded MP3…it sounds awful! I play the Native American Flute a little too, but not very well; I don't possess much musical talent. I love all animals and many times have been called an "animal whisperer," especially with dogs and cats. I was a landscape, nature, and wildlife photographer and digital artist for ten years until I sold all my gear and retired from the hobby in early 2017. A lot has fallen away since the awakening, even my love of listening to music to some degree. It seems I've become a "silence junkie." I enjoy writing, and I still really groove on traveling. I suppose I'm still trying to figure out what I'll be when I grow up!

I: Perfect, thanks Phil! Please share one unusual thing about your daily life, or life in general.

P: (looks puzzled and pauses) Well, here's one that most people I know find odd. For the last twenty years or so, I've generally eaten once a day, and that's almost always lunch, as I don't like eating late. My motto is "eat to live rather than live to eat." This topic came up while I was visiting The Abbey of Gethsemani for the first time in February 2009. During a wide-ranging conversation with Father Damien who was the "Guest Master" at the time, my once-a-day eating habit came up. He wasn't surprised at all and told me that in their tradition, this was called a "monks fast" and that monks of various persuasions had been eating this way for more than one thousand years! I know eating once-a-day flies in the face of current medical advice, and I'm not recommending it to anyone; I'm just sharing what's worked for me.

I: Interesting. As lunch is your only full meal of the day, do you eat a lot to carry you through?

P: No, just normal portions. And while we're on the subject, it may shock and/or disappoint some of my readers here to discover that I'm not a vegetarian. I don't eat much meat, but I do eat some: mainly chicken, turkey, and a little seafood. I almost never eat beef and pork though. I'm living proof that there are no hard and fast rules about Self-Realization, which I feel is a really good thing, as lots of folks put undue pressure on themselves to live up to some perceived standard **before** they can awaken, and it just ain't true.

I: I have a question for you about politics and your affiliations, if any. Given the volatile nature of today's political climate, you're certainly free to pass if you'd rather not go there.

P: I don't mind talking about politics or the very important issues that we all face as a civilization. They need to be discussed…desperately. First, I think many of the people who go into politics do so with the hope of making their respective cities, states, or countries better, and God Bless 'em for trying! Second, I've always been fairly apolitical but that's not to say that I don't pay attention to what's happening in the political arena. Third, as a registered Independent, I appear to be a member of a rapidly vanishing breed in this day and age of hyper-polarized politics. I'll support *anyone,* Republican or Democrat, as long as what they are proposing makes some amount of sense to me.

Talking big picture now, what we're seeing in politics is the same as what we're seeing with everything else. *Everything in manifestation is a reflection of the consciousness that is present in This Moment.* It's hard to argue that **any** of our systems or isms are working anymore. Not only do we have age-old, ignorance-fueled madness throughout the world, but now we have technologies on our doorstep that are incredibly exciting on one hand, and yet on the other hand, there is no way for *anyone* to predict the impact they will have once fully developed and set loose. Not long ago it was announced that "living robots" had been created! While these "xenobots" are less than a millimeter wide, their likely impact on the world is unfathomably wide. Their potential benefits *and* detriments ought to be front-page news, but of course they're not. Please don't get me wrong, I love science and the possible benefits to humanity that it offers. But take AI for instance. DARPA [Defense Advanced Research Projects Agency] is the leading nation-state developer of it, even collaborating with Google on "defensive" AI systems, *but to what end?* It seems to me that the underlying issue at hand isn't a political one any more than it is a systemic failure of our social, or economic, or educational, or religious, or any of our other institutions out there. **The problem stems from our sense**

of separation. The illusory fear that it's us – or "me" – against everyone else who doesn't share our/my assessment of *how things should be*...given the ego-mind's view of reality, based in part on one's background, intelligence, nationality, belief systems, and, of course, consciousness. This is why I feel certain that, to some extent, institutions of all kinds are going to have to fall apart before we as a civilization can put them back together. Only this time, put them together more consciously, with a long term view of sustainability and not simply for shortsighted gain. Not for "my" benefit while billions starve and/or barely survive in abject poverty. I don't know when or what the last straw tipping point will be, but given what I see, it already is falling apart. Our collective insanity – ignorance of our Unity – is simply *not sustainable* for much longer. And anyone thinking the world can continue to go on this way has their head buried in some very denial-based, unconscious sand.

By writing *Grace Happens,* I hope to inspire people to make the maximum spiritual effort they can, however they can. It's not as if we cannot evolve. *We can't decline to participate in life because We Are Life!* But **how we participate** is the blessed opportunity of and in Each Moment. The more awake we are, the more our world is ministered, and I'm not talking about this abstractly or philosophically. At some point **today**, over 1.5 billion people won't have access to clean water and nearly as many don't have electricity. Get this – there are well over 2 billion people who still don't have toilets or indoor plumbing and presently, roughly 20% of the earth's population consumes 80% of its natural resources! Here in the U.S., we make it national news when some guy competitively eats 70+ hot dogs in 10 minutes, while it's estimated that somebody loses their current opportunity to evolve from hunger or hunger related issues every 10 seconds. Setting all that aside for a moment, *as a species we can't even stop killing each other!* **We have to evolve**. Hoping our elected officials fix everything by just spending money or, as we often see, "declaring war" on a problem, never works. A global shift in consciousness is needed, and it has to begin with *all of us* awakening to the highest degree possible.

If awakening can happen to a yo-yo like Phil, then it can surely happen to anyone! [I briefly thought about calling the book *Autobiography of a Yo-Yo* but in the end, I didn't feel that title would do the material justice. Needlessly, an "AYY" would've most likely pissed-off a few humorless SRF hardliners too.] While we do what we can for people within the contextual field of daily life, ultimately the greatest gift we can give anyone is our own evolving consciousness. Paramahansa Yogananda said, "Reform yourself and you will have reformed thousands." **This** is one key reason why I strived so diligently on the spiritual path. I deeply care about our planet, about future generations, and about *diminishing suffering* to the greatest extent possible. **This** is why I committed all those years ago, come what may, to "the inner evolution toward spiritual perfection." **This** is why Yogananda's quote is the first one in the book. Through my journey and small example, I pray that people will feel the urgency of the condition of our planet and ultimately Realize their Oneness in and as All That Is. By doing this, our world evolves for the highest good of everyone.

I: I so appreciate you taking that question, and your sentiments. Given how entrenched the world is in how things are, and how the divide between the "haves" and the "have nots" keeps widening, what will it take to make the rich and powerful change their ways of operating? What incentives do they have?

P: I wish I knew. Like anyone else, I can only speculate. As I previously mentioned, doing all we can to awaken our own consciousness is the most meaningful and important place to start. Unfortunately, my observations are that while many, if not most, want to go out and change the world, not very many want to do the much tougher work of changing themselves. That's not surprising I guess, and it seems to have been that way throughout all of history, hence Jesus reportedly saying, "The harvest is plenty, but the laborers are few." I do feel that we are in the portion of the ascending Yuga cycle known as Dwapara and therefore I remain optimistic overall. [In his book, *The Holy Science,* Swami Sri Yukteswar calculated that this current Yuga began around 1700 CE.] That said, I cannot imagine the deeply entrenched Kali Yuga consciousness that is fueling the insanity we see in the world today going down without some sort of global crisis and upheaval forcing it to. The greedy and power-hungry are probably not going to change their ways otherwise. Please keep in mind though that this is just first and third chakra consciousness; there is no "good" and "evil" or "right" and "wrong" here. I have no idea what will spark the change. It will probably be a combination of things, mostly on a global scale, but I really don't want to speculate on that here; it's not particularly useful and again, I just don't know any of this for sure.

What I will add is that things are so off-kilter that I think it will require some sort of what many would call Divine intercession. Most of the world's major religions have this in their mythologies. There is the second coming of Christ, the Hindu Kalki Avatar, The Maitreya Buddha, the Muslim Twelfth Imam, and probably many more than I am not aware of. Maybe, if or when the Shift really hits the fan, there will be a Highly Evolved Being that will appear – if he or she is not here already – to show civilization a way of living that works long term, and help usher in a new era. As consciousness is the manifestation of infinite potentiality, that sort of thing <u>is</u> possible but again, it's just conjecture on my part. I want to keep this interview primarily focused on what I can *experientially* speak to and not merely harangue and/or speculate on, so that's probably enough on this topic.

I: Thank you for opining on these subjects, Phil; I know they're not what your book is really about. While I know that all this is just your best take on things, I do think that there will be people reading this that will be interested in how an awakened consciousness views our current global situation.

P: Well, *just because someone is awake, doesn't mean they are correct about everything* – I make mistakes! In order to answer <u>all</u> your questions, I'm just sharing my best guesses. I'd add that regardless of how manifestation unfolds, the sparks of consciousness that are sufficiently awake need to <u>Be</u> the light of awareness in every way possible. It all adds up; it all matters. Everything is interconnected. It's all one homogenous, unified field of conscious intelligent energy. There's a timeworn axiom from somewhere that states, "with each thing improved, all of creation is improved," and it is literally true.

I: Well put. Before we talk about the awakening, I'd like to explore why you wrote the book. In our pre-interview conversation, it was clear that on top of being a very private person, you also don't seem to have any aspirations to become a spiritual teacher. And yet, what was written was *a very personal account*. Sharing it all now with the world seems to run counter to your wish for privacy.

P: (sigh) Yes it does. I've found that post-awakening there are no desires or goals in life. By desires, I don't mean the occasional wish for ice cream. And by goals, I'm excluding normal practical matters. Ego-driven desires, however, are the type that bring karma, and have a certain amount of "stickiness" to them. When these are or are not satisfied, feelings of ease or dis-ease arise. As I am not being driven by personal desires and trying to attract everything that feels good in life and pushing away what doesn't – a strategy that never works in the end by the way – there now is just a deep trust of What Is-As It Is. From this, "impulses" or "urges" arise naturally and often spontaneously. These, in turn, fuel actions with no need for any specific result. Destiny = What Is. This is how *Grace Happens* came to be. Beginning in September of 2019, an urge to somehow share the blessings I've received started nagging at me and eventually broke through while I was on my desert retreat in Arizona. It feels as if there are three central reasons behind the impulse to make my awakening journey known: 1) There are very few as-it-is-happening accounts of awakenings available and therefore, sharing my experiences might be helpful to someone. 2) This is a way to sincerely thank everyone and everything that helped me through my awakening. 3) I hope to inspire those who read the book to <u>remember</u> their inherent Oneness in and as All Things and by doing so, be a light unto our world.

I: Would you please tell us about the book's dedications?

P: Paramahansa Yogananda is my Guru, and his organization and techniques were critical to my eventual awakening. They weren't the only factors by any means, but they were the biggest. If I am writing any book of this type at all, it's going to be, at least in part, dedicated to them.

Nevertheless, while my path worked, it didn't prepare me at all for what came after. In addition to the support of a few close friends, coupled with Nisargadatta's wisdom, Adyashanti made a colossal difference. Finding Adya's audio archives was like striking gold, and while there were many things that he spoke to that were very helpful, there were three key areas that assisted me the most: 1) Knowing that there is nearly always **ebb and flow** to the bliss and deep feelings of perfection in everything that I was experiencing was invaluable. This is the "I had it, I lost it" stage. Realizing this allowed me to relax when the honeymoon stuff would wane, which in turn made the overall process flow much easier. 2) Bliss is, not surprisingly, intoxicating, but it also is *just another level of consciousness that one can become attached to and be stuck in.* Spiritual aspirants can't wait to give up the "hell" of egoic separation consciousness, but Adya helped me to see what I hadn't considered – that we must surrender "heaven" too. Bliss, and the highest expressions of one's personal self-ness, also must be relinquished, in order to abide in the natural state. 3) Adya provided a clear view of the various aspects of the mystifying terra incognita that I found myself in and with it, practical tactics and strategies for traversing it. This last item is a big reason why *Grace Happens* was written. While awakenings never unfold in exactly the same way, generally there are some shared characteristics.

I: You mentioned "bliss." We read and hear so much about this in spirituality, but there doesn't seem to be a clear understanding about what it is. Could you define bliss?

P: I don't want to attempt an entire exposé on bliss as it's so subjective. I guess it's probably worth telling people what my experience of it was like early on though, and as concisely as possible, this is it: a fluid mix of joy and peace with a dash of euphoria.

I: That works, thank you. My next question is, was there ever a time that you felt as if awakening was on the near horizon, possibly through some type of premonition or experience?

P: Not really, no. And I think that's an exceptionally fortunate thing.

I: Why is that?

P: Given what transpired over the two years after The Kiss, especially during the first nine months, if I would have been given a blow-by-blow description of it all in advance, I might have thrown myself in the ocean. Perhaps not literally, but I really would have been searching for, and wondering where the necessary courage to face it all was going to come from. The rebirthing stage was without a doubt **the most** challenging and disorienting time in this life. Having read the awakening accounts of Bernadette Roberts and Suzanne Segal, I know it can be worse, but still, I wouldn't wish what I went through on anyone. As I mentioned earlier, this is one of the reasons I am "coming out of the awakening closet." If even one thing in this book makes awakening just a tad bit easier for somebody, then it was worth all the effort.

The Kiss manifested out of left field, completely blindsiding me. Generally, I think that's how these types of things go down. Nevertheless, early on in my spiritual journey I was told on three separate occasions that awakening was my destiny in this incarnation. Also, in the twelve months prior to The Kiss, there were two events that in hindsight, I'd now say pointed to a looming cataclysmic Shift of some sort. At the time, however, there was no way I could've recognized what it would be.

I: If you would, please share these with us.

P: Very early in the new millennium while living in Atlanta, I had the good fortune to have three separate darshans with Sri Karunamayi. During the last two, she stated as unambiguously as possible that "moksha" was what I incarnated for and that if I stuck to the path, it would inevitably happen. Hearing that was fantastic, don't get me wrong, but in the back of my mind there was still some doubt. Then, during a pilgrimage of sorts to Southern California in 2005, I had the privilege of a private meeting with Brother Anandamoy at SRF's Mount Washington headquarters in Los Angeles. I had met with Brother once before in 2001 when I was thinking about becoming a monk – in retrospect one of my more unconvincing ideas. Needless to say, I didn't become one and both I and SRF were better off for it! That being the case, my second meeting with him was one I will never forget, and while much of what was discussed isn't germane to what we're talking about here, he did indicate to me that Self-Realization was on my near horizon. While he communicated this encouraging news a bit more cryptically than Sri Karunamayi did, he left no doubt in my mind that if I stayed true to my path, The Universe in and as Phil was going to awaken in this lifetime.

In regards to the two somewhat strange experiences that happened much closer to the awakening, the first was in late September of 2016, about one year prior to The Kiss. I had recently settled into my new home in Temecula and I was out shopping for groceries. I'd been at my new job for about two weeks and I already had the feeling that it wasn't going to turn out to be what I had hoped for. It is odd how we're always able to remember certain events as if they happened a moment ago, and this is one of those. After shopping, I was standing outside my car when I had the *strangest feeling*. Now, I am seldom lacking for words and on top of that, I've had several years to reflect on that moment. Even still, I've never been able to come up with a satisfying description of how I felt in that moment. Some fear was there I suppose but I didn't feel afraid. Some uncertainty about the future was present…a certain foreboding maybe. I was acutely aware in that moment that I was feeling something that I'd never felt before and I couldn't put any words to it. All I could say, then or now, was that it felt as if I was heading toward something I'd never encountered or imagined.

In January 2017, a friend emailed me out of the blue, inquiring if I was OK. He said he was asking because his spiritual teacher – who hardly knew me – all of a sudden asked him if I was OK and then stated that I was entering a period of "spiritual crisis." Through various friends in SRF, I knew his teacher had an exceptional reputation, along with a certain siddhi known as etheric vision. I emailed back stating that the organization I had recently gone to work for turned out to look worse than worms on a waffle iron. What's more, I was on an indefinite medical leave due to possibly serious physical issues. Therefore, "crisis" seemed like a reasonable description to me! And, as these types of things so often do, it all got worse before it got better. At times like these, it's critical to remember that **crisis = opportunity**. Often, what appears to be "the bottom" is the perfect catalyst we need to evolve, and that's what the first nine months of 2017 turned out to be for me.

I: Very interesting. How are you able to explain Sri Karunamayi and Brother Anandamoy both being able to, apparently, see this one aspect of your future?

P: I can't. There are some who have what in the eastern spiritual traditions are called siddhis – extraordinary powers – and these can manifest in both awakened and unawakened people. I have no doubts by the way that both Karunamayi and Brotherji were awake. If memory serves, there are allegedly eight primary powers that can manifest; don't ask me what they all are. Clairvoyance may be one, although I don't think one just decides to peek ahead for funsies. Instead, that glimpse is provided by The Universe for a purpose. Additionally, there is ongoing research into a possible link between psychic phenomena and quantum entanglement, but the jury is surely still out on that.

I: Regarding the likelihood of awakening, what or how did you feel about it during your sadhana?

P: I hope this doesn't sound arrogant, as that's not how I felt, but my inner attitude or assumption was always, **why not** me?! Logically, I knew that I Was One With All Things, and while I never took it for granted, my eventual awakening did feel inevitable! I also found it helpful to evoke what Yogananda said about Enlightenment – The Natural State – being our "birthright," and that, all you need to do is "improve your knowing." I adamantly took this approach throughout my sadhana.

An example of this – not to mention an unforgettable experience – took place with Sri Karunamayi at the aforementioned darshan. Shortly before the proceedings began, things were relaxed, with lots of people standing around talking. Sri Karunamayi was seated, smiling and looking around, and occasionally waving to somebody. Unexpectedly, she held up the microphone and quipped, "Everyone here today will become enlightened." I was aghast as everyone looked up briefly, laughed at the notion, and then went back to their conversations! Well…as earnestly as I took my search for enlightenment, this was no joking matter, so I sat there with an unhappy look, feeling hurt. She was looking off to her left as I was sitting there feeling somewhat slighted, and suddenly she froze. In the next instant, the smile vanished from her face. Slowly, she turned until she was looking me right in the eye, and in my mind I heard her say, "For you, I mean it." She then nonchalantly turned away to wave at someone, as if nothing had happened! Needless to say, this gave me a lot of confidence.

I: Fascinating stuff! Switching gears now, in your book and in our previous talk, you used the term "non-duality," as in "non-dual awareness." I know this isn't a philosophy book and that you don't make any claims of being a scholar in these areas, but in terms of your post-awakening experience, what is non-duality to you? It seems as if non-dual teachers and teachings are very in-vogue these days, so if you don't mind, I'd like to hear your insights.

P: You are correct; this is not a philosophy book. There are plenty of those already, and even if the world was clamoring for another, I'm not qualified to write one. Also, I'm not a teacher of anything, let alone a non-duality expert. Ramana Maharshi is generally considered to be the towering icon of 20th century Advaita but actually, he never studied it in his life until well after his Self-Realization! Once he was stabilized in the place in consciousness that he was, and once he got settled in Arunachala [Tamil Nadu, India], he was able to read some of the ancient Vedic texts, along with Masters like Shankara. These so completely corroborated his awakened experience that he began using them as teaching tools. While I'm not setting out to teach per se, I too found that post-awakening, the awareness-experience was best pointed to by non-duality-based verbiage along with, to some degree, the terminology that comes from Zen. The fundamental principle of Advaita that my experience confirms is that non-dual consciousness is our natural state.

Now, there are different flavors of non-dual thought and honestly, I don't fathom the nuances between classical Advaita Vedanta and the current New Age non-duality and Neo-Advaita schools, with their postmodern doctrines of relativism and ostensible lack of Absolute Truth. What's more, I don't care. From my perspective, debating all that has nothing to do with Being awake. I'm not disparaging philosophical explorations or these particular paths. I'm just saying it all strikes me as mind-play and *for me*, it has nothing to do with living an awakened life. I don't know what else to say on the subject so I'm going to punt the ball back to you.

I: That works. OK, as concisely as possible, please describe what awakening is like for you now.

P: There now is an intimate and visceral awareness-experience of Being One with Everything. It feels as if The Universe is me. Conversely, there is an experiential knowing that I Am No One or, in other words, no-thing in particular. There is no sense of doership, no inner world, and no separate I. This Beingness is self-authenticating or, put another way, my Unity in and as All Things is self-evident. No outside validation is necessary, and there is no "outside!" There is an eternal unknowing that is lived, and through it, knowing is revealed. There is an unshakable conviction that the awakened state deepens eternally; we never stop evolving. Egoic desires and attachments give way to joyful surrender and trust in What Is. Love and compassion become the impetus for one's actions, which arise naturally out of deep internal Stillness, with no agenda or goal. Awakened consciousness becomes a physical embodiment – with one foot in eternal, unchanging Awareness and one foot in the Present Moment of manifestation, in service of All Things. Reality is experienced as quite ordinary and yet, it is also intensely felt as wondrous, awe-inspiring, and sacred.

I: That's perfect Phil, thank you for that. I'd like to go in the opposite direction now and take a few minutes to discuss what awakening isn't and/or hasn't done in your experience.

P: Sounds reasonable. There <u>are</u> a lot of misrepresentations, misconceptions, and fantasies out there in sunny spiritual land regarding what post-awakening life is like. As awakening is beyond the mind's ability to conceptualize, this is certainly understandable. In no particular order, I guess some of the big myths are: 1) That it's complete and immediate. 2) That we all of a sudden are in total bliss forever. 3) That we are suddenly given deep cosmic insights into the nature of damn near everything. 4) That everything in life starts to go "right." 5) That all our stubborn personality traits that are viewed as "bad" just shrivel up and in embarrassment, slink away. 6) That all our past karma is instantly vaporized. 7) That we will suddenly be a lot better at all the stuff we weren't so good at before. 8) That we'll instantly have magnetic personalities and then people from all walks of life will be irresistibly drawn to us – especially the opposite sex, or the same sex – whatever floats your awakened boat. 9) That we'll be able to attract whatever we want into our lives like they do in the movie, *The Secret*. 10) That Ascended Masters will start hanging out with us on their days off. 11) That we will start looking incredibly holy, even first thing in the morning. 12) Celibacy? No problem y'all! Love it!

There are plenty more; those are just a few of the standard-fare ones. It's not like one or more of those *couldn't* happen, but as I really want to keep my observations and suggestions based in personal experience, I can honestly say that none of those have happened for me. And ya know, truth to tell, I am still coming to grips with the fact that I'm not a supermodel magnet. Imagine that! Well, at least I can corroborate all the truly blessed things that <u>do</u> come with an awakening, so that's a positive!

I: Ha! That is quite the list. Thank you for clearing those up! (chuckles) I have a few more for you along those lines. How, if at all, has your personality changed? Are you always composed and peaceful now? I guess what I'm getting at is, are there things in life that make you impatient or mad? If so, what are they and did these things irritate you before the awakening? Similarly, on top of all that, how do you view sex now?

P: (yells and pounds the table with fist) **I can't stand being asked these types of questions!** (smiles) Just kidding! For this, I can only speak to my experience but no, my personality hasn't changed much. I may be more outwardly quiet than I was before but it's hard for me to tell. Perhaps close friends of mine could better answer that. It seems that, post-awakening, I am still jam-packed with an irrepressible, marginally dubious, and very often irreverent brand of humor! It looks as if *personality* doesn't have much, if anything, to do with an abiding dropping away of the ego-mind. Our general likes and dislikes continue to some degree, unless of course they don't. I can and still do yell for my favorite sports teams, although the amount of cussing and flying spittle has been reduced by nearly 100%, which makes me more likely to be invited to sporting-event parties now! Outwardly, I'm not much different in this respect than I was before, but inwardly, there's really nothing that truly cares. I mean sure, I'm always going to want to see the Red Sox beat the ever-livin' snot out of The Evil Empire [a.k.a. the New York Yankees]. However, *all of it now is just seen as an aspect of the passing play of form*. It is and always will be impossible for me to look at any of this stuff as I once did. And actually, that's a truly blessed thing! I've noticed jumping-up-and-down excitement never happens anymore either, although I certainly appreciate things more than I ever have before. I'm perpetually amazed with wonder and awe at the littlest of things, whereas before I often wouldn't notice. Excitement is mostly gone though, and while this might not sound appetizing, suffering has also fallen away, making for a much more peaceful and joyous passage through life.

That said, *awakening doesn't mean that one ceases to feel!* From my experience, I feel even more intensely! There are two reasons for this: 1) There's no sense of separation between me and anyone or anything else and, 2) There are no defense mechanisms around the heart anymore. There's no fear about what the spiritual heart feels anymore, or how deeply it feels. It just is what it is and does what it does. So with that, the entire gamut of feelings is possible, and I'd posit that it is both natural and healthy to feel the entire range. That seems to be an essential component of our humanity and I am very big on not denying one's humanness. Only the ego-mind does that. Consequently, just as I don't take sporting events – or anything else for that matter – too seriously anymore, I most of all don't take *Phil* too seriously! I still care…but without any need for life to unfold in a particular way.

As far as what specific things still occasionally set Phil off…well, he's never had much patience for automated phone directories, although on this he can't be the only one! I totally get why companies use them – saving money – but they can be pretty irritating, especially now that their voice recognition platforms want to do everything for you, often making it a challenge to figure out how to actually speak to a human. What else? There have been times, usually during the course of my work, where I haven't suffered fools gladly. This has subsided some though. Certainly, I don't mind people that don't know something. Hell, I don't know much of anything beyond I Am! Nevertheless, it is still hard at times to tolerate people who just don't give a rip, and by that I mostly mean some of the professional associates I've worked with. Over my career, I've observed a decline in the general work ethic of the labor force and with it, a growing sense of entitlement. Those two combined sometimes raise my blood pressure. The single most notable change, however, is that if something does ignite Mount Vesuvius, it almost never lasts for more than a few minutes, and with that, I'm not stewing on it later. Either one is in the Present Moment or one isn't. As I am, it leaves little to none of it sticking. I guess that's a good way to put it – nothing "sticks" because there's "nobody home" for events to stick to. I've also noticed that there have been times when, even as the mind-body known as Phil is getting irate about something, there is awareness there impersonally witnessing it, so it really can't take over. Now, this utterly ruins a satisfying old-fashioned blow-up, but I've found that the trade-off is more than worth it!

As for sex, I find it quite possibly *the most overrated thing in the world*. Conversely, along with consuming tasty foods and beverages, sex may be the most fun, natural, and healthy aspect of humanness there is. If your real questions are, "Do I still find people sexually attractive and do I still get horny?" the answer to both is yes. Early on, I used to think that celibacy – sometimes referred to as "Brahmacharya" in eastern religious practices – was required for awakening. As it turned out, at least in my case, it wasn't. What's more, *I don't think celibacy is required for anyone to awaken!* While the practice may be useful in purifying the body-mind, and the urge may naturally fall away during sadhana and/or post-awakening, attempting to ignore and/or artificially stifle such a natural and powerful feature of our humanness is asking for trouble. One surely doesn't have to look very hard at certain religious/spiritual institutions around the world for evidence of this. From my perspective, *aversion and indulgence* are simply two sides of the same coin, and that doesn't go for just sex. In some spiritual practices, sex is actually used for awakening. Therefore, as I view it, both options can be helpful…or not, depending on one's karmic predilection. Let's put all our cards on the table here – there are *innumerable* "horny celibates" in the world wearing monastic and priestly garb. On the other hand, sex and other sensory indulgences do carry the potential for addiction and depleting vital energies. On this, I recommend the proverbial middle path, unless one or the other options clearly make themselves evident. Ultimately, it's just energy and an indispensable aspect of the human mind-body organism we all utilize, so making a huge deal out of sex either way seems both unnecessary and unhelpful. There's far too much anxiety, guilt, shame, and all the rest over such a perfectly natural thing, and in my view, none of it is useful. We need a more, dare I use the word, *enlightened* attitude towards sex. There may well be places in one's sadhana – a.k.a. Life – where it's useful to take a break from it or, to indulge in it. My advice then is to listen to your heart, trust the process, and just say **no thank you** to all the fearful stigma surrounding sex.

While on the platform you've kindly given me, LGBTQ+ modulations of consciousness shouldn't be discriminated against doing *anything* in life, including church service or monastic vocations. A sad and needless example of this [at the time this was written] is an international spiritual organization near and dear to my heart prohibiting gays from teaching their Sunday school classes. Does the expression of homosexuality make one *incapable* of teaching children? Or worse, make one a pedophile?! This is the 21st century for God's sake! I am bringing these issues up, not because I have a personal axe to grind, but because I deeply care – about those who are discriminated against and about the organization. I'm directing these remarks to those in spiritual leadership positions here. Groups like this are losing many fine individuals at a time when people aren't exactly hammering down the doors to get in. Their longstanding policy of "don't ask, don't tell" is just that…except they "ask" and then penalize those who "tell" honestly, and this is something I've witnessed. When interviewing for potential monastics, this organization provides a list of qualifications that must be met prior to arrival, but they aren't up front about what *disqualifies* a candidate. I've known some incredibly competent and loyal members that jumped through the preliminary hoops, and once onsite, were given a list of questions, including one about their sexual orientation. Up to this point, everything's been honest and aboveboard, but here's the skullduggery: anything but a heterosexual checkmark gets you immediately kicked out of their program. Couldn't that at least be stated up front so these individuals don't waste their time, and so they don't have to experience the hurt and disillusionment that arises from the shock of finding out this way? It'd be the honest thing to do, but of course they don't want this discriminatory policy anywhere in writing, and for obvious reasons.

There are numerous polls that show church attendance here in the U.S. is declining and I think it's obvious as to why: these institutions are not *evolving*, and that's what is needed. The wake of a boat doesn't determine its course! Come on people, let's end this type of Kali Yuga crap once and for all. Your organization will be far better off for it in the long run.

Personally, I don't even view people as white or black, straight or gay, male or female. While these differences exist – the multiplicity of manifestation – non-dual awareness doesn't latch onto outward appearances and their illusion-based labels. Early in the awakening, there was the awareness-experience of simply seeing people as souls, in and as Soul. I find it disheartening to hear all the pleas for unity, well-intentioned though they may be, as the term itself implies bringing two or more separate elements together. In the end, everyone and everything are already One, but we're not able to see this obvious fact in ego-consciousness.

I view sexual preferences as an impersonal, karmic predisposition for any given individuated modulation of consciousness, akin to one's color of skin or hair. Why would *anyone care*, let alone condemn, what somebody's sexual orientation is, as long as it's consensual and doesn't hurt anyone? That being said, one's sexual orientation might very easily become an *identity*, just like one's ethnicity, gender, age, or anything else, hence our need to be vigilant of that pitfall while on the spiritual path. Along with attachments and desires, identities have to be tossed over the side as well! I feel the Conversations with God [CWG] material has some of the clearest, most commonsensical views on sex, and how it relates to spirituality, that I've come across. In these spiritually groundbreaking and refreshing texts, the term is made into an acronym. S.E.X. stands for Synergistic Energy eXchange. I also quite like the word "sacred" instead of Synergistic. In either case, given this description, everyone is continuously having S.E.X., albeit not always physically! In regards to physical intimacy, I cannot think of a better description than this – two modulations of consciousness exchanging energy synergistically/sacredly. *What difference could gender possibly make in this?* Here now, let's bravely reexamine outdated and hurtful views and policies, and fearlessly evolve… individually, organizationally, and societally!

I: Very thorough and interesting! Your answers are a fascinating blend of humanness and, um…

P: It's just consciousness manifesting, my friend.

I: Fair enough. One last question on this. You mentioned what does and doesn't carry over after awakening. In your list, you said that karma isn't "instantly vaporized." After reading about your "karmic purge," I can't help but wonder where all that karma goes and, if some remains, might that be why certain former personality characteristics endure?

P: Those are both excellent and large questions! Since I don't <u>know</u>, all I can provide you and the reader with is my sense of it in This Moment. Karma is an integral *concept* in eastern spiritual traditions. I think the most concise definition of karma is this, courtesy of Nisargadatta Maharaj: "**An accumulation of unspent energies, of unfulfilled desires, and fears not understood**." Adi Shankara taught that both karma <u>and</u> reincarnation fall away after one has awakened but again, I don't experientially know that. The one thing I will add is a pointer that Ramana used. It's one that I really like, and I have seen and still do see this with post-awakening Phil. Ramana used the metaphor of the karmically bound ego being like a plugged-in and running electric fan. Once the plug is pulled from the electrical socket – this is analogous to a transcendence of the ego-mind – then the fan is done functioning. However, the blades continue to spin and take time to stop. This is how he viewed and explained karma. Nisargadatta said that there are two types of karma. One type can be mitigated by Grace but the other has to be burned while our individuated consciousness is in-form. So after awakening, there's a "run-off period" and there seems to be no way to tell how long that will take. I observe this run-off like everything else. It's impersonal, transitory, and occurs naturally.

I: And once this is complete, is there anything?! Is there <u>no</u> karmically bound ego of any kind left?

P: Again, you are probing philosophical and metaphysical questions that I just can't answer. It's not because I don't want to but because I simply don't know. In some of the eastern teachings, it is said that there must be a shard of ego or, put another way, a psychological construct, to act as an "interface" between the soul – individuated consciousness – and the mind-body it uses. For effect, I sometimes refer to the latter as a "meat suit" but most people don't seem to care much for that description! Ramana used the metaphor of the moon. Most people's ego is the full moon on a clear and dark night. The remaining ego of awakened consciousness in-form is analogous to a sliver of the moon on a clear day in broad daylight. That analogy intuitively seems to work for me.

I: All right then. Based on our pre-interview discussions, it doesn't seem that you place much importance on your personal history or your spiritual experiences.

P: No, I suppose not. It's hard to describe, but everything that came before the awakening almost seems like a dream. I guess this isn't to be wondered at, given the first 57 years were lived in varying degrees of the "dream state" to borrow a term used most by the author known as Jed McKenna.

The avant-garde playwright Eugene Ionesco beautifully described how I often feel about life before the awakening when he stated, "I am not quite sure whether I am dreaming or remembering, whether I have lived my life or dreamed it. Just as dreams do, memory makes me profoundly aware of the unreality, the evanescence of the world, a fleeting image in the moving water." Or, as Chuang Tzu famously wrote after waking up from a dream he had: "I do not know whether I was then a man dreaming I was a butterfly, or whether I am now a butterfly dreaming I am a man."

Obviously it all happened and my memory of that period is still intact to the degree it is, and the skills and lessons learned from that part of this life are all there and can be accessed and utilized. That said, qualitatively, the place that I am living from now and the Directness of Perception that comes with it is so radically different, it almost seems as if the pre-awakened time of my life was someone else's or…a dream within a dream.

I: Listening to you talk about your life pre-awakening, the tone in your voice sounds a bit melancholy. Do you have regrets?

P: Regrets? No. There were a great many unfortunate actions taken though. By "unfortunate," I mean actions that were perceived as hurtful by others. For the record, I am *truly sorry* for all those who were hurt by my lack of awareness. There were countless times I was an unfeeling and unthinking dolt. Some of the stupid shit I did (pause) well, I guess it gets back to one of the fundamental messages in this book – if awakening happened to me, then it sure as hell can happen to you, or to anyone! And the really hopeful thing is that it indeed will, inevitably, happen to everyone. That's what The Universe – [localized] Consciousness – seems to be doing at all levels…waking up to Itself. If we can look back at our less than savory actions and ask ourselves, "given what I know now, would I do it all the same way?" and honestly say "no," then it's a lesson learned and we move on. *Everyone is doing the best they can from where they are,* so regrets are not only useless, but they also provide the ego-mind with a reason to stay in the past, negatively reinforcing itself, rather than Being Here Now. However much one might like to do certain things over, especially when others are hurt by our actions, what happened **had** to happen and the proof for that is those events **did** happen. One might regret "mistakes," but *are they mistakes* as in "bad"? Or, are they simply Universal Consciousness perfectly unfolding in that moment? By what measurement could we judge? It all depends on how one contextualizes the actions and events in life. As is clearly illustrated in the CWG material, introspecting and utilizing the spiritual method or process of "recontextualization" can be very useful, *as long as it isn't used to justify and possibly even perpetuate unhealthy actions!* There is simply no way to know what our actions may do to help another understand something, even the ones we deem hurtful or bad. Everyone's seen someone do something dumb that helped them learn what works and what doesn't. To fully understand *why* things unfold in the way they do would require complete knowledge of every single thing in the universe since its beginning – if it even has one – and that's obviously impossible. *Causality is just a concept!* The CWG material illustrates that as we recontextualize our actions, we learn that asking "why" is not only irrelevant but it is also disempowering, as it feeds into egoic victim consciousness, which again is a way for the ego-mind to fortify identity…any identity will do! The critical question we must ask ourselves is not "why" but rather "what" as in *what do I choose to learn from this* and *what do I choose to become from it?* I think that's how we get our psychological house in order, so to speak, so when something like awakening does come knocking, we're better prepared to receive it. In this context, it's impossible to see this process as anything other than *the necessary ripening for awakening to happen.* Ultimately in my case, it all worked! Awakening happened. I can't say that this type of stuff is rolling around in my consciousness any more but certainly, early on in my spiritual journey, recontextualization was a very useful tool.

Digressing slightly, even if we <u>could</u> go back and act more consciously in certain situations, righting wrongs as it were, what would the ramifications be? A different me? A different reality? A different Universe? There was a fantastic *Star Trek Next Generation* episode titled *Tapestry,* when Captain Picard dies and is allowed to go back in time by an omnipotent being known as Q. Upon returning to his youth, he is able to change the "mistake" he made and avoid the cause of his death. Unfortunately for Picard, the man he then became and the life he would have lived were, for him, far worse than death! Not only was it a brilliant piece of science fiction writing with some tremendously funny moments, but also a lesson in letting the past go, embracing <u>all</u> the aspects of our humanity, and accepting What Is in this eternal Present Moment – even one's physical death. We take responsibility for our actions, learn from them, and then let 'em go. It was what it was. In the end, there are no regrets <u>and</u> no justified resentments. Post-awakening, for me it's certainly not that I don't <u>care</u> about What Is in This Moment but rather, I don't <u>mind</u>. That's where acceptance and peace lie. Then, if there are aspects of the perfection that need our aid – and there are no shortages of those in the world – then those become aspects of the perfection that we strive to improve!

I: In terms of what would be thought of as extraordinary spiritual experiences, were there many leading up to the awakening?

P: "Many" is a relative term. I suppose one could say that I had a fair amount, but as they were unique to my process, they're not likely to be significant to the reader, who has their own process percolating. Some though could be viewed as milestones, and thus be considered foundational elements of the awakening. Like so many do, early on, I lived for these experiences, but now I tend to view them with a "grateful indifference." Gratitude for What Is, in this case the experience, but indifferent as to what happens or whether it happens at all. In the first couple of years after The Kiss, there weren't many at all but that's OK. I feel they can *sometimes* be an impediment, regardless of how wonderfully powerful and temporarily transformative they may be.

I: How can they be an impediment?

P: Well, first, all experiences are transitory. Even the greatest of them come and go and while they may be wonderful, even transformative to a degree, they still don't last. So let's say we have a biggie, however one defines big. Once it is over, what do we generally do? We can't stop thinking about it and, I know this was sometimes true in my case, we can't stop talking about it either. I've always had an inner urge to authentically share with likeminded souls, as is hopefully evidenced by this book. Sharing these types of experiences may be beneficial for someone else, or not. Egos have a way of twisting these things around and suddenly the other person wonders, "how can I get that, why hasn't it happened to me, how can someone like him or her deserve that?" and more. They may have been perfectly OK with their sadhana and now, or maybe even quite a ways down the road, this junk comes up and it's not useful. Then there's the other side of the coin. The person who had the experience can't figure out what it means – a big one in my case – or they're wondering if/when it'll happen again, or why it hasn't happened again. You get the idea. Some people are karmically programmed for lots of spiritual fireworks and others aren't, so it's best to not compare. I'm not saying that one shouldn't share them either. Good lord, countless amazing experiences have been shared in teachings and books over the last 2,500 years, this one included! Done well, this type of sharing can be a symbol of hope and inspiration to others. Those inspired might be just starting out, or maybe they've been on the path a long time and are feeling stuck in one of the inevitable "dry periods." I don't think irreparable harm is done either way, but as with any process, spiritual or otherwise, there are inherent caveats and pitfalls and one obviously would do well to be mindful of them. Why walk into a pothole or cul-de-sac if you don't have to? Awakening is challenging enough! I am a firm advocate of making the process – *any process* – as easy and straightforward as one can.

I: That all makes sense, but people are always curious to hear about the types of experiences and events that led up to an awakening such as yours. Would you share something with us? For example, what was your first spiritual experience?

P: The first, what I would call a "spiritual experience" in this lifetime, is also my first memory, which was between the ages of one and two years old.

I: Wait…how old?!

P: I can't be exactly sure but I was able to crawl and climb out of the crib somehow, so that's my best guess. In any event, I remember it as if it happened this morning! I was lying on my back and able to see my crib, the ceiling, and the early-morning light coming through the window to my left. We lived in a tiny one bedroom house until I was five years old. My sister, who is twelve years older than me, had the bedroom and my mom and dad slept in the living room on a hideaway sofa a few feet from me. This first experience was one of pure beingness, as I obviously knew no language and accordingly, I had no thoughts – just Pure Awareness. As I reflect back to that moment now, I would describe it as Pure Perception of the "Is-ness" or "Suchness" of the Now. Due to my ability to vividly remember it, in a sense it was a spiritual gift; a precursor to the natural state of awakened consciousness! After some amount of time, I climbed out of the crib and over to where my parents were sleeping. Quietly sliding into bed with them, I fell asleep and that's all I remember until I was three or four and in nursery school.

I: Earlier you mentioned "biggies." Would you care to share your first big one?

P: Well…ah, I was a lot older for that one. Ten, as I recall. (smiling)

I: Seriously? Come on now!

P: What can I say? These things just happen. I guess that's why one of my current favorite expressions is – "Life Happens." And hey, (smiles) it's more accurate than the other four-letter word that is frequently heard prior to "happens!"

I: I can't argue with that.

P: All right, so this was the first "big one." The body was fairly ill with asthma and allergies throughout my childhood and, to a much lesser degree, my teenage years. I have always had the sense that, prior to this incarnation, I asked to take the karma early on and get what I could out of the way. Perhaps we have no choice in these matters, but regardless, I never felt like a victim of my poor health and that, to some extent, we as souls have a vote in how our earthly process will unfold. I obviously **don't know** this but it is a feeling I've always had. In any case, my dad was in the kitchen area working and I was lying on the living room sofa doing nothing but struggling to breathe. I remember being so tired of the asthma and having to consciously fight for every breath, something that everyone else I knew took for granted. One moment I was on the couch, right hand cupped over my mouth and nose in a way I unconsciously did. As I came to find out many years later, that hand position is a type of mudra. Anyway, in the next moment I was out-of-body! I could see my dad, my physical body on the couch, and my astral body, which appeared light grey and luminous. I could see 360 degrees and I could also see my astral body from where I was lying on the couch. I was, so to speak, simultaneously the seer, the seeing, and the seen, in what might be best described as an *undifferentiated* experience of reality. There was no thought, no feelings and no fear; just a knowing in the ground of my being that I was not the body and from that moment on I never feared death. I cannot say how long I was out-of-body, as there was no sense of time, but at some point I had bodily consciousness again and spent some time lying there, trying to assimilate an experience for which I had no prior knowledge of, or words for. I don't remember how long that lasted either but eventually I got up and told my dad about what had happened. All I remember about that conversation was that he genuinely seemed to believe me, but he also appeared a bit frightened, and didn't seem to know what to do or say. God bless him; given similar circumstances, I imagine most parents wouldn't have fared any better than he did! I do remember that I deeply appreciated him believing me instead of dismissively blowing it off as a mere dream or even worse, turn me over to some clueless therapist and their always-at-the-ready prescription pad.

I: Amazing! At the age of ten, you realize that you are not the body and that you don't fear death! Nevertheless, let me ask you this – has that ever been put to the test? Have you ever actually faced your possible physical demise?

P: Yes, I have. Twice. It would take too long to go into all the details and they're really not important anyway. The short versions are, when I was 26 I ran into a burning house and saved a dog. The second was during my time as the operations manager at Hidden Valley just after my 52nd birthday. I piloted a suddenly brakeless golf cart down a very steep, winding road at 40+ miles an hour and crashed it headfirst into a heavy metal gate, which was memorable. Both times, there was absolutely no fear at all. Instead, there was great clarity and deep calm. Like awakening, the spontaneous astral projection at age ten was just Grace happening, and having no fear of death was my experiential knowing and lived experience from that point on.

While on this topic, I was blessed to have been a hospice volunteer and trainer off and on for nearly twelve years, and looking back, I now see why I chose that one, out of the multitude of volunteer opportunities that were available. This out-of-body experience left me with/as a calm, genuinely unafraid, and reassuring presence around those who were *actively transitioning,* and it seemed that on some level, they were able to sense it. Not all, certainly, but some. In all candor, I have always felt that I received much more from those who were transitioning than I was ever able to give to them. The dying can be direct, potent, and sometimes poignant teachers, if we have the courage to meet them where they are and be able to look death straight in the eye, as they are doing.

I: With their time on earth short, all the BS goes right out the window, doesn't it?

P: Yes it does. And in the often short time that they have, spiritual breakthroughs of all kinds may happen. Transitioning is an important, sometimes beautiful opportunity to evolve on many levels. And interestingly, while I have no fear of this body's ultimate demise, I found that more than a few of my clients didn't either. Generally, I've found most people don't worry about death nearly as much as they worry about what it's going to take to get there.

I: That makes sense. There are a lot of terminal diseases that impart pain and anguish along the way.

P: True, although pain management has come a long way, as has hospice care. The medical profession's understanding and acceptance of hospice is also maturing, thankfully. Not surprisingly, I suppose, clients who had some type of faith-based belief system tended to worry less about what comes after than those who didn't. Dr. Elisabeth Kubler-Ross, one of the pioneers in hospice care who also developed the well-known five stages of grief model, said something quite profound that I want to add here: "It's not the end of the physical body that should worry us. Rather, our concern must be to live while we're alive – to release our inner selves from the spiritual death that comes with living behind a facade designed to conform to external definitions of who and what we are."

From this, it seems that dying isn't such a big deal; anyone can do it. The *test* is living! What's more, when discussing their upcoming death, I found our hospice clients' biggest fear *prior* to death was usually centered on the loss of control, and this shouldn't be surprising, as **control** is an essential pillar on which the separate self stands on. The fear-based desire to have everything possible in our lives "under control" is one of the fundamental tenets of the ego-mind and why nearly everyone I've met dislikes change. Since *life* and *change* are one and the same, keeping things predictable and controlled are about as feasible as holding back the ocean tide with a fork! At best, it's a defense mechanism, and at worst, it demonstrates an utter lack of trust in The Universe.

Back to the hospice patients I assisted, their biggest fear about what comes *after* death was that there is **nothing**. No existence at all – Annihilation. While I don't know, my sense is that at the subconscious level, the ego-mind recognizes that it is an illusory construct and that its identity with/as the body means that as the body dies, so it too dies. Since the ego-mind cannot see what's beyond, it infers that there's nothing beyond. Hence the very real terror many feel about nonexistence after bodily death. In my experience, the existential annihilation of the ego-mind was excruciating, which is a great reason to get it out of the way before physical death occurs!

If I may, I'd also like to read an insightful comment on this topic by the Tibetan Dzogchen Lama Sogyal Rinpoche who wrote the well-known and regarded book, *The Tibetan Book of Living and Dying*.

I: By all means, go ahead.

P: As a preface, Sogyal was highly respected around the world before ultimately falling into disrepute over abuse allegations that came out in 2017. Sadly, he was not the first teacher of his stature that had these types of issues arise. They point to a vital detail to remember: after awakening happens, it doesn't mean that there isn't karma remaining [leshavidya] that has to be burned off, or that all other facets of one's character and temperament are suddenly and miraculously perfected. Adyashanti sometimes talks about this, and that it's an unrealistic expectation – on the part of those who might be awakening *and* on the part of those around the person awakening – to suddenly think someone's imperfections will just disappear. While Sogyal transitioned in 2019 with an undeniably tarnished legacy, his [alleged] transgressions don't, at least to my mind, invalidate the genuine service he provided to others, or the wisdom that he imparted through his life's work. I don't judge...it just was the way it was and hopefully people learn from it.

With all that aside he insightfully said, "Perhaps the deepest reason why we are afraid of death is because we do not know who we are. We believe in a personal, unique, and separate identity – but if we dare to examine it, we find that this identity depends entirely on an endless collection of things to prop it up: our name, our "biography," our partners, family, home, job, friends, credit cards…It is on their fragile and transient support that we rely for our security. So when they are all taken away, will we have any idea of who we really are? Without our familiar props, we are faced with just ourselves, a person we do not know, an unnerving stranger with whom we have been living all the time but we never really wanted to meet. Isn't that why we have tried to fill every moment of time with noise and activity, however boring or trivial, to ensure that we are never left in silence with this stranger on our own?"

I: That does help illuminate the issue, Phil. Before moving to my next topic for our discussion, is there anything else that you'd like to add about death? After all, it is the one experience we all have to face, and possibly the most vexing mystery there is.

P: I would like to add something, but it's a Reality that most people are probably not able to hear.

I: And that is?

P: Nothing is born and nothing dies.

I: (pause) Please continue; that *is* going to take some explaining.

P: First, as the CWG material correctly points out, it's not "life and death" as is so often heard. <u>Birth</u> is the opposite of death. Second, **Life**, which is synonymous with Consciousness, **has no opposite**. If you are wondering how something can have no opposite, that is a limitation of dualistic thought. Third, one could easily infer that The Absolute [not an actual "thing"] is the opposite of Consciousness but that would make It "relative" to something and It is beyond the *mind-projected concepts* of duality and relativity. I'm not sure that the interconnectedness of Being and Non-Being can *precisely* be put into words! With this, Awareness and Consciousness are terms often used interchangeably. However, I view them as different and in the same way Nisargadatta [usually] did. Consciousness, from which duality, matter, and ultimately life are derived, emanates *from* Awareness, so all of Manifestation then is, essentially, instantiated Emptiness. The primordial, pristine, uncaused, unconditioned, and unstained Absolute, **actualizes** Beingness, so fundamentally there is only The Absolute or, in theistic terms, God as The Unmoved Mover. The awakening brought a Direct Perception of Beingness – the Nature of Reality – as One Unified "Happening." As the Ground of Being – Conscious Manifestation – emanates from Non-Being, it is also true that, as the enigmatic yet beloved Indian avatar Meher Baba put it, "All that is happening is not happening – and nothing ever will happen."

I: Whoa…that there is deep. (pause) Birth and death being opposites that way makes sense though!

P: (smiles and nods head) Yes, it really does. And as I just mentioned, another word for Life is…

I: Consciousness.

P: Yep. And how can that possibly cease to exist?! Manifestation or "Lila" – The Divine Play, as it is referred to in non-dualistic Hinduism – is, so far as we know, eternal. Infinite conscious energy, imbued with Divine Intelligence, is always changing form, and forms are obviously impermanent. Yet Its **essence**, the Non-Being Awareness of The Godhead, forever remains untouched, both at the macro-level and…in us. Consequently, this must be **our essence** too! When Ramana Maharshi was on his deathbed, his distraught devotees were crying for him to not leave them. In one of the most powerful and direct teachings he ever gave, he asked them – I'm betting with some feeling of exasperation – "Where could I go?" Ya gotta understand that when people are truly staring death in the face, the vast majority of the 7+ billion people in our world today are seeing it with body-identified ego consciousness [That is, over 99.5% of the population, according to the data in Dr. Jeffrey Martin's book, *The Finders*]. Even when they subscribe to a belief system that embraces some sort of afterlife narrative, it still feels as if *they* are dying. Ramana also taught what I stated a few minutes ago – *nothing is born and nothing dies*. With The Kiss, the ego-mind shattering Realization that came first was, I Am No One. Almost immediately after, like a tidal wave, it became clear beyond what words can convey that if I Am No One or, put another way, that I Am No Thing in Particular, then by definition that must mean that I Am Everything! Meher Baba aptly said, "It is not so much that you are within the cosmos as that the cosmos is within you." How does All That Is cease to exist?! One of the integral byproducts that often accompanies awakening is this Realization of Interconnectedness and Unity, which in turn brings the deep peace that comes with the knowing that death is not to be dreaded…any more than birth is! One's body identification ends. The Absolute Motionless and Silent No-thing-ness of The Godhead <u>is</u> **All There Is**. It Is You!

I: That's a heck of a lot to think about. (pause) Well, OK then, I have to ask you this. If everyone and everything is fundamentally the Awareness of The Godhead, then what is it that is separating me as an unawakened modulation of consciousness from you as an awakened one?

P: Nothing.

I: Here we go with the nothingness stuff again. Phil, my brain still hurts from that last discourse.

P: I don't mean "nothing" as in The Absolute Nothingness of The Godhead.

I: Well, to what nothing are you referring to then?

P: This one – there is **no-thing** that differentiates between awakened and unawakened modulations of consciousness. **Who** or **What** is there that could "be" one or the other?

I: I'm hanging out in the wind here Phil; I'm going to need more than that.

P: The idea or perception of one being "awakened" or "unawakened" is illusory, my friend. Only the egoic separate-self sees reality in that dualistic way. From the perception of/in/as Unity, *there is no awakened or unawakened anything*. In All Beings, I <u>see</u> the underlying Primordial Awareness – The Godhead. There are no separate and objective things "out there" and we now know this from quantum theory and biocentrism as much as we do from metaphysics. Rumi reportedly said, "The world is full of waves and the sea is indivisible." You're seeing waves while **I Am** the Sea. While one may be able to accept this intellectually, it unfortunately falls far short of the

Direct Perception post-awakening. After transcending the ego-mind, there is now an awareness-experience of Unity at the essential level of Beingness. It's not that maya's veil of illusion isn't still there, it's that now I simply see through it. Fundamentally, *there is no one* to be (un)awakened! When Phil affirms, "I'm awake" he sure as hell doesn't mean to imply that he is…and you ain't! He just means that he's Realized there is no separate me, or you, or anything else. Those egoic and sense-based distinctions simply fall away, like clouds dissolving in the sky. The intimate awareness-experience of and as Unity, is what I awakened into – the Absolute and inherently Empty, Interconnectedness of All That Is.

Let me share an applicable quote from Nisargadatta with you on this: "Right here and now, you are in the realized state. But you try to judge it through desires and mind concepts, hence your inability to apperceive it and abide in it." From this, my friend, we see the most direct way out of "the cage of Samsara" is to Recognize that, here now, **there is no cage** and there never was one!

I: I'm starting to get it now. So my perceiving someone or something as anything different than what I Am – including awakened and unawakened – is just looking from the separate self.

P: Yes! However, if one doesn't experientially know it, if it hasn't been Realized yet, then an intellectual-only understanding of it doesn't do one much good. If the illusion of the separate self hasn't been abidingly transcended, then *where we are living from in our daily life doesn't change.* It just becomes yet another concept. To help make the point, I'm going to split Oneness into twoness. **Relatively**, there are certainly differences between us all, and the various levels of consciousness are undoubtedly the most fundamental. But from the perspective of the **Absolute**, our *essence* is untouched and always the same. Samsara is Nirvana and Nirvana is Samsara. They look different, and the experience of these seemingly separate realities is different to be sure, but those are just illusory appearances. In the end, here and now, they are always and essentially One.

I: You know, somehow hearing that makes me feel a lot better! It's amazing to see how the egoic-self divides, labels, and judges everything. One more thing comes to mind with this. You mentioned "various levels of consciousness." Would you expand on that?

P: Sure. My initial understanding of the concept of levels of consciousness, LOC for short, was brought about by my interest in the work of Dr. David Hawkins. While Hawkins' work was possibly derivative of prior rudimentary examinations into the topic, to my knowledge he was the first to map out the levels of consciousness and expound on its qualities as it evolves through human form. It's too large of a subject to be adequately explained here in this interview. Briefly, he posited that as individuated modulations of consciousness evolve through and as humans, there are corresponding attributes that gradually ascend. For example, we see how we evolve past densely-filtered-consciousness emotions such as shame, guilt, fear, and anger and evolve into the clearer-consciousness levels such as trust, forgiveness, love, and peace. Corresponding to these is a 1-1000 logarithmic-based scale [which Hawkins admitted was numerically arbitrary]. For instance, 200 is where power transcends force, 500 is where love transcends the intellect, and 600 is where awakening begins.

Moreover, these attributes reflect how one views and interprets the contextual field that one is in and is. The most succinct way of stating this that I know of is one of my all-time favorite quotes attributed to Anaïs Nin, who said, "We don't see things as they are, we see them as we are." Just fantastic! From my point of view, Hawkin's map of consciousness is *fundamental* to a macro-level understanding of one's "involution," to borrow an important term from Meher Baba's classic, *God Speaks*. I feel his first three books were the most important to this area of consciousness research, with the third, *I: Reality and Subjectivity*, being Doc's tour de force.

However...he also posited a method of verifying these levels [levels being a loaded word], through the practice of muscle testing. There's been much work in this area of kinesiology and with it, I feel there's a lot of merit. That being said, the accuracy – and therefore validity – of his calibrations need to be viewed with a critical eye. After all, just as we all do, he and his testing partner(s) appear to have had their positionalities. I mean, no one is perfect, right?! The overall premise of there being varying degrees of beingness in/as consciousness rings true in my awareness-experience, but the potential pitfall is that the calibration process and corresponding LOC chart may invite one to compare one person to another. This, then, may possibly foment feelings of superiority or inferiority. Either of these two viewpoints are a function of the ego-mind's illusory separate-self and therefore, if utilized and adopted blindly, may lead to divisiveness and the sense of separation rather than unity. In other words, the ego's identity is reified rather than diminished. I certainly don't feel Doc ever meant his calibration technique to be misunderstood and utilized in that way, but it may be a fair criticism of this aspect of his work nonetheless.

In one of Doc's books, he listed a lot of spiritual teachers and their corresponding LOC numbers. I feel what led to some real consternation amongst friends I had was seeing their favorite teacher or guru at an LOC that didn't match what they had in mind and as a result, they often called the whole thing hogwash, thereby throwing out the baby with the bathwater. To me, I chalked these anomalies up to human error and/or some preexisting bias on the part of Hawkins and/or one of his team.

I: Good, enough of that then. Shall we move to the next topic?

P: Of course, fire away!

I: You mentioned service as an element of your sadhana. What other aspects did it have?

P: As a disciple of Yogananda, the techniques he left were fundamental to my practice. As he left more than most people have the time to do, my core was meditation, and within that the technique of Kriya yoga was paramount. With this, I read a library of metaphysical books, listened to countless hours of spiritual talks, watched innumerable mystically-oriented videos, practiced introspection, cultivated devotion, went on retreats, became ever-more comfortable with solitude and, as already discussed, provided service to others – Karma yoga. In part of his hallowed prayer, Saint Francis wrote, "For it is in giving that we receive." Through this, he was pointing to our Oneness. Literally, what we do for others we are doing for us! Parallel with all this, I attended spiritual services, satsangs and lectures, took in darshans, and soaked up the loving fellowship of like-minded souls. There were a couple of instances where entheogens [psilocybin] were employed. If used with intention, reverence, and respect, these *may* foment breakthroughs of different types. As it turns out, and as Ram Dass publicly demonstrated during his early seeking years, they are not a technology that in and of themselves produce an abiding awakening. I'm not saying it's impossible, as anything can happen of course. I'm just saying that entheogens don't have a demonstrable history for being a reliable method for awakening. That, plus there are possible health risks that have been associated with the indiscriminate use of these types of agents. All of that aside, throughout my sadhana, I gradually learned to surrender "control" of "my sadhana" – a decidedly necessary step.

I: Is there anything else that you'd like to add about the nature of sadhana?

P: I've never come across a more succinct or true description of what sadhana is than what Nisargadatta Maharaj said about it: "Sadhana is a search for what to give up. Empty yourself completely." Now <u>that</u> cuts right to the heart of the matter! Wu Hsin, a prolific quote machine if ever there was one, also had a fantastically apropos comment along these same lines:

"Awakening occurs
Not when there is no more
To be added
But instead,
When there is no more
To be taken away."

I: Those are beautiful! I don't want to veer off track too much, as I still want to circle back to an area of your spiritual experiences that we haven't completely explored yet. But before we go any further, please take a moment to talk about the Gateless Gate.

P: For me, the proverbial Gateless Gate refers to the *illusory* barrier standing between individuated unawakened and awakened consciousness. I think another good representational phrase for this is "Event Horizon." From my pre-awakening viewpoint/identity as a seeker, the gate seemed all but insurmountable. Once awakening happens, one looks back and sees that there never was a gate. Rumi beautifully pointed to this when he said he'd been knocking on the door only to discover that he'd been knocking from the inside! I too experienced and described it similarly [see email dated 3-24-18 in chapter 3]. I also really like how Nisargadatta straightforwardly put it to a seeker: "Having never left the house you are asking for the way home." (laughs)

I: (smiling) In our discussions about sadhana, I'm assuming that we've been talking pre-awakening. Is sadhana different post-awakening? Is there sadhana after awakening?

P: Excellent questions, but I can only tell you how it's been for me. Post-awakening, Life Itself became my "ashram without walls." While this is true for everyone, regardless of whether Self-Realization has happened or not, this wasn't my lived experience until after The Kiss. I found that once I had, more or less, acclimated to the non-dual state, everything flowed much easier, given there was no "self-direction." In other words, there was no ego-mind getting in the way. The spiritual path is like a rocket ship taking off for outer space. In the beginning, fighting against gravity – eons of karma and sanskaric impressions in the aspirant's case – it takes an enormous amount of thrust just to achieve liftoff. Until it clears the earth's gravitational pull, the rocket is battling its way up and out, much as we do in our sadhana. Once the rocket ship clears the earth's gravity, it really picks up speed and soars with much less thrust or, in our case, <u>effort</u>. In my case, this is where tremendous leaps began happening, seemingly with no effort at all on my part. If I may, in order to answer your questions fully, I'll summarize how my sadhana unfolded post-Kiss.

I: Sure, that'd be great.

P: For nearly two years [beginning in September 2017], there was nothing in the way of "practice" happening. For the first nine months, with one important exception – the karmic purge that I wrote about – there was so much disorientation, so much energy moving around, no friggin' personal will…I mean…it was all I could do to navigate through it! I wasn't able to do anything more than survive and learn to live in the world again, so no traditional practice was happening. After I started working, it took another six months or so to become comfortable functioning in the business world again from/as non-dual consciousness. Finally [around April 2019], I began to feel an "inner movement" and started reading spiritual books again. I read, and this time actually understood, Nisargadatta's *I Am That*, followed by Rupert Spira's exceptionally articulate *The Nature of Consciousness*. Let's see, then came Alistair Shearer's classic on Adi Shankara, *In The Light of Self*, along with several others over the next nine months. In September, I left my job, as they unexpectedly sold 12 of the 16 hotels I was supporting, so I spent two months back at my cherished Hidden Valley Ashram, which was just magical. By the second anniversary of The Kiss, it felt as if I had truly come full circle…and was now beginning another! Formal sitting meditation started happening again as well, but there was no schedule or routine; it always arose spontaneously. Of course, the fundamental change was that there was **no one** "doing" it and with that, there was absolutely no goal <u>for</u> doing it, other than the joy <u>of</u> doing it. Meditation became like listening to music or dancing. Unless one is a professional, one doesn't <u>do</u> either for any reason. They're just fun and a natural expression of the consciousness that one is. Entering a more mature awakened state just after my two-year anniversary of The Kiss [October 2019], I was also immeasurably blessed to receive my second darshan with Mother Meera in Los Angeles. Subsequently, I spent time with family for the holidays before heading to the desert, where [the original draft of] this book was written. During the last four months of 2019 [and throughout 2020], there was a palpable and unmistakable "deepening" in/of/as consciousness [or, an "ascent," depending on how one prefers to visualize it]. Whereas I found awakening an "up and out" movement, this deepening process felt more "down and in."

Here now, the peace and stillness of a deeply meditative mind have become the norm throughout my entire day and activities. This, I now know, is our Natural State. Both actions and speech arise up from and out of a deep inner silence, with little-to-no thoughts. Sadhana <u>is</u> All of Life, and has become an "experiment" of/in/as consciousness. Energetic impulses arise out of the nowhere and into the now here and then, hmmm…let's see what happens! So, that's how sadhana-life flows now. I just show up every day, and The Universe does the rest. Despite the world's outward appearances, It's All Perfect, Just As It Is.

I: Regarding thinking, you do have <u>some</u> thoughts, right?! I mean, it's not like there's just nothing all the time? I get that *you can think* but it's hard to imagine having none at all. And if you do still have some thoughts, is there a time or activity where you have more? Or, is there a place where you have a lot less? For some reason, maybe because I can barely remember a time when I didn't have **any** thoughts at all, the idea of being totally thoughtless is almost incomprehensible to me.

P: Thoughts do still pop up/in and float by, sure. Nevertheless, there are long stretches where there aren't any. In 2019, I read Jean Klein's wonderful book, *I Am,* and he wrote something that, to this point, seems to be the most precise way of describing how this deepening into Stillness has been for me. He said, "It is not the mind which attunes to the I am but the I am which absorbs the mind." It frequently feels as if the mind is being swallowed by an infinite field of black, *motionless* Silence. That probably doesn't sound attractive to most people but I'm here to tell ya that unfathomably deep, utter Stillness is the most beautiful state of Presence I know of. The late Jesuit priest Anthony de Mello appropriately said, "Silence is not the absence of sound, but the absence of self." At times, the Silence is deafening. I guess that's why, when you were asking about my interests and all that at the beginning, I said I was becoming a "silence junkie." **Being** in and as that Silence is like, (teary-eyed pause) it feels as if I Am resting in the arms of God. The eminent 13th century poet Rumi reportedly said that "Silence is the language of God." It is the "I Am" that Nisargadatta was always encouraging people to sense and dwell in. As far as I can tell, this motionless Silence is The Absolute that eternally IS. It is Pure, unobstructed and unconditioned by thoughts, or ego, or mind – **Awareness**. In Dzogchen, this Primordial, Pristine Awareness is called *Rigpa,* in which Pure Presence resides.

(pauses to wipe eyes) To answer your other questions, and so I don't come across as being too cosmically heavy again (smiles), thoughts do intermittently float across the screen of my consciousness. And yes, there is an activity and time of day where thoughts are the most active, and I would say almost invariably so. This will probably sound weird, because it's always struck **me** as weird, but for whatever reason(s), when I'm in the shower – ordinarily a morning thing for me – there are nearly always thoughts happening!

I: In the shower???

P: Yes, and please don't bother to ask me why, because on this I really am clueless! I mean, I couldn't even hazard a guess. Conversely, the mind almost immediately goes silent, and I mean Still, in noisy and/or crowded places like supermarkets and airports. It's almost become like a defense mechanism.

I: Amazing! If you ever figure those two out, please let me know! I keep wanting to get to my next question but you keep bringing up things I hadn't considered, and they lead to other questions.

P: Hopefully that's OK.

I: Oh, yes…no grumbles here at all! It's truly fascinating stuff. My new question for you is this – you mentioned "experiments of/in/as consciousness."

P: Yes.

I: So as you're already awakened, what or where could these experiments lead to? I mean, what more is there? Isn't awake…Awake?!

P: Those are more great questions. When it comes to this topic, I am often reminded of the perplexing Zen proverb: "After reaching the mountaintop, keep on climbing." I am not sure how useful it is in answering your question however! Here's my best take on the issue for what it's worth. We Are Already Complete and yet, through my awakening journey, I Realized that the evolutionary process of **everything** in manifestation is always deepening, so this naturally includes us. Consciousness is, in a sense, becoming an ever-clearer, more pure and gifted expression of Spirit. We are always becoming ever-more refined tools for and as The Divine. This is no joke – the illumined spiritual Masters throughout history were all examples of what we will eventually become! The "experiment" is just showing up every day and being completely available to the Divine Impulses we receive through the perfect unfolding of Spirit.

To your questions, yes, awake is awake. As I understand the term, "awakening" means that there has been *an abiding transcendence* and then, *a dropping away of the ego-mind as a separate self,* along with *being established in/as non-dual awareness.* That being said, in an infinite universe, so too must the spectrum of awakened consciousness be infinite. Accordingly – and fortunately from my perspective – there is no culmination of our evolution. I say fortunately because it seems to me that if there were some sort of static endpoint, no matter how rapturous, it would eventually get old. I mean OK; I could see hangin' out in the clouds in bliss playing my harp or surfin' the net for a few hundred billion years. But doing that…or anything…*forever?!* Maybe it's just the restless spirit in me, but if we're talking *eternity,* at some point I'm going to want to grow and explore again. The good news is that I'm certain this scenario is groundless, as it became abundantly clear to me during the early stages of the awakening that this is simply not the case. In saying all this, I understand that I may be dashing some hopes here, as I've known some spiritual seekers who expected that once they crossed the awakening finish line, they'd alight onto some cosmic podium on Hiranyaloka [purportedly a spiritually advanced astral planet] and receive their Self-Realization merit badge from God. If She's busy that day, some Ascended Master with a slender social calendar probably gets the gig but hey, whose complaining! From there, they can kick back for eternity, their taxes are never audited, and life is perpetually groovy. On a generous day, I might call these hopes a less-than-fully-mature understanding. On a not so generous day, I would most likely call it bliss-bunny escapist fantasy. As a reminder to our audience at home, **who/what** awakens?

Consciousness. And as consciousness is infinite, so must be the depths of awakened beingness. Look at some of the localized modulations of consciousness throughout history. I have no doubts that Paramahansa Yogananda, to cite an obvious example, was a far more awakened manifestation of consciousness than Phil is to this point. In the same way, Homo sapiens are much more awake – a more *evolved expression* of consciousness – than an animal, which is more awake than a plant, which is more awake than a rock, and nearly all rocks are a heck of a lot more awake than 99% of those now serving in our civilization's political arena…Ah jeez (slaps forehead) did I *really* just say that?!

I: Yes Phil, you did. And we're keeping it in the interview; no redacted copies will be published!

P: Well…that's all right. I'm sure they've been called worse things than that. Be that as it may, the same then must be true for awakened modulations of consciousness. Phil is awakened, but he would be the first to acknowledge that Ramana Maharshi, or Nisargadatta Maharaj, or Saint Francis of Assisi – to name just a few of many! – were "deeper" in the ocean of consciousness than he is in this moment. So too might it be said that Jesus, or The Buddha, or Krishna were in deeper waters than the three illumined sages I previously mentioned. While I'm in no position to judge or rank their differences, that's just how they have always appeared to me. At any rate, and as we've already spoken about, there *is* a post-awakening sadhana that takes place... unless it doesn't. It depends on The Universe in and as the mind-body that's awakened. And here's another paradox. How can there be "more" of Self-Realized Beingness? An awakened soul is consciously One With All That Is. There is no *more* to be had and yet, from where I am here and now it's clear that somehow there is!

It's been my observation that those who are genuinely awake don't have any issues with these paradoxes. I think they're awe-inspiring! For those who want all of this to fit nicely and cleanly into a linear and logical conceptual box, I would suggest that there is still clarity that has yet to unfold. Regarding the concept of eternal evolution, my bottom-line understanding is this: we are "verbs" – Dynamic Processes, Dependently Arising, and Absolutely Interconnected. We are *not* "nouns" – lumps of organic matter that sheathe an ego-mind, which is identifying itself as a psychosomatic apparatus separate from everything else. Consequently, awakening must also be verb-like! It is an *eternal, ever-evolving unfolding,* and if it weren't, I think that would be the worst news imaginable. Does that in any way help or answer your questions?

I: It does, and did. Thank you for giving all of my questions your best shot, especially when they might fall outside of your direct experience.

P: You're welcome. Just like everyone, I do the best I can from where I am! (laughs)

I: (laughing) True enough, true enough. OK, so this is the question that's been patiently waiting "on deck" to use the baseball parlance that you sometimes employ.

P: Baseball is great for that! I often use baseball metaphors at work too. Let's not forget there are also time-honored baseball parallels for measuring successes in one's love life! (smiles)

I: Whoa...now I'm sorry I brought it up. Ahem. Moving right along, let's go back one more time to your spiritual experiences. My question is, other than those you've already mentioned, what if any events do you feel had a bearing on the awakening?

P: Holy smokes…all of them! Not only what would be considered spiritual experiences but truly, *everything and everyone* in this life contributed in some manner to the awakening. All of creation is a manifestation of consciousness; nothing happens in a vacuum and consciousness is what awakens!

I: But isn't there anything that you look back on as being a *critical* stepping-stone to awakening?

P: I don't know how one would know that for certain. There's a maturation that's taking place on levels we're not even aware of, and when an individuated spark of consciousness has evolved sufficiently, awakening happens. It's a natural and impersonal unfolding of consciousness. Whether we do or don't do a spiritual practice, as far as I can tell, it all comes down to ripeness, although it does seem that having a dedicated practice definitely increases one's ripeness.

(silent and long pregnant pause)

P: I'm getting the sense that you'd like something more than that.

I: (laughing) Yes!

P: Well, (sigh) all right then. I guess what might be considered the most direct precursors to awakening started in…I want to say about 2002. While living in Atlanta, one Sunday afternoon I decided to go to the Ignatius House. Our Atlanta SRF group conducted a silent retreat there in 2000, and I used to return occasionally to sit by the river, meditate, and enjoy the vibe. Right before leaving my home, I felt energy in my crown chakra for the first time; it kind of felt like champagne bubbles rising. Méthode Champenoise, not Charmat! By the time I got there I felt *drunk*. I didn't know what the heck was happening! I found a bench by the water and not being able to stand any more, I laid down on it and slept for a short time. Thankfully, I was in a safe place. When I awoke, everything was Still internally; it seemed as if everything was moving slower. It was amazing! There was a deep awareness of the present moment and it lasted a couple of hours. I started calling this state "no-mind," derived from the Japanese martial arts/Zen term "Mushin." A couple of years later, during one of my many visits to the Meher Center in Myrtle Beach, South Carolina, the same sort of thing happened again only much more intensely. While meditating in Baba's bedroom on a Sunday morning, I felt three distinct raps on the top of my head where the crown chakra is seated.

I: Did it hurt?!

P: No, (chuckles) it kind of felt like it does when a doctor taps your knee with a rubber hammer. But *oh baby*, when I walked out of there it was as if I was three-sheets-to-the-wind intoxicated. The crown chakra was buzzing and the inner stillness was incredibly deep. There were no thoughts at all and I couldn't do much for several hours. As my sadhana went on, the amount of thought was being reduced. A couple of years later, I was with SRF friends visiting other friends in North Carolina. While meditating together on the first night, I again felt a rap on the top of my head in the crown chakra area. There was just one this time but it propelled me into the same state as the two episodes I just told you about, this time lasting all weekend. From there it was so gradual that I never really noticed the ongoing reduction of thought until one night, while living in Naples, Florida I was suddenly aware that it was as if I was in the deepest meditation that I had ever experienced. And this is the bizarre part. At the time, I was the General Manager of a very high-end, fine dining restaurant located in a 4-diamond hotel. And…it happened on a busy Friday night on the dining room floor, right in the middle of the dinner rush!

I: Were you able to function normally?

P: Unlike the instances before, I actually was. I guess there had been enough time acclimating to it so it had become more or less natural. I started using the comparison of the ocean and its depth. So, ordinary consciousness would be analogous to the surface of the ocean which always has some movement but is often pretty choppy and can end up a hurricane. About 60 feet down there is a lot less movement, and at the bottom of the ocean, it's Still. It just Is, so to speak. And that is what this was like in terms of thought reduction. Most of the time I was 60 feet down with just a few thoughts passing by, like clouds floating across a mostly empty sky. While it was rare back then, there were a few times when the mind would be bottom-of-the-ocean Still.

I: How long did this go on, and how do you feel it directly relates to the awakening?

P: It still is like that to this day. Now of course, there is a Unitive Beingness and an intimate Directness of Perception that did not exist back then. However, as I previously described, some thoughts do happen now and then. I have recently begun to feel that the term "motionless" is the best pointer for how it is nowadays, which I got from Ramana Maharshi. After the Naples incident, and with the reduction of thoughts never really going away, I communicated several times over the years about it with an SRF monk who I am very close to, along with learning what I could about it. During that time, I particularly found Eckhart Tolle's teachings to be quite helpful. Eventually, the monk and I both concluded that if the awakened state was a movie theater, then I was most likely hanging out in the lobby with my Coke, popcorn, and ticket already in-hand for my reserved seat. From the time things got very still internally in Naples, more or less a near-abiding state of no-mind, to the time of the awakening it was…about ten years I guess.

I: I can see why you might feel these were likely "runner-up events" to the awakening.

P: Well, again, everything and everyone in this life – and in All Lifetimes – were "runner-up events" to the degree that they were. Biggest picture, everything that's ever taken place in the entire universe since the Big Bang was a related-by-marriage factor! But yeah, one might conclude upon some modicum of reflection and analysis that a deeper state of conscious awareness was being accessed and acclimated to during these events. That, and an obvious stimulation and activation of kundalini, especially in the crown chakra.

I: Let's talk for a moment about kundalini and the energetic component of awakening, all right?

P: Sure. There are a few books listed in the Soul Food section that cover this subject. Given that, plus the importance of this subject, and due to the fact that I'm no expert, I'd like to stick to how it was for me, if that's OK.

I: Of course.

P: I wrote about this in some of my emails, so what I'd add here is that this energetic phenomenon appears to be the single most common denominator in the awakening process. In part, there looks to be a necessary energetic "rewiring" of the brain and bodies – physical, astral, and causal. The other part seems to be the result of not having an egoic-structure to sustain. It appears that doing this 24/7 takes up *a lot of energy*. With ego gone, the energy is rerouted and utilized in other ways.

On another related note, while I am certain there are qualified teachers of kundalini yoga in the world, to my mind people doing this are in potentially hazardous territory. I've heard Adyashanti say that he's had more than a few people visit him who had been under the tutelage of supposedly qualified teachers and, sure enough, whatever they were doing got the energy flowing. However, when that happens, all kinds of issues can flare up and when they do, the teachers don't always look so astute. Subsequently, there Adya is, trying to help them put Humpty Dumpty back together again. As Gopi Krishna discovered and later famously wrote about, kundalini turns out to be a lot like toothpaste; it can't be put back in the tube…at least not very easily or very well! Through my experiences with both Kriya yoga and my particular post-awakening process, I have felt what a wildly powerful and unpredictable force of nature sister kundalini is. Therefore, my sincere recommendation is just don't screw with it. And if you do, then please take it s-l-o-w!

I: And yet, from my admittedly limited understanding of it, Kriya yoga is working with kundalini too, channeling it through the sushumna somehow. As you said earlier, that was a fundamental method of your pre-awakening sadhana. How is *this* OK when other practices may not be?

P: Well, if you are going to the place down the street with the kundalini yoga sign out front, how do you know what you're getting? The technique of Kriya yoga that Yoganandaji brought to the west has been around for millennia, and SRF introduces the practice of it into a student's spiritual routine very progressively and, I would also say, watchfully. The monks and nuns who are counselors in the organization are adept at determining how one is progressing and whether the student is ready for an increase. Additionally, and SRF claims importantly, one doesn't start Kriya until a formal Guru-Disciple relationship has been established. In doing this, Yogananda himself is, in effect, assisting the Kriyaban and this is an incalculable advantage over someone trying to learn it out of a book or at a yoga studio. Now certainly, I'm not here saying that no SRF student in history has ever had a problem arise! Even under the best guidance possible there are physical and psychological factors that might negatively affect someone doing Kriya, not to mention karmic factors as well. It is impossible to know unequivocally how someone will fare with *any* method. Just as there are risks in life, there are also risks on the spiritual journey. It's not exempt from casualties any more than any other aspect of life. That's why I am saying – just be damn careful. From my own experience, there is *nothing* more sublime than the activation of kundalini. As I wrote about at the end of chapter three, each Kriya loop felt better than 10 orgasms, and there were nigh on 600 that day! Of course, that one experience was more Grace Happening rather than the result of a typical Kriya session but still, I have had kundalini rushes while doing Kriya that have literally put me on the floor, which is the main reason why I got a bench and started meditating Zen style! (laughs)

I: Seriously?

P: Yes, very seriously. In 2009 while living in Asheville, North Carolina, a bliss rush – I'm not sure what better description to use – arose and there was no body awareness until my nose hit the deck. As I was meditating in a chair, I apparently went straight down and face-planted on the floor. If the room wasn't carpeted, I would have broken my nose for sure, as that was the first thing that hit. I guess that is why the yogis of yore advocated the full lotus posture, as it kind of locks one in place. Due to my age when I started meditating, plus the wear and tear on my hips and legs from my years in martial arts and playing rugby, doing the full lotus thing just wasn't going to happen. Meditating while sitting on a chair seemed perfect until this started manifesting. While I have fallen forward from my bench in a kneeling position, it's not far enough to cause bodily damage.

I: Good heavens, I never thought about meditation as a contact sport before!

P: Well, as the T-shirt saying goes: Meditation – It's Not What You Think! (laughs)

I: Ain't that the truth! (laughing)

P: I guess I'd like to sum up the subject of kundalini with this – I'm definitely not saying that there aren't capable, qualified teachers out there. Nor am I pitching Kriya yoga the SRF way, or any other way for that matter. What worked for me may or may not work for someone else. I wouldn't ever presume to try and sell a spiritual methodology or ideology to anyone! All

I'm saying is to just be very careful. OK? Kundalini merits being treated with respect. If one fries their circuits so to speak, it might be irreversible, which in turn may cause a hell of a lot of physical and even emotional pain and problems. One can certainly awaken without going through all of that.

I: Duly noted. If there was someone who, after reading your book, asked you where they should start their spiritual journey, what would you tell them? Would it be Yogananda's Self-Realization Fellowship, which you've been a member of for all these years?

P: Oh dear, this could possibly get me into trouble with some of the SRF faithful out there! Well...first of all, I doubt that someone who knows absolutely *nothing* about spirituality would be reading this book, but if I was approached by somebody asking about beginning a spiritual path, I'd have some questions for them first, before exploring the plethora of available options. That all having been said, would SRF be my default and/or only suggestion? No, it wouldn't, and here's why.

First, let me be clear – Yogananda and his teachings work! *I awakened through them.* But as we spoke about earlier, while Kriya and meditation was the core of my practice, one can't dismiss Meher Baba, who was *definitely* working for me. One can't forget the various teachings that resonated within and subsequently were adopted. And one can't ignore my life experiences, which also went into the stew. The long list of ingredients that went into my awakening mix was unique and unrepeatable, *just as yours is.* So while I would obviously be delighted to talk about Yogananda and SRF, I think it would be more helpful to our hypothetical seeker to ascertain what their inclinations might be. Jumping straight into Kriya, or Zazen, or Self-Enquiry, or whatever, might be a bridge too far. I'd probably suggest that they dip their toes into a number of things, through the myriad of books and websites that are available, which might well include Yogananda's *Autobiography of a Yogi.* Of all the 20th century's spiritual books, it certainly was one of the most influential. But maybe the *Conversations with God* material, or Eckhart Tolle's *The Power of Now,* or Michael Singer's *The Untethered Soul,* or possibly something from the late Dr. Wayne Dyer might be more appropriate for a newbie. Among some of the other icons, Deepak Chopra has certainly done his fair share over the years. Given the bazillion books he's authored, it's a wonder that he's had time for anything else in life. I can't imagine how he's done it. I don't know if it's really an "introductory" book but his *How To Know God* is brilliant. There have been so very many illumined teachers and splendid authors in the last 150 years alone, and we are all very blessed for it!

While I have appreciatively mentioned Yogananda, SRF, and Kriya a lot throughout this book, I don't want readers to think that I am pushing it as the path to take. As odd as this may sound, while I am *in* SRF, I am not *of* it. And the same would be true if I awakened via some other spiritual Master or teaching. When one awakens, one transcends the need for such things…unless they don't. It is certainly not that one goes beyond a teacher or teaching, but instead, the ego-mind that identifies with a path, or a teacher, or a practice, *dissolves*. The late – and greatly missed – Ram Dass used to correctly point out that all methods are traps and that they are designed that way. He also used to illustrate that, paradoxically, our practices don't really work unless we allow them to trap us. Enlightened Masters like Yogananda certainly understand this when they're signing people up. They are a trap because in the end, at the Event Horizon of awakening, *everything has to go,* and that necessarily includes what helped get us there. One Zen Master explained it to his students this way: "You have to swallow the fish and then spit out the bones." Having said that, early on the path, this isn't a subtlety that's always useful to hear, or necessarily important to know unless, of course, it is. There are fundamentalists in all religions and spiritual organizations that might call this blasphemy or heresy. Let 'em call it whatever they want, it makes no difference to me. But in This Moment, from the non-dual awareness known as Phil, the highest compliment possible to any teacher or teaching is this – *they aren't needed anymore.* Why? Because they did their job – *they worked!* And for doing so, we gratefully and eternally tip our cap to them, acknowledging their unique and vital role.

I also want to be very clear in this aspect of my message as well. I am not telling anyone to quit their practice! In my experience, devotion to one's path, coupled with joyful spiritual effort, is critical to awakening, especially early on. *There is a great deal to be said for discipline and determination!* But after many years, one's sadhana can also just become a **lifestyle**, and yet another identity, which only holds us back. As Adyashanti often asserts, the ego is like a shapeshifter. Please don't let it trick you into "being" a "seeker." All egoic identities are false!

Let me read the following from Nisargadatta to you: "When effort is needed, effort will appear. When effortlessness becomes essential, it will assert itself. You need not push life about. Just flow with it and give yourself completely to the task of the present moment, which is the dying [into] the now." And: "This process or readjustment is what you call sadhana. Ambition is personal, liberation is from the personal. In liberation both the subject and the object of ambition are no longer."

I: Again, very beautiful.

P: It is. (long pause, gazing out the window) You know, I'm suddenly feeling a strong energetic impulse that wants to add one more important dash of spice into this particular stew, if that's OK.

I: By all means.

P: It is truly wonderful, not to mention an incalculable blessing, to find a spiritual orientation in life. I actually see it as receiving a very special type of Grace, without which earnest sadhana doesn't begin. Often, it feels as if we're becoming *alive* for the first time. I know that's how it felt for me! Speaking from my experiences early on, I think it's both common and very natural to take ourselves, *our identity,* and place it into the path we choose at the time. We want to be a part of something larger and wiser, and that is completely understandable. I cannot express how thrilled I was when I joined the SRF group in Atlanta. I was around like-minded souls that not only supported me in my nascent spiritual journey but also provided me with friendship, understanding, and loving support in activities outside of SRF too. Some of them became – and will always be – *my family*. I'd not really had that in my entire life, especially as I had been moving around so much due to my career. It was a tremendously exciting and wonderful time. **It felt as if I had come home!** If you are searching for a transcendental path or spiritual fellowship, I definitely encourage you to be alert for these types of feelings. They show that you are very likely on the right track! If you have to force something like a spiritual path – or anything for that matter – it might not be the optimal thing for you at that point in time.

However, as we progress – **if we are progressing** – we discover that the path of Self-Realization is a journey that must be walked by oneself, especially near the end. I would say "alone" but we never truly walk the path alone, as that is just an illusion of the separate self. Still, there may come a time when we have little to no need for spiritual community. To grow is obviously necessary but to **outgrow** is also – but perhaps less obviously – necessary. For me, after just a few years it became a decidedly more solitary path. When this happens, if we have truly assimilated ourselves into the spirit of a teaching and not just its outer trappings, we then find that one day we are not a part of a teaching as much as **it becomes a part of us**. We take what uniquely works for us and make it our own. It then becomes an expression of us – our consciousness transforms – rather than how it was in the beginning, when we are trying to look and sound and act like whatever it is that we are now a part of. Then, and especially if there is a Guru-Disciple relationship, sadhana becomes an extremely personal and intimate thing. This is where *attunement* to one's spiritual Master really pays off. And if your particular path doesn't have a guru, that's OK too. As the ancient adages go: Life Itself is the Guru; God, Guru, and Self are One. This is where one's sadhana becomes laser-like focused and only what is truly required to progress remains, until the inevitable time comes when even that must be surrendered. Please, always remember this – the seeking never ends. Instead, *the seeker dissolves*. For those "seekers" reading this who have been on a spiritual path for a long time, this can be a very difficult-to-see stumbling block – letting go of what's magically gotten us so far from where we started. The **end goal** isn't to BE a virtuoso meditator, or a mystic, or a saint, or a sage, or a monk, or a yogi. All of these are just more fucking identities! The **end goal** is to be free from delusion!

Nisargadatta unequivocally asserted, "The search for Reality is the most dangerous of all undertakings, for it will destroy the world in which you live." Given this vital admonition, how much are we truly willing to give up to awaken? Are we ready to sacrifice the finite for the infinite? During the "rebirthing" months, especially when I was out in the desert, I kept saying to God, "even this…even that?" as the last of the ego-mind's core attachments were being (un)mercifully ripped away, or so it felt at the time. The price of awakening is *everything* – but there's no way you can know what everything means *until you're paying it*. No two awakenings are identical, so yours might be easier than mine was. Nevertheless, in this lifetime, during what I described as the "rebirthing" process, I never felt more **alone and vulnerable**. (pausing, a few gentle tears start to fall down Phil's face) The *annihilation* of egoic identity is the only Real Death we face. Even now, just describing this viscerally brings back the utterly bereft feelings of existential despair and fear that I felt.

While I probably wouldn't feel that all of this is vital to share during my first meeting with our hypothetical beginner, I will share this with all my spiritual sisters and brothers who still find themselves "seekers" on the path 20-30-40 years on...or longer. Inevitably, it seems that all spiritual paths come down to one crucial act – **surrender**. This necessarily includes your cherished and long-held-on-to spiritual teachings and teachers – because *you* can't ever "get there." Your beloved teacher and techniques can't carry you across the finish line, although they certainly would were it possible. You cannot finally, once and for all, set the ego-mind aside because there is no ego-mind to set aside; it's a fiction. And you cannot set this aside because there is no you to do the setting aside. In other words, *there is nothing to be set aside, and there is no doer to do it!* As is postulated in Zen, at times the best way forward is to "take the backward step." Try letting go of the steering wheel! In our complete, undeniable inability to attain awakening, in the final, ego-mind-shattering understanding that there is nothing "I" can "do" to make enlightenment happen – *then* Grace may descend upon us, in and through our naked and total vulnerability. And after that – when non-dual Awareness IS – **this** is when The Real Voyage of Discovery begins!

Why continue to suffer? Why live in the dream state? Please, don't just settle for walking a spiritual path. The ego-mind will happily do that forever! *Our final step on the path...is to give up all steps!* Like the brave little salt puppet at the beginning of this book fearlessly dissolving into the sea, we must willingly lose all we imagine we are...to Realize What We Are!

I: (long moment of silence) I'm not even sure what to say.

P: (wiping tears) Sometimes we're better served by not saying anything and just letting Silence have Its Way. (long pause) If we are done with all the questions, let's wrap it up and call it a day.

I: I actually don't think that I have anything else, Phil. I do want to say thank you so very much for our time together and more importantly, for your authentic candor, insights, and wisdom. It has given me a lot to ponder, as I am sure it will for everyone who reads your book.

P: Well...thank you too! (tired smile) All I can add is that "my" candor, insights, and wisdom come up from and out of the Stillness within. Just like you, Phil watches it happen. It's not only a sincere privilege to have been here today with you, but also Phil's unending privilege to be the mind-body conduit for Spirit to share Its wisdom and love with you. And not only with you, but with everyone Phil meets, and with everyone who reads *Grace Happens*.

Paradox

"You will never achieve spiritual enlightenment.
The you that you think of as you is not you.
The you that thinks of you as you is not you.
There is no you, so who wishes to become enlightened?

Who is not enlightened?
Who will become enlightened?
Who will be enlightened?

Enlightenment is your destiny –
more certain than sunrise.
You cannot fail to achieve enlightenment.
Were you told otherwise?
Irresistible forces compel you.
The universe insists. It is not within your power to fail.

There is no path to enlightenment:
It lies in all directions at all times.
On the journey to enlightenment, you create and
destroy your own path with every step.

No one can follow another's path.
No one can step off the path.
No one can lead another.
No one can turn back.
No one can stop.

Enlightenment is closer than your skin,
more immediate than your next breath,
and forever beyond your reach.

It need not be sought because it cannot be found.
It cannot be found because it cannot be lost.
It cannot be lost because it is
not other than that which seeks.

The paradox is that there is no paradox.
Isn't that the damnedest thing?"

~ *Spiritual Enlightenment: The Damnedest Thing by Jed McKenna*

> *The pathless path*
> *is the path always under our feet*
> *that has no extension.*
>
> ~ Longchenpa

EPILOGUE:
The Road Goes Ever On

In the original draft of the book, the Q&A interview was the ending. Due to the pandemic, however, an extra sixteen months went by: February 2020 until June 2021. Despite the hardships that many felt, myself included, I am incredibly thankful that this pause took place because so much more transpired that I can now tell you about. As a result, this epilogue came into being, and I feel it is the rightful conclusion to my story.

Unlike the previous chapters, this final section delves into my deepening perceptions by subject first and chronology second. It represents a variety of themes, some of which are philosophical and some of which are personal in the extreme. A few of these have been touched upon to varying degrees already, while others are wholly new because they are recent developments in my spiritual unfoldment. Like my early emails, many of my budding insights from this period are still a bit raw and thus not thoroughly grokked. Yet, since my first correspondence written the day after The Kiss, for reasons unknown to me, there has been an inner push to be as transparent and authentic as possible about my awakening. On a deep, non-conceptual level, it has felt compulsory to share how the Process has unfolded, along with the considerable challenges that have arisen from it – to lay bare everything and accept the worldly vulnerability and consequences that come with this. I won't pretend that this has always been easy, but I remain committed to it nonetheless.

For context, my unforeseen "2020 Airbnb Tour" brought continually changing (and stunning) scenery. With my fledgling employment search dead prior to arrival, I spent nearly nine months in Arizona: six in the magical red-rock-

and-vortex haven known as Sedona, one in Flagstaff, and forty days in Lake Havasu City. From there, I returned to southern California, where I currently reside. Most of the year was spent in seclusion, generated partly by my inner work and partly by the captivating and unprecedented machinations of the newly-born COVID-19 era. During this time, there was a strong energetic impulse toward a spiritual progression that I could not foresee, all of it unfolding in the effortless Flow that I am in and – I Am.

Before we begin our deep dive, please note that within the numerous book passages cited, the bracketed comments and italics are mine. With that, I want to open with a remarkable quote from the deep writings of the late Bernadette Roberts, a former Carmelite nun and contemplative in the Catholic tradition. In her highly-acclaimed book, *The Experience of No-Self: A Contemplative Journey,* she wrote the following:

> This [spiritual] journey then, is nothing more, yet nothing less than a period of acclimating to a new way of seeing, a time of transition and revelation as it gradually comes upon "that" which remains when there is no self. This is not a journey for those who expect love and bliss, rather, it is for the hardy who have been tried by fire and have come to rest in a tough, immovable trust in "that" which lies beyond the known, beyond the self, beyond union and even beyond love and trust itself.

The Nature of Illusion

The cosmic weaver of the illusory dream state is known in Advaita Vedanta and Dzogchen as *maya*. In eastern spiritual traditions, maya is seen as the incomplete, purely physical and mental reality in which one's everyday consciousness is ensnared, hence the metaphor of a dream often being used to describe it. The nature of the illusion is built into the very fabric of Beingness Itself, so consequently it's an essential conceptual element of what we're waking up from.

Over the years, many "spiritual seekers" I have known (Phil included) were under the impression that they were somehow in a duel to the death with this omnipresent veil of delusion in order to *achieve* Self-Realization. But are we really? Like the ego, is sister maya Real, or just a mental construct – a *relatively real* optical illusion – created by conditioned mind? If she's the latter, then what power does she actually hold over us, save what our minds project onto her and allow? From my post-awakening awareness-experience, I have realized that everything – the entire multiverse – is a projection of and happens in **Mind**. Max Planck was one of the goliaths of 19th and 20th century classical physics as well as one of the founding fathers of quantum theory. He alluded to the probability of illusion being an epiphenomenon of mind when he stated, *"We must assume behind this force the existence of a conscious and intelligent mind. This mind is the matrix of all matter."* To grasp the nature of maya, perhaps all that's needed is a change in perspective. To transcend maya, perhaps all that's necessary is to still the mind! This easy-to-say but challenging-to-do technique (a.k.a. meditation) allows access to the "gap" between sensory input and cognition, ceasing the continual *superimposition* of one's endless mental commentary (labels, comparisons, judgments, – the finite) onto the non-dual Unicity of the infinite. Even in the midst of our hectic lives, never-ending challenges and hardships, and the world's pervasive distractions, the clear light and stillness of our innate Buddha Mind remains a portal into infinite Reality itself. This silent, uncaused, and unconditioned Reality is **You**, forever existing in the gap between thoughts. This primordial emptiness also underlies the form and apparent substance of a universe that our senses and mind erroneously infer to be real.

For my money, no one in history expounded the Nature of Reality (i.e. The Empty, Illusory Display of Samsara and Nirvana) any clearer than Adi Shankara, the renowned Indian Master of Advaita Vedanta from the eighth and ninth centuries CE. Please consider these excerpts from Alistair Shearer's masterful work, *In The Light Of The Self: Adi Shankara and the Yoga of Non-dualism:*

> "Reality is a paradox for the normal mind," begins the Master [Shankara], "and this is why we have to employ the concept of maya if we are to understand it. This maya is often misunderstood, because it transcends our common-sense logic which tells us that a thing is either 'this' or 'that' and cannot be both at once. Maya – now what is this maya?" … "Now, to understand this question of maya, let us consider the moon reflected in the water down there. If you look closely, you will see that the moon is not really immersed in the water, yet nor is it wholly outside of it. We cannot say that the moon is actually in the water, because it is a mere reflection; but on the other hand, we cannot say that it is not there, because, even though a reflection, it manifestly is there, right

in front of us. Like that, if we are to be strictly accurate, we must say that the world of maya is both real and unreal at the same time. It is like a mirage, a divine mirage." [Longchenpa pointed to this when he reportedly said, "Nothing is as it seems, neither is it otherwise."]

"… phenomenal appearances are very curious! On the one hand, they exist of course; no one could deny that. But at the same time they have no abiding reality: they are impermanent, utterly evanescent. There is a permanence in life, but that status belongs to the non-dual Being alone, which is unmanifest and hidden, out of sight and beyond sense perception. Because Being is hidden behind the scenes so to say, the ordinary uncultured mind is quite unaware of it, and therefore such a mind falls into the grip of the world and becomes subject to the binding power of creation. What then is the status of this maya? We can say *it is the transitory dimension of life, superimposed upon the Divine* which in itself lies forever beyond all time, space and causation. As human beings, our noble destiny is first and foremost to transcend the insufficiencies of the ever-changing realm of maya, and thereby live our natural inborn identity with that Divine directly. Only then shall we avoid undue entanglement in the superimpositions that obscure it. And it is only by being free of this entanglement that we shall be able to understand and enjoy the world of variety aright, which is to recognize it as the Divine made manifest." … "Strictly speaking, *maya is not a force … it is a concept.*"

Even though I've shared this maxim earlier in the book, its importance bears repeating – no matter how it may look, *sadhana is inherently a process of subtraction*. Might maya's reputed sway over us then be yet another false notion to release, as we drop the baggage of *relative* appearances and Realize Absolute Truth? In Jed McKenna's unconventional yet superb book, *Spiritual Warfare: Book Three of The Enlightenment Trilogy*, I truly feel he correctly and succinctly sums up our "battle" with delusion: "Maya has every advantage except one – Absolute Truth. Maya doesn't exist; Truth does."

Every Awakening is Unique

I want to reiterate that *everyone* is blessed with a unique journey and awakening. What I have been sharing so far, along with what I'll be imparting moving forward, may not ever fall into your experience. The Luminous, Conscious

Manifestation that is **Beingness** expresses Itself in infinite ways. Therefore, the notion among some spiritual seekers that there is only one possible realized state doesn't hold up. The infinitude of everything manifesting must include awakening too, both in how it happens, and in how **What Is** appears. That being said, the prospects are that there will be some shared commonalities. For a comprehensive perspective on the varieties, qualities, and psychographics of awakening, the best collection of verifiable data I know of is found in *The Leap: The Psychology of Spiritual Awakening* by Steve Taylor. Importantly, the book's scientifically-based research also clearly delineates between a genuine awakening experience and psychosis. For those who may be uncertain about which one is manifesting, this can be invaluable. I should know, I was one of them.

Given that each journey of Self-realization is unrepeatable, most accounts of abiding awakenings demonstrate that one generally awakens at the level of the gut, the heart, or the head, each with their own perceptions of reality. These spiritual centers can awaken singularly or together, in any order, over any span of time. Why, when, and how they activate is beyond my current comprehension. Furthermore, I've never seen or heard this fully explained by anyone. In any event, along with our distinctive attributes contributing to the variations of awakening (innate and learned skills, personality traits, natural inclinations, karmic predilections, etc.), different spiritual traditions and their respective practices also tend to foment different facets of Truth. Examples of this could be a Tibetan Dzogchen Rinpoche describing Reality as the Dance of Samantabhadra, and that Emptiness is the underlying Nature of Reality. A Sufi Sheikh might describe his experience as the Lover and the Beloved becoming One, eternally merged in a shoreless Ocean of Bliss. An exponent of Vedanta could point to her non-dualistic, Direct Perception of This Moment as Beingness…and then say that there is no one who awakens. What's more, all three of these would be, in their own way, accurate! I find it nothing short of awe-inspiring that Spirit expresses Itself through an infinite number of modulations of consciousness that clearly have qualitative differences in Pure Perception, hence there being so many magnificent expressions of awakened consciousness throughout history!

Energy and Changing Times

Beginning in March 2020, and intermittently continuing to this day, I began feeling immensely powerful energies that were seemingly saturating the physical plane of reality. As a result, they became an unexpected companion of my sadhana, and in hindsight, I am confident that they played a pivotal role in accelerating the maturation of my awareness-experience. I mostly notice these energies in the late-evening/early-morning hours, and they feel like I am being plugged into a "charging station" (as one friend described them) and amped up with high-voltage energy, unable to sleep. My reason for sharing this is that it felt intuitively, both to me and to some of my friends, as if this was happening at the level of the body-mind and on a planetary scale. I am all but convinced that these "Shiva" energies are vibratory catalysts coming from the inner planes, and that they are contributing to the unprecedented global changes that we are all witnessing. Furthermore, it appears to me that they are exacerbating the extreme duress that so many are experiencing today. For those who are more conscious, it appears that these catalysts are fueling spiritual evolution. Yet for those less conscious, it is possible that they are hitting blockages in their chakras and creating energetic instabilities and mental confusion. This may even be contributing to the surge of destructive behaviors such as mass shootings and irrational hate crimes (among many other things) that we're seeing today. Concurrent with these mystifying but palpable energies was an imposed segregation (due to COVID-19), and perhaps these two variables together are stimulating the upheaval we see in almost every aspect of our planet and society today. While I am not ascribing causation, I do believe that there is a correlative factor. Perhaps, this is one aspect of the Global Consciousness Shift that many (me included) have anticipated with hopefulness for years. However, before things can get "better," sometimes they get "worse," and there is obviously no way to know how things will unfold in the coming years. During these crucial and historic times, I suggest being as present and centered as possible and not succumbing to the fear-based hysteria that pervades the media and social narrative. The consciousness that we bring and *are* is the best remedy, not only for our inner peace, but also for the evolution of our species and the preservation of our planet.

Solitude

For many, solitude can be an unwanted, difficult, and even terrifying prospect, as we have recently witnessed around the world due to the lockdowns. Let's face it, as Blaise Pascal observed and commented on, few people want to be in isolation; our entire Western society is geared toward the opposite. However, for those desiring and/or experiencing spiritual advancement, solitude can be a gift. Personally, it has always been one of the most fertile contextual fields for my evolution, and during the first nine months of 2020, I was blessed with near-total seclusion.

One unforeseen accompaniment to this was uncommunicativeness, and this may have caused (and may still be causing) some of my family and friends to feel as if they have been shut out of my life. This began in mid-February, when I returned to the SRF ashram after my retreat. Unknowingly, I'd become so finely tuned during my retreat that I found urban areas and their associated vibrations and noise to be tremendously difficult to bear. There are, of course, apocryphal stories of isolated yogis assiduously shunning people and villages after an extended interval in a cave or forest somewhere. This is because the yogi can be, at least for a while, vulnerable to courser environments and their accompanying energies, but I never considered that this might befall me. Astonishingly, I even experienced this energetic dis-ease at Hidden Valley, which had been an important spiritual sanctuary to me for years. Overall, it took about two weeks before I began to acclimate to the world again, and before I knew what had transpired, COVID arrived, SRF closed its facilities, and I was heading to Sedona. From then on, it simply felt compulsory to turn within and tune out the world as much as possible. While I wasn't refusing to answer messages, my replies were brief and I wasn't initiating many of my own. I sincerely apologize to anyone reading this who may have felt slighted.

Another unforeseen accompaniment to my seclusion was that I fell into a predominantly *transcendent* space rather than an *immanent* one. A different way of describing this would be that I was more firmly fixed in the Empty-Spaciousness of The Absolute, instead of the Heart-centered Presence that comes with being accepting of, and seamlessly integrated into, our humanness. Maybe yet a simpler way of saying this is that I was more seated in the Formless rather than in Form. To illustrate this, I was once described as "doe-eyed," meaning that every so often I had a somewhat unfocused, distant-looking gaze. There were often pregnant pauses between someone's question and my response, which came with a deeply interiorized countenance. "Being" was definitely happening more than "doing," but spiritually speaking, *they are both equally important!* I realize that dividing form and formless, along with being and doing, creates duality where there is none, but I don't think these fundamental aspects of Reality can be pointed to in a way that avoids this dualistic convention.

I'm mentioning all of this here, as these sorts of things can and sometimes do arise during our spiritual journey. Should any of this happen with you, it is prudent to have one or two people in the loop. Especially when you are awakening, or acclimating to an awakening that's already emerged, whatever direction The Divine Hand points to is worth going in, so long as no one is harmed of course, *which includes you!* While I am admittedly not a shining specimen of the Buddha's middle path (whatever that may be), it is most likely the optimal road to take…unless it isn't.

An Impulse to Serve

In early August, my immersion into Dzogchen naturally ended and so did the near-total solitude that I had been enjoying. With this, came an unmistakable Impulse to start "getting my hands dirty," as in engaging more with people. However, this was not a generic impulse. Instead, it was extremely specific: the urge was to share my experiences and insights with those who were *actively awakening* or with those who seemed to be very close to it.

My decision as to who I would share with was accomplished primarily through a complete trust in The Universe to organize such things, in conjunction with my intuitive and discriminative capacities. I surely wasn't looking to teach professionally, as that would add remuneration into the mix, which I don't want (there's certainly nothing inappropriate about that though). Nevertheless, if sharing my story could conceivably support someone during their journey, then that felt like dharmic and immensely privileged seva. Incredibly, it was only *two days* after the Impulse arose that I received an email from an ex-monastic friend who I hadn't heard from in many months. In his message, he stated that in his role as an energetic healer and hatha yoga instructor, he'd been working with somebody for several years and that this person now appeared to be awakening. As all other avenues had been explored, he asked if I would consider helping. Wow! The improbable timing of these sorts of things never ceases to amaze me, nor do they go unnoticed. So began an extraordinary and wonderful relationship of mutual spiritual growth with this individual, in addition to two others who I had already been corresponding with. Due to privacy issues, I won't share specifics about my communications and satsangs with these precious souls. In any event, I will describe the spiritual growth that all of this brought to me, as well as what their insightful feedback helped me to see and understand, three plus years after The Kiss.

Transmission

During and after some of our satsangs, it was reported to me on a semi-regular basis and in various ways that "transmission" was happening through/from Phil. During my nine-month rebirthing period in 2018, a retreatant at Hidden Valley that I didn't even know told me that he'd felt "strong waves of peace" emanating from my room. Due to this and similar events later on, hearing the same thing now from all three of these close friends wasn't shocking. Still, there was no one *doing* it! What's more, I was almost never aware of it, so I have no reason to thump my chest about any of this. I view transmission (and siddhis in general) with grateful indifference. My gratitude is for this mind-body being utilized in such a beautiful way, while my indifference is because there is no doership. The point to remember is that with no actual separation between anything, there are no spiritual energies or vibrations (i.e. shakti, chi, prana, etc.) coming "from" one individual and being "sent to" another.

Like many terms in our spiritual lexicon, "transmission" carries a fair amount of misconceptions. Due to the limitations of the person-to-person belief, I am inviting you here to approach this in a more nuanced fashion, from what I feel is perhaps the most complete and detailed definition of transmission. Please consider the following two passages from Keith Dowman's excellent translation and Dzogchen commentary, *Original Perfection: Vairotsana's Five Early Transmissions*:

> The essence of the transmission is simple, direct perception. In the timeless moment of the here and now, there is no space for projection and filtration and no time for evaluation, reflection, and judgment. In

this lies natural perfection. Herein lies the secret of nondual reality. When we speak of nondual mysticism, what is indicated is nothing but the clear light intrinsic to everyday perception; yet this perception and this function of awareness bring ultimate resolution to the human condition. All its dichotomies and contradictions are resolved in the unitary light of awareness in itself. If it can be said that conception and action exist, surely there is no gap between the initiation of the act and its actualization. The unitary moment is its own reward. Time and space are resolved in the all-inclusive wholeness of the moment. The quandaries of embodiment are resolved in each moment. The paradox and antinomies of gender are resolved in the unity of the moment. This is transmission of the Great Perfection that does not impose a new, conditional structure upon the mind but reveals what is already, primordially present. It comes by way of confirmation, then, of what has always been known: that the nature of being, the nature of reality, and the nature of mind are immanent as consummate perfection.

There is nothing in this transmission that can be grasped or conceptualized or cultivated or practiced. To assimilate it into the logical intellect and spin it out as a philosophy or doctrine is to nullify its purpose, just as the magic of poetry is lost in analysis. The transmission itself is a timeless event, like every moment of experience, arising as spontaneity, without cause or condition, so it cannot be developed into a yoga or a meditation practice. It cannot be turned into religion: there are no tenets of belief; neither devotion nor faith is a condition of its revelation; and no ritual interprets and structures it. It is simply an existential understanding of the here and now.

The Harmonization of Wisdom and Love

I feel it's worth repeating here that my awakening happened first in the mind (wisdom) and then immediately after in the heart (love). During the first nine months after The Kiss, aspects of the gut (existential death) were unavoidably addressed too, but it seems as if most of those challenges were already out of the way. Whether this particular opening sequence was due to pre-incarnational efforts, pre-awakening sadhana in this life, my aggregate karmic package, my guru, some or all of these, or something else altogether, I do not know. I do know that from the opening bell, my awakened awareness-experience was predominately mind/wisdom based. While calculating an exact proportion is obviously not possible, once everything had settled down and my awakened Beingness had matured (somewhere around the two-year anniversary of The Kiss), my best guesstimate was that the wisdom aspect outweighed the love aspect by 75% to 25%. This undeniably imprecise approximation was primarily based on intuitive feel, along with feedback from the friends that I was in regular contact with. Eventually, I believe, our deepening into/as awakened consciousness leads to the Mind-Heart (i.e. Wisdom-Love) facets of our individuated Oneness **balancing**, thereby functioning together in an ever-more refined harmony. It is also worth remembering that this rarely, if ever, happens at the beginning of one's awakening. Based on this, coupled with my own experience, it is reasonable to expect that at least a portion of your post-awakening life will be these two dancing together. Again, it is these fundamental aspects of awakened consciousness that Nisargadatta Maharaj pointed to when he impeccably stated, "Love says, 'I am everything.' Wisdom says, 'I am nothing.' Between the two my life flows."

After walking the spiritual path for a time, we often begin feeling one or more aspects of the Unitive State. In my case, the first that manifested was the feeling of peace, as in, "The peace of God which passeth all understanding." The reason this peace lies outside of our limited human understanding is that it isn't dependent on "outer" conditions for it to arise and perpetuate itself. It is present and felt irrespective of what's happening around us or to us. Over time, this peace beyond my understanding became the feature of the Divine that was most predominant. The final quarter of 2020, however, brought a different quality of Spirit that, while felt before, had never been known so intensely – Divine Love.

In the latter stages of my Dzogchen period, and during my interactions with friends undergoing their own awakenings, my inner balance between Wisdom and Heart neared a more equitable distribution. Unlooked for and at seemingly random times, I began feeling profound waves of love welling up, through, and over me. These waves varied in intensity and were borderline rapturous. The peak of this was in November, during my forty-day sojourn in Lake Havasu City. While in a meditation with my friend, a wave of Divine Love passed through me that was so strong my body shook repeatedly. Unable to speak, move, or open my eyes, I felt another wave approaching, and as it permeated every cell of my body, I shook again even more. Finally, a third wave passed and the feeling of love in my heart (and chest area in general) was so immense, so dazzlingly powerful, that I prayed for it to stop, as I thought it might cause my physical heart to fail. There was **so much** love that body-consciousness and everything else fell away, and Unconditional Love was all that existed. With this came the realizations that Love is omnipresent and What We Are is Love.

While reflecting on these miraculous experiences, I recalled these lyrics by the American band Kansas from a noticeably spiritual song off their 1976 album, *Leftoverture:*

"Here I am, I'm sure to see a sign
All my life I knew that it was mine
It's always here, it's always there
It's just love and miracles out of nowhere
Love, and miracles out of nowhere"

Transmuting Energetic Residues – Karma

It was during my interactions with the above-mentioned awakening soul that the next theme of my swiftly-evolving sadhana emerged, and I feel that it is the other side of the metaphorical Divine Love coin: taking on karma. Intuitively, it seems that this was made possible by my heart opening up to such a degree. I wouldn't say that I was taking on "the karma of others," as there are no "others" in Oneness. Regardless, both individual and mass karma exist in Samsara, and its energy is present in both the gross and subtle realms. Truly, I never dreamed of being a vehicle for this! What's more, I readily acknowledge that there is no way to know any of this for certain, hence the importance I place on listening to and trusting my intuitive sense, as the mystically-oriented experiences I've had were never accompanied by explanatory memoranda from on high.

My first experience of this happened out-of-the-blue back in 2008, when a prayer of mine was answered after asking to take on whatever karma I could from my mother in her last few days in the body. Although this prayer was granted, the physical ramifications were so severe and my memory of the experience was so dark, I felt that I would never attempt it again. My assumption had always been that karmic ingestion, transmutation, and elimination was the sole province of illumined spiritual Masters. Moreover,

I do not consider myself on par with them. Due to my reverence for the Masters, to state to the world by way of this book that this body-mind organism is "eating karma" seems outlandish at best and delusional at worst. However, when I began writing *Grace Happens,* my commitment was to Truth, whatever It looked like. Anything less would be a disservice to you, since *everything that's happened to me can happen to you as well.*

The next occurrence of this came without warning twelve years later while I was spending time in Flagstaff with my friend. I suddenly found myself not feeling well and needing to lie down. The body became hot and then quickly went cold. There were three separate waves of "yuck" that passed through, several minutes apart. This *yuck* came into my lower torso area, worked its way through in an upward direction, and then exited around the third eye chakra. The best way to describe the pain that had my body shaking in a convulsion-like manner is to say that it was like trying to pass an energetic kidney stone. Anyone who's had the normal variety of kidney stone (I'm one of them) knows what genuine pain is and sadly, these were in that same-pain ballpark. During the "passing" stage, tears were streaming and less-than-delicate language was sometimes uttered, while in between I was mainly trying to catch my breath and center myself in the event there was a next wave. My friend was obviously concerned and sitting nearby in order to be of assistance, as neither of us knew what was happening. Yet even as all this was unfolding, we both somehow felt that this was a blessing. My friend later reported feeling on an energetic level that "something was being removed." In the aftermath of this, I found myself incredibly thirsty and later on ravenously hungry.

Unlike the first experience with my mom, I was now genuinely undeterred. From a place of love, the next day I affirmed to The Universe that if I was indeed ready to be utilized in this unique and sacred way, then I asked that It use me well, and to please give me all that I am able to take. And so It has. After the Flagstaff experience, there were, on average, three of these events per month, always with a week or more in between. At the time this is being written, I am incapable of doing this at will. Moreover, I have no goal of making this something that I can turn on whenever the mood strikes. Even if I could manage to initiate this, it would be crazy, as I have *no idea* how this affects the physical and subtle bodies. As is true with so many other facets of our sadhana, I feel these types of considerations are best left to

Divine Intelligence. "Trusting the Process" is not just a new-age tagline – it's **essential.** If I do need to know some aspect of this, then The Universe will make it known. As St. John of the Cross extolled, I've become accustomed to "walking in the dark."

The ensuing occurrences of this phenomenon generally were not specific to one individual; they felt more like energetically cleansing an area. On the other hand, there have been a few that were specific in nature, sometimes with visual glimpses of the places and people involved. Mercifully, the convulsions and other extremes became less severe as time went on. It's as if this body-mind organism has become more capable of handling karma or, put another way, more able to process these "energetic residues." Perhaps the best way to describe this is: once I would begin to feel ill and lie down in surrender, it sometimes felt as if there was a dark, energetic skin enveloping my body. At other times, it felt like pieces of small-shaped energy were somehow being consumed, converted, and expelled. During this period (several months), there was a recovery window that ordinarily took about a day or so. By mid-2021, the convulsions and recovery periods were gone. Here now, it is as if this body-mind apparatus has become something akin to an electrostatic air cleaner, in that throughout the day I feel energy spikes randomly puncturing the body, much like an air cleaner zapping large dust particles. These spikes can be felt anywhere in the body, with zero warning. The upside to this is that I'm not writhing in bed, but the downside is that there is no way to steel myself against the incoming "energetic shrapnel," as it happens so randomly. Most of these don't hurt but instead just produce a reflexive contraction in the stomach. When these spikes do bring discomfort or even genuine pain, it actually feels somewhat blissful immediately afterward. It's a serviceful privilege and I wouldn't have it any other way.

Samadhi

Another portion of my journey that I feel necessary to disclose is the event in/of/as consciousness that I am calling *samadhi*. This disclosure carries a caveat, however. Like the term "enlightenment," samadhi comes with a lot of different interpretations, so while it may have baggage, I believe this is the best word to describe what occurred. As this is not an academic essay, I will not explore this philosophically any further except to say that samadhi is frequently described as a "complete absorption" that is sometimes experienced by those on the spiritual path, usually during deep meditation. This is where no part of one's mind is left to maintain the awareness of anything other than the object of one's meditation. The *absorption* that was happening with me, however, was not on an *object* in meditation; the duality of subject-object perception had vanished. This was on/in/as an Absolutely Black, Motionless, and Silent No-thing-ness. The Void. The Uncaused, Unconditioned, and Unmoving Infinite Plenum of Pure Potentiality.

At some point in my immersion into Dzogchen, interludes of "nothingness" started happening. These would typically be five to fifteen minutes in duration. Rather than nothingness, maybe a better pointer is – **Nonexistence**. I only knew these interludes from either end, as there was *nothing* in between. I was only able to approximate the length of these by checking the time afterwards and then trying to recall when it began. During the samadhi, there was no sense of time or duality. No perceiver and no phenomena to perceive. Just Plain Nothing. This is why I would describe these samadhi interludes as a **nonexperience**, because as the concept is characteristically defined, an experience requires an observer and something to observe. In this, there was neither.

During my subsequent introspections, I pondered on what exactly was aware of The Void. As there was *no one* not experiencing *no thing*, then *who* or *what* was reporting what I'm describing as "Absolutely Black, Motionless, and Silent No-thing-ness?" The answer is obviously awareness. But then, can awareness be both aware and unaware at the same time? Well, based on what I was (non)experiencing, it seems that it can, which was both a revelation and a paradox. If you remember the epigraph from the Introduction, Nisargadatta described this as "Pure Awareness not aware of itself." Beingness, which I often refer to as awareness-experience, can either be: 1. *As something* (the separation-based subject-object of the waking or dreaming state), 2. *As nothing* (the "I Am No One" aspect of Unity consciousness) or, 3. *As everything* (the "I Am Everything" aspect of Unity consciousness). However, based on these samadhi non-events, there seems to be a fourth possibility as well: Beingness *as not anything*. Said another way, it is non-dualistic Unity awareness-experience without experience! (Some of my understanding of how best to verbalize all this was aided by a talk given by Hameed Ali.)

Now, you might be asking the same questions that I've asked myself: "What does this mean?" and, practically speaking, "What benefit is there?" Likewise, "How do these non-events affect everyday life?" To all these questions, I can only offer one unsatisfying answer...I don't know. There was a feeling that perhaps my subtle bodies were being rewired and therefore being "enhanced," but that's purely speculation. As the year went on, these samadhis would spontaneously arise two or three times a month with increasing duration, lasting up to approximately one hour. In one case, during a shared meditation with a friend who was "circling the drain," the nonexperience of no-thingness happened to us both at the same time. In other words, we dropped into samadhi together. Frankly, I didn't even know this was possible! I also must concede that I cannot verify or even speak to my friend's nonexperience. Nevertheless, we were both aware of each other on "the edges." To rephrase, we both remember dropping off together and then opening our eyes within seconds of one another. Without relating my nonexperience, my friend described the exact same thing. Furthermore, after each of these samadhis, it took some time to come back to my normal waking state of consciousness. I would describe this like the feeling of interiorization one has after a deep meditation, only this was that feeling *on steroids!* The amount of time necessary for me to "reboot" varied, depending on the length of the samadhi, and during this shared samadhi of about one hour, it took me a couple of hours to reengage fully. It took my friend about twenty-four hours.

The Falling Away of the Unitive Self

As I mentioned in previous chapters, my initial awakening brought with it a visceral awareness-experience of there being no separateness between Phil and the rest of world. Yet, despite not being identified as a separate self, there was still other (i.e. alterity). I am not pointing to the multiplicity of/in/as Manifestation. Even though there is Oneness, there are also infinite individual expressions of that Oneness. This was something else. With more distance in my rearview mirror, a paradox had appeared. How was Beingness Whole and simultaneously aware of and experiencing otherness? It was as if the Unitive State that arose from my awakening was not complete somehow.

During my ongoing meditation/communion with The Universe, this was the question and conundrum I offered It. In time, I came to recognize that the initial phases of Oneness and the Unitive State are inherently transitional and evolve over time. While this is impossible to explain satisfactorily, as it is such a subtle point of difference not readily apparent in ego consciousness, I concluded that if there was still other, then there still must be a self, i.e. some subject-object split that had not yet been transcended. Moreover, this understanding came, in part, through the breathtaking wisdom of Bernadette Roberts in her book, *The Path to No-Self*. In this sometimes abstruse yet uniquely profound manuscript, I found unmistakable parallels between what she wrote about and what I was beginning to experience. The ensuing two excerpts from Bernadette's book merit consideration here, with her "butterfly" being the newly awakened:

> What we have to admit is that any state, however ecstatic or delightful cannot be maintained for any length of time without it growing commonplace and unspectacular. We have to face up to the fact that the transformation is over, the wedding and honeymoon are over, and we must now put these experiences behind and move courageously into a new life beyond transforming union. From now on, we look back on the transformation process as the child looks back on its embryonic stage. Life in the chrysalis was very secure, the mechanism of transformation was a path in itself, but once the butterfly emerges, this secure path comes to an end, and the butterfly is virtually on its own. Then it must fly into a new space, into the unknown – go forth to the full exercise of the mature unitive life.
>
> The moment we step into this new dimension, we have already begun a life beyond transformation, a life which few people realize is actually a stage unto itself; a vital, crucial preparatory stage for yet further change and transformation. Because no one realizes this, the stage has been given little coverage, has not been seen in its true perspective and, therefore remains little understood. One reason is that to have perspective – on anything – we need distance; that is, we must have passed through a stage before we can look back and see it for what it is.

From our never-ending evolution, Bernadette posited that one eventually and necessarily moves **past** Unitive Beingness into what she and various other spiritual teachers call "No-Self." More importantly, *my experience now confirms this*. Those familiar with the map of consciousness that the late Dr. David Hawkins espoused would view this as the difference between levels of consciousness in the 600's (awakening sage) and 700+ (the consciousness strata of enlightenment). I stand by my comments in this book's Introduction about preferring the word "awakening" to "enlightenment." However, here now, it appears as if there may be a valid distinction between the two terms.

Bernadette pointed to an "inner flame" that eventually burns the Unity Self out, leaving only No-Self. In emails beginning around June of 2019, I mentioned that after nearly two years of seemingly no inner movement, there began faint stirrings deep within. Initially, it felt as though the awakening process had left a pile of ash – what I thought were the remains of the now burned-to-the-ground ego-mind structure. By the two-year anniversary of The Kiss, these stirrings felt like a small burning flame, but its source of fuel, along with its purpose for burning, was unknown. By early 2020, the flame had become a raging fire that resulted in *Grace Happens* being written. In This Moment, I sense that the flame's purpose (these pointers are metaphorical and not to be taken too literally) is to consume the ash. And *the ash* is the remaining essence of the existing Unitive Self. The ensuing passages are how Bernadette artfully described this:

> [Its] sole purpose is to interiorly consume its unitive partner. ... this flame is an intense living, not a living *for* God, but a living *with* God. It is a totally subjective experience, the experience of the whole self living to the fullest extent of its potential which, somehow, is not enough.
>
> I finally decided that, since the flame had no way to the outside, it would simply have to explode someday. I had no idea what would happen then, but was sure it would be something wonderful – the ultimate of all possible expressions! Eventually this explosion did occur, but it was nothing like I expected – it was just a puff! A silent puff and the flame went out. With this, however, the entire unitive center disappeared, and what remained was absolute stillness and silence. There was no movement at all, and also no sense of emptiness, because now there was no longer a "within" and therefore nothing left to be empty.
>
> The essence of the unitive life, then, is the gradual imperceptible death of the self, a death made possible because the self is secured, anchored in God so that it has no fear of living fully, accepting all the suffering, heartaches, and trials that come its way. The mechanism of the self's

dying is built into its life with God – we give all, He takes all, and when all is gone, He alone remains. Without this unitive life we cannot possibly give up the self; there would not be sufficient security, love, trust, or even a sufficient reason to do so.

In time … we discover that we can only be pure mediums of God when there is no self remaining. This phase, then, is the time when God is burning out and consuming the self in a way we never thought possible; in truth, it is an imperceptible dying of the unitive self.

January 5, 2021 (the birthday of my guru, Paramahansa Yogananda) held perhaps the most sacred occasion of this lifetime. I view only The Kiss and my Karmic Purge nine months later as equal in significance. Due to the exceptionally intimate nature of the event, I feel it appropriate to share only a few details. Yoganandaji, Meher Baba, and other Masters central to my spiritual evolution in this incarnation were present, in what felt like an initiation into enlightenment. The awareness-experience of "otherness" dissolved, and the realization "everything is me" gave way to "I Am Everything." It felt like an expansion, although this is not entirely accurate to apply to Consciousness, as Its nature is infinite (where could It expand to?). Before this Shift, there was a spherical center of "I" without borders; there was interconnectedness, but "I" was localized. Now it feels as if I Am Everywhere. There is no localization, no "other," and no "things" left for me to be the totality of. The infinite Universe is "I," and if I have a body, That is it. The Shift from Oneness with other to Oneness without otherness was subtle. So subtle, in fact, that it took a while before I really noticed the difference and even longer before I attempted to verbalize it. There was no epiphany in a rainbow-filled sky while the angels sang *Stairway to Heaven*. Yes, there was my unforgettable moment with the Masters, but subsequently, as Bernadette wrote, the "unitive center" fell away like a "silent puff."

Reflections after Enlightenment

Beginning my spiritual journey, it was with the singular purpose of attaining moksha – of becoming enlightened. Then, I'm sorry to say, I envisioned leaving. Ignobly, I wanted out. I'd had enough of the world's illusion-based insanity, enough of the never-ending struggles of life, enough suffering. I was going to "achieve" enlightenment (whatever that was) and then exit stage-left into well-deserved glory and eternal bliss. Everyone else would just have to slog it out for countless incarnations just as I surely had. In the beginning, unbeknownst to me, there was little compassion for my fellow wanderers in the dream state and few thoughts about aiding others. If this sounds familiar, that's because it is. This "I've damn well had enough" point is where many begin their spiritual journey, and I was no exception. The desire to leave this worldly existence is very common and totally understandable. Moreover, in my egoic mind, I was confident that I had all the "right" stuff: my guru and his techniques, the single-pointed focus to succeed, the willingness to sacrifice the tangible finite for the promise of the infinite, an unshakable sense of destiny, and countless iterations of Life's blessings perfectly lined up, all designed to ultimately confer enlightenment on me. On January 5, 2021, everything came together effortlessly, and here now I Am Home, *knowing that I never left*. What I didn't know all those years ago at the "beginning" of my sadhana, and what I surely never imagined at the "end" of it, was that, as a modulation of awakened Beingness, there was still an all-important decision ahead to make.

One week after the sacred events of January 5, I awoke to a feeling of **dread** in the air. There was a palpable feeling that this might be my last day on earth using this body-mind organism, and the one friend around me at the time clearly sensed it too. Brother Death felt nearby and there was no shaking this premonition. That night, I quickly fell asleep and, almost immediately, was out-of-body and in a dimly lit, narrow corridor about twenty feet in length. As I began to rise, at the end of the corridor was the world and all that I love most. There was a spotlight on it and the choice was clear: do I wish to stay or go? I knew this was my long-hoped-for chance to leave this nutty world and shout *hasta la vista baby!* However, instead of rising, I moved toward the end of the corridor and then instantly awoke, realizing that I would stay in the body for whatever remaining time is given to me. The egoic Phil that started out all those years ago would have been shocked and dismayed at my decision to stay, but then again, he was beginning his journey as many do – from a place of self-centeredness. What would also have distressed him was that "Phil" didn't survive the awakening and, thankfully, there was no way that he could. What remains now is The Universe in and as Phil, and It saw both paths of service – without a human body working on the inner planes, or with one in the physical plane – and unflinchingly chose the latter. That which I love most in the world was more important and it wasn't even close.

There are always consequences stemming from our actions, even proverbial "right action," and I want to share my observations with you. As we come to a close, let's review the major costs of my awakening. First, the spiritual journey and its inevitable conclusion – an abiding, transcendental shift – tends to be messy, confusing, and at times seemingly crazy to those around us. Resultantly, in practical terms there has been a worldly cost. Stemming from my decision in 2012 to leave the corporate world and manage an ashram for free, my career was derailed, and the awakening has only made this worse. And yet, despite these worldly setbacks, I find myself embracing *whatever it takes* to evolve, both spiritually and as a human, and bearing my soul about it all at the same time.

Second, while there is no separation and Unity in every moment, there is a feeling that I'm alien to a world that everyone takes for granted as normal and real. This feeling of not fitting in was present long before the awakening and it persists. Before, my ego-mind intensely wanted to be understood, and that felt like my personal cross to bear; now, it's simply accepted as **What Is**. In human terms, perhaps the highest price I paid was that some of my highly-valued friendships dissolved. Conversely, some friendships deepened and new ones formed, so in this respect, awakening is no different than any other major life-changing event. Stop for a moment and honestly ask yourself these questions: if no one ever knew you were enlightened, would it matter? Alternatively, if they did know, how would you feel if they never once cared to ask about it or worse, just dropped you without a word from their lives after many years of close friendship? I have dealt with these and wisdom <u>does</u> allow me to experience them as part of the perfection of The Universe. In all honesty though, I admit that this has and sometimes still does bring sadness. Be that as it may, I fully realize that there is no good/bad or right/wrong in all of this. It seems that the longing to be "seen" – to genuinely be understood and accepted – is a part of humanness, with or without awakening. Maybe this longing stems from the intrinsic divinity that's hidden within all of us. Maybe the people in our lives who we want to see us cannot, in part because we ourselves aren't willing to embrace and share our own divinity. I really don't know, but it's something to ponder. Perhaps, this longing to be seen is yet another reason this book was written.

The third major result I've observed is that the news of the world hurts more. A hell of a lot more. This comes not from a heightened sense of empathy and compassion, although these are present too, but instead from the indescribable living awareness-experience that the events of the world **are me**. While the aspect of consciousness known as Phil isn't perpetrating the atrocities we see and hear about every day, those who commit and are victim to senseless acts of violence are *not other than me* either. Because of this, an insight came in May 2021 that I had unknowingly walled-off my heart to a certain extent and was operating mostly from the wisdom aspect of the mind. Ram Dass once unequivocally said that living in wisdom only is a "cold place." How had this happened to me? Now that I was experientially One with/as the world, at some level I felt unable to endure its collective suffering. As a result, I insulated my heart, which impeded compassion, and I unknowingly harbored anger about this deep within. Upon intense introspection and dialogue with one of my dearest friends, I expressed concern that there may be some sort of personality flaw or possible karmic impediment present. In the final analysis, however, I concluded that I was still having difficulty harmonizing the heart facet with the wisdom of the mind. While *my essence* – primordial awareness – was not affected (It never is!), my *embodiment* of It was affected, and that, dear reader, seems to be our eternal challenge. Whether in a human body-mind now, or in some other physical apparatus residing on another planet down the road, regardless of our level of consciousness, Life is always providing us with a contextual field in which to evolve. It's The Dance and it's a humbling process…but it is the only game in town. So like you, I do my best from where I am.

The Nature of Reality

Here now, if there is any "identity" Phil has at all, it is this: I Am That – The Absolute – as well as the infinite expressions of consciousness in manifestation that It gives rise to: The Multiverse Itself. But even as I write this, I find that this too is subtly evolving! It seems that I am moving even more into the "cloud of unknowing" and that even this "I Am Everything-ness" that arose in January is being supplanted six-months later by the intrinsic Emptiness of All Things. Throughout this book, many times and in many ways, I've pointed to what non-dual Unitive Beingness has been like for me, both early on and as the awakening matured. However, as consciousness continues to unfold, I would now describe the "core" of my awareness-experience as *the absence of Beingness*. Free from motion, thought, or disturbances of any kind, in this "space" there is a total absence of pain, pleasure, or suffering. It is, in a word – empty. The heart still feels and the body still does what it does, but this Empty Void seems now to be omnipresent...and that means in and as me.

To better understand this, I have recently been immersed in Buddhist writings on Sunyata (i.e. ajata), and this concept is at the heart of Ramana Maharshi's teachings, among many others. Please consider the following two explanatory excerpts from *Emptiness* by Robert Wolfe:

> Advaita tells us that reality is "not two". Ajata tells us that it is "not even one". Ajata translates as "no creation". [Or, "not caused."] This means to say that nowhere has anything ever come into being. Therefore, the entire universe (or universes) – and everything therein – has no reality. In other words, the ultimate condition is nothing, or nothingness. Advaita is to ajata, as milk is to cream. In advaita, we come to realize that "all that is, is That," or the Absolute. Ajata is where we subsequently come to realize that there is not even That (or the Absolute).
>
> "Dependent co-arising" is the form of "emptiness is form". While all forms are considered to have a beginning and an ending, not anything we regard as a form is self-standing, or self-created; a form may be considered to be a cause of something, or else an effect of some other thing. In fact all that we consider to be forms are actually a creation or conception by one form in particular, the human "mind". The point is that all forms are dependent for their presumed existence: all things, it can be said, are dependent on some other thing (or things) for their "arising" – your self included. So all forms, dependently-arising as they are, have no "self-nature"; are not independently existing phenomena. In other words, each thing is empty of reality as a fixed entity throughout the passage of time: all things are transitory, mutable, dependent upon extraneous causes or conditions. In short, "form is empty" of reality. That emptiness of reality is what form actually is. Emptiness itself does not "exist" (nor non-exist), we might say, "in a vacuum". It is what form is when we recognize that no forms can have self-nature. But if there were no appearances of forms, the emptiness of reality in forms would be meaningless. Thus, you might say, emptiness is "necessarily" the being of forms which (co-dependently) appear. Form is emptiness, emptiness is form.

This is about as counterintuitive as can be, but this is now "my" Am-ness. Beyond logic and concept is an inner Emptiness that I See as What Is. In the Q&A, I talked about Meher Baba teaching that nothing has ever happened, is happening, or will happen, and while I had a firm conviction about that at one level during the interview, it wasn't a lived experience until now...and it's been a game-changer. When addressing the concept of cosmic illusion (maya) at the beginning of this epilogue, I also relayed Max Planck's quote about mind being the matrix of all matter. From the "place" of Sunyata, it is seen that *the entire "external" world is fundamentally a vibration of the mind.* Unknowingly, one first creates out of their mind and then sees what the mind itself has created. If the mind is inherently nothing (no-thing in particular), then what reality is there to that which the mind perceives? The last passage that I want to share with you on this deeply essential topic comes from David Godman's biographical trilogy of H.W.L. Poonja titled *Nothing Ever Happened.* In these, Godman recorded the following summary of Papaji's views on ajata:

> You have never allowed yourself to experience the emptiness that is empty of all objects. Instead have the conviction, "I am in emptiness right now. Emptiness is my nature." Nothing will be left – no gods and no universe. This is the same nothingness that must have preceded "the gods" and their "creations." Nothing has ever existed. This, ultimately, is the only truth. Whatever else you read in the scriptures comes from a different perspective, a relative perspective which assumes the reality of ideas such as birth, death, bondage, and so on. I will tell you the bare truth: there is no birth, there is no death, there is no creator and there is no creation. This is now my conviction, my experience. What is seen does not exist. I know the truth that nothing has ever happened. Nothing ever existed at all. No one exists, nothing exists. This is the truth. In reality, nothing has ever been created. Absolute non-manifestation is the only Truth. That place is my real home. It is where I always am.

As extraordinary as some of what I've written about here may seem, to me it feels like all of it was just a natural unfolding of what began with The Kiss. However unlikely, in the end, all of this was *inevitable.* The place in and as consciousness I find myself now is miraculous beyond my ability to share and yet, day-to-day, it still often appears quite ordinary. Despite the never-ending worldly challenges, there also is an inner peace and joyful acceptance of This Moment that isn't dependent on anything "outside." Feelings of love, compassion, and understanding pervade each moment, along with an unshakable awareness that our essence is forever untouched – *eternally unstained* – by events in our lives and in the world. Regardless of the trials inherent in our humanity, freedom from suffering is possible. Enlightenment is Liberation from Samsara.

As I near my four-year anniversary of The Kiss, the eternal, ever-new "voyage of discovery" manifests, both in and as the guy writing this, and in everything else…you included. It truly has been an immense privilege to share with you my journey of awakening. Here now, my sincere prayer is that you too will awaken from the suffering that's inherent in the dream state. Once more and this time say it with me: We Are That Which We Seek! Realizing this, we then remember the Truth in Matsuo Basho's sagely adage – "Every day is a journey, and the journey itself is home." This has been Grace Happening: An Awakening of Consciousness. Thank you so very much for *taking the ride,* dear friend, and God Bless You!

Lokah Samastah Sukhino Bhavantu

May all beings everywhere be happy and free, and may the thoughts, words,
and actions of my own life contribute in some way to that happiness,
and to that freedom for all.

No matter what spiritual path you've walked or what teachings you've followed, they must lead you back to no path and no teaching. A true teaching is like a blazing fire that consumes itself. The teaching must not only consume you, but consume itself as well. All must be burned to ash, and then the ash must be burned. Then, and only then, is the Ultimate realized.

~ *Adyashanti*

APPENDIX:
Soul Food

There is certainly no scarcity of gurus, spiritual teachers, mystics, sages, prophets, visionaries, shamans, life coaches, spiritual healers, mediums, intuitives, monastics, priests, and the like in today's new-age marketplace. Finding the genuine article that also resonates in one's soul is often a daunting task for many. I attribute the ease with which I found Yogananda and his teachings to our meeting each other during my previous incarnation while living in Boston. This pre-existing link made it a simple matter of him waiting until I was ready-to-go this time around.

I think Ram Dass put it best when he stated, "A teacher points the way; the guru is the way." Paraphrasing here, he went on to say that the guru is a mirror who reflects back to the disciple where their work is. In addition to my guru-disciple relationship with Yoganandaji, I have been doubly blessed to have had Meher Baba actively involved in my evolution. My only explanation for this, other than "good karma," is that I was such a rough assignment that I needed more than one Master to help awaken me! I can well imagine a conversation between these two great Beings going something like this – Yogananda: "Please...you take him for a while, I need a vacation from all his silliness!" Baba: "OK, (sigh)...but you owe me!" While some struggle with the notion of having more than one Master at a time, I have never had any problem with it. First, they are not in competition for the most followers. Second, they too are a part of Oneness (God, Spirit, Source), with each being a different facet of the same infinite diamond. Third, I'll take help from anywhere I can get it. After all, that's their chosen vocational gig! As

I understand it, loyalty to the guru is simply an unswerving commitment to Realizing Truth, not to a particular (non)physical form.

Regarding my spiritual teachers in this life, there have been too many to count, as *everyone* in Life is a teacher if one is conscious enough to realize it; hence, the Hindu and Buddhist term "Upa Guru," who can be *anyone,* versus a "Sat Guru," who is a Master karmically dedicated to the spiritual evolution of the disciple. **Life itself** is the teacher (that's really what the Manifestation of Consciousness does) as it reflects back our individuated wave of consciousness and, in doing this, creates the contextual field in which we evolve. God, Guru, and Self are One – *in and as* All Things!

With that said, I thought it might be useful to include a list of those who have inspired and guided me most in life, as all have been referenced throughout this book. Listed alphabetically by their first (or only) name, I've also included website addresses when possible and a bit about when and how they aided my journey. As with any search for a guru or teacher, one must be careful to use one's discrimination and intuitive heart, never taking anything for granted. I always placed what I heard against my own experience and/or intuition and never blindly followed anyone or any teaching. Any supposed teacher asking people to do otherwise should be a warning to be very, very careful. As in any area of life, charlatans abound. Even the genuinely awakened have fallen to the temptations of glamor, so it pays to look before leaping. I feel one of the best measures of a guru or teacher is the people they attract, and the awakened souls (if any) that come from their lineage and teachings. The ensuing list is not all-inclusive by any means. However, these are the Masters and teachers who had the greatest influence on my sadhana and ultimate awakening. As such, I endorse them all implicitly.

The Masters

Ibn 'Arabi: There have been many towering spiritual giants who have profoundly aided my awakening over the years, but the seven included here stand above all the others for the most important reason that I know of: all of them *deeply touched my heart.* The first spiritual luminary detailed here – al-Shaykh al-Akbar ("The Greatest Master") – was the last to be added to the list because I had a deep immersion into Sufism, and Ibn in particular, near the culmination of this book's editing process. When Meher Baba recorded the greatest Sufi Perfect Masters ever, Ibn was included on it, and when it came to penetrating logic, 'Arabi is often mentioned in the same breath with Adi Shankara. Ibn was a mystic-philosopher, scholar-teacher, poet, and *prodigious* writer as well, having authored some 300 books. His two universally acknowledged masterworks are *The Meccan Revelations (Al-Futuhat al-Makkiyya)* and *The Ringstones of Wisdom (Fusus al-hikam)*, both of which I'd place alongside any of history's great mystical tomes. The Muhyiddin Ibn 'Arabi Society is the best place that I know of for more about this lofty soul: https://ibnarabisociety.org/.

Longchenpa: Formally known as Longchen Rabjam ("Infinite, Vast Expanse of Space") and Drimé Özer, this 14th century Master was one of the clearest and deepest authors, scholars, and realized luminaries in all of Tibetan Buddhism. He taught not only from an academic position but also from a profound experiential Beingness. Considered the most important writer on Dzogchen teachings, *The Seven Treasuries* and the *Trilogy of Rest* are regarded as his foremost works. At times, I sensed a tangible connection with Longchenpa and felt as if I've been blessed by his transmission.

Meher Baba: I probably have not written enough in this book about Baba's incalculable help throughout my journey, along with some of the miraculous experiences with him, and with him at the Meher Center in Myrtle Beach. His books *God Speaks* and *Discourses* are both deep and amazing, although the former is, by Baba's own admission, not exactly easy reading. Meticulously chronicled in Dr. William Donkin's manuscript, *The Wayfarers,* Baba's many years of working with the spiritually advanced but stuck-in-consciousness God-Intoxicated ("Masts," a Sufi term pronounced "musts") was fascinating and unique to Baba as far as I know. While it has been said that "his ways are unfathomable," Baba is, for me, as great as they come. I liken my relationship to Baba as him being my favorite uncle. There are many websites dedicated to him but these two are probably the best places to start: http://www.avatarmeherbaba.org and https://www.mehercenter.org.

Meister Eckhart: This thirteenth and fourteenth century German theologian, mystic, philosopher, and priest of the Franciscan and Dominican Orders is my favorite of the Christian Mystics (along with Saint Francis). Other than the Christian-based language that he necessarily used, in some ways his sermons sounded more like a Zen Roshi's dharma talk (satsang) than anything else, and I find it somewhat miraculous that he wasn't burned at the stake for heresy. An internet search will bring up lots of information on him (many books have been published about him too), but my principal source for his teachings comes from an exceptionally well-done set of audio recordings by James Finley, Ph.D. titled *Meister Eckhart's Living Wisdom: Indestructible Joy and the Path of Letting Go*. This set can be found and purchased on the voluminous and wonderful *Sounds True* website: https://www.soundstrue.com/store. I found this in early 2017 but didn't really start getting into it fully until my stay at Hidden Valley in September of that year. As events unfolded, this is what I was listening to when The Kiss happened and as a result, it will always hold a special place in my heart.

Nisargadatta Maharaj: He was a wild, sometimes fierce and confrontational Master. He was also always loving and compassionate underneath it all. Nisargadatta is, along with Ramana Maharshi, the best-known 20th century exponent of non-duality. *I Am That* is a must-have collection of dialogues between him and the seekers who visited him in his small apartment in Mumbai, and it's a bona fide spiritual classic. His teachings were, perhaps, the most direct and narrow of any that I am aware of from that era and therefore generally not for the spiritual newbie or faint of heart. An excellent way to learn about Nisargadatta is an audio study course by Adyashanti. I don't know of an official website for him, but an internet search will readily produce a large amount of quality information.

Paramahansa Yogananda: He is my guru – my Spiritual Master. What higher tribute is there? It is impossible to share just how much he has shaped this incarnation in its evolution toward awakening. The intellect is simply incapable of processing and/or comprehending what an awakened soul of his stature and evolution does and is capable of doing, especially when one is attuned. His *Autobiography of a Yogi* is perhaps the most read spiritual account of the 20th century, and often cited as the seminal book read by those on a spiritual path. Furthermore, his expansive commentaries on The Bhagavad Gita, *God Talks With Arjuna – Royal Science of God-Realization,* as well as on the life and teachings of Jesus of Nazareth, *The Second Coming Of Christ – The Resurrection of the Christ Within You,* are definitive in my view, and mind-boggling in scope. Here is the SRF website: https://www.yogananda.org.

Saint Francis of Assisi: Described by Meher Baba as the most advanced Master in the Christian tradition save Jesus himself, my connection to Francesco goes back to when he roamed Assisi and the world at large. One of the clearest, most succinct quotes on the fact that We Are That Which We Seek was articulated by St. Francis when he reportedly said, "The One you are looking for is the One who is looking." There is so much available on him that I cannot point to a definitive website. However, I do recommend these two books as a starting place, both based on his teachings and about his life and work: 1) *There's a Spiritual Solution to Every Problem* by Dr. Wayne Dyer and 2) *Saint Francis* by Nikos Kazantzakis, a fabulous historical novel that truly gives the reader the feel of what life with Francesco was like during the time he walked the earth. Wayne Dyer also recorded a wonderful DVD set that included a visit to Assisi titled *Experiencing the Miraculous*.

Modern Day Sages

Adyashanti: Through two of my dear friends, Adya thankfully came to me in October of 2017, absolutely and miraculously right on time. It is impossible for me to imagine what the post-Kiss transition would have been like without his teachings, particularly with the issues around the loss of personal will and the "I have it, I lost it" phase. Adya is more or less a combination of Zen and Advaita, with a huge dose of no-nonsense, straight-to-the-point discourse. These, then, are all compassionately couched within his direct and considerable experience. Adya's audio and video libraries are available for purchase on his website: https://www.adyashanti.org.

Alan Watts: My first spiritual teacher, Alan was a highly-regarded author, as well as a respected scholar with amazing oratory skills, all served up with mischievous wit and irreverent humor. From the age of about thirteen on, Alan opened my eyes to the eastern spiritual traditions. He is widely accounted as one of the 20th century's foremost disseminators of Buddhism in general and Zen in particular. I found his acclaimed manuscript, *The Book: On The Taboo Against Knowing Who You Are*, to be an all-time classic and a must-read. While Alan reportedly had his struggles in areas of life that many of us do, he'll always hold a very special place in my heart. Website: http://www.alanwatts.org.

Eckhart Tolle: I initially discovered Eckhart due to his international bestselling book, *The Power of Now*. However, I actually got into him more due to his second book, *A New Earth* (which also sold like wildfire, especially after Oprah's book club recommendation). As the concept and experience of inner stillness (no-mind) moved to the forefront of my consciousness and in my sadhana, he greatly assisted me in understanding what was unfolding within. His website: http://www.eckharttolle.com.

Francis Lucille: Francis is an internationally respected non-duality teacher. He was a student of the distinguished European Advaita Vedanta teacher, Jean Klein, and the teacher of another prominent modern-day non-duality educator, Rupert Spira. In 2017, a monastic friend suggested that I attend one of the free satsangs that are generally held each weekend in Francis' beautiful home in the hills overlooking the Temecula, California valley. Since then, I've enjoyed attending his satsangs whenever I was in his area. Francis is the author of three exceptional books, and many of his talks may be found on YouTube. You can find out more about Francis, his satsang schedule, and his conducted retreats online: https://francislucille.com.

Neale Donald Walsch: The *Conversations with God* material, specifically books 1-4, *Communion with God*, and *Home with God: In a Life That Never Ends* are as good as it gets in my reality and resonate about as true with my inner sensibilities as is possible. The first three "conversations" books had an immense impact on me, as I found them very early on after my Shift at age 38. I was fortunate to meet Neale on a few occasions and get to know him some. Along with Ram Dass, I have always deeply admired Neale for being so authentic and open about his life's challenges, along with his (perceived) faults and foibles. Being able to do this, particularly in the highly public role that he and Ram Dass operated in and from, isn't always easy. Based on their honesty and ability to willingly embrace their humanness, I have always challenged myself to do the same. For all things Neale and CWG, this website is the best place to start: http://www.nealedonaldwalsch.com.

Ram Dass: I have immense love and admiration for this man. While his books are what many gravitate to, for me it was his lectures that worked best. Prior to his stroke, he was, in my estimation, the most eloquent and beautiful speaker I'd ever heard. Remarkably blunt about admitting to "his stuff," deeply insightful into all aspects of the path, and rich with stories about his time with his guru (Neem Karoli Baba) and the many other spiritual glitterati that he knew, I have listened to his many lectures for countless hours. Reflecting back on the 60's and 70's, together with Alan Watts and George Harrison, there was probably no one more responsible for disseminating the eastern spiritual traditions to the western world than Ram Dass. Anyone not familiar with him should watch the wonderful documentary movies *Fierce Grace* and *Becoming Nobody*. Both of these films are educational and very touching biographical looks at his remarkable incarnation that sadly (for all of us) ended in December 2019. While he will surely be missed, his spirit lives on, and his website has many resources that will continue to sustain his legacy: https://www.ramdass.org.

Rupert Spira: UK born and based, Rupert is an internationally known teacher through his lectures, satsangs, and books, all rooted in the lineage of Jean Klein and Atmananda Krishnamenon (who both advocated the tantric approach of Kashmir Shaivism, in addition to Advaita Vedanta). Along with his teacher, Francis Lucille, I find Rupert to be one of the most lucid and precise disseminators of non-duality in today's marketplace. I read his book, *The Nature of Consciousness: Essays on the Unity of Mind and Matter,* in the fall of 2019 and was deeply impressed. The internet has much more information about him: https://rupertspira.com.

Thomas Merton: Possibly the most well-known and influential Catholic (Trappist) monk of the 20th century, he was also an exceptionally prolific and highly-regarded author, as well as an international advocate for peace and interfaith ecumenism. Maybe most importantly, from my perspective, he was a contemplative and mystic in the truest sense of the words. His legacy was what fomented my two weeklong individual retreats at the Abbey of Gethsemani in February and June of 2009. In addition to all his books, original audio recordings of Merton (mostly from his meetings at Gethsemani) have also begun to be released, and for anyone into Merton, these are wonderful to finally be able to listen to. Also, on the *Sounds True* website, James Finley (a novice at Gethsemani under Merton's direction) has an exceptional set of audios titled *Thomas Merton's Path to the Palace of Nowhere*. Sites to peruse: http://merton.org and http://www.monks.org and https://jamesfinley.org.

Wayne Dyer: Stumbling upon Wayne by "chance" and then watching one of his PBS lectures in December of 1998 led to my Shift that I've written about;

and the rest, as they say, is history. Wayne's teachings were significant early on in my journey, as he was a highly articulate and entertaining writer and speaker. Importantly, he provided me with a vocabulary for my newly found spiritual interests and experiences, which then assisted me in communicating to friends and family what was happening. He had a talent for taking spiritual texts and concepts and explaining them for those who often were not steeped in the esoteric. He did this in a simple, knowledgeable, and fun way. In return, many were exposed to truths they otherwise might have overlooked. Consequently, he helped raise the consciousness of the planet as a whole and assisted countless people individually as well. He was a wonderful man and I miss him. His webpage is: https://www.drwaynedyer.com.

Recommended Resources

All authors and/or editors are listed alphabetically by their first names, and anything with an * is bibliographical, as passages from it were quoted in this book. Explore and enjoy!

Adyashanti:
1. The End of Your World: Uncensored Straight Talk on the Nature of Enlightenment*
2. The Impact of Awakening: Third Edition*
3. I Am That: Exploring the Teachings of Nisargadatta Maharaj (audio study course)
4. Experiencing No-Self (audio study course)
5. Uncensored Straight Talk (audio study course)
6. Awake In Uncharted Waters (audio)
7. Enlightenment Unfolding (audio)
8. Coming Down The Mountain (audio)
9. The Shedding of Identity (audio)
10. The Infinite Shining (audio)

A.H. Almaas:
1. Luminous Night's Journey: An Autobiographical Fragment*
2. Runaway Realization: Living a Life of Ceaseless Discovery*

Alan Watts:
1. The Book: On the Taboo Against Knowing Who You Are
2. The Way of Zen
3. You're It!: On Hiding, Seeking, and Being Found (audio)
4. Out of Your Mind: Essential Listening from the Alan Watts Audio Archives (audio)

Alistair Shearer:
1. In The Light Of The Self: Adi Shankara and the Yoga of Non-dualism*

Anam Thubten:
1. The Citadel of Awareness: A Commentary on Jigme Lingpa's Dzogchen Aspiration Prayer

Andre Doshim Halaw:
1. God Is Nothingness
2. No-Mind: Realizing Your True Nature

Andrew Newberg and Mark Robert Waldman:
1. How Enlightenment Changes Your Brain

Arthur Osborne (Editor):
1. True Happiness: The Teachings Of Ramana Maharshi

B. Alan Wallace (Translation and Commentary):
1. Heart Of The Great Perfection: Düdjom Lingpa's Visions Of The Great Perfection
2. Buddhahood Without Meditation: Düdjom Lingpa's Visions Of The Great Perfection*
3. The Vajra Essence: Düdjom Lingpa's Visions Of The Great Perfection*
4. Fathoming The Mind: Inquiry And Insight in Düdjom Lingpa's Vajra Essence

Bernadette Roberts:
1. The Path To No-Self: Life At The Center*
2. The Experience of No-Self: A Contemplative Journey*

Bonnie Greenwell:
1. When Spirit Leaps: Navigating the Process of Spiritual Awakening
2. The Awakening Guide: A Companion for the Inward Journey

Chögyal Namkhai Norbu Rinpoche with Adriano Clemente:
1. The Supreme Source: The Fundamental Tantra of the Dzogchen Semde Kunjed Gyalpo

Chögyal Namkhai Norbu Rinpoche with John Myrdhin Reynolds:
1. The Golden Letters: The Three Statements of Garab Dorje, First Dzogchen Master*

David Carse:
1. Perfect Brilliant Stillness: beyond the individual self

David Godman (Editor):
1. Be As You Are: The Teachings of Sri Ramana Maharshi*
2. Nothing Ever Happened: Volumes 1-3*

David R. Hawkins:
1. Power vs. Force: The Hidden Determinants of Human Behavior
2. The Eye Of The Eye: From Which Nothing Is Hidden
3. I: Reality And Subjectivity

Deepak Chopra:
1. How To Know God

Dorothy Hunt:
1. Ending The Search: From Spiritual Ambition to the Heart of Awareness*

Eckhart Tolle:
1. The Power of Now
2. A New Earth: Awakening to Your Life's Purpose

Francis Dale Bennett:
1. I Am That I Am

Francis Lucille:
1. The Perfume of Silence
2. Eternity Now
3. Truth Love Beauty

H.W.L. Poonja:
1. The Truth Is*

Ibn 'Arabi/Balyani (Translated from the Arabic by Cecilia Twinch):
1. Know Yourself: An explanation of the oneness of being

Ilie Cioara:
1. The Silence Of The Mind
2. The Wondrous Journey: Into the Depth of Our Being
3. Life Is Eternal Newness
4. I Am Boundless

James Finley:
1. Meister Eckhart's Living Wisdom: Indestructible Joy and the Path of Letting Go (audio)
2. Thomas Merton's Path to the Palace of Nowhere: The Essential Guide to the Contemplative Teachings of Thomas Merton (audio)

Jean Klein:
1. I Am*
2. The Book of Listening
3. Who Am I? The Sacred Quest
4. The Ease of Being
5. Transmission of the Flame

Jed McKenna:
1. The Enlightenment Trilogy: Books One* and Three*
2. Dream State: A Conspiracy Theory

Jeffrey A. Martin:
1. The Finders

John Allen Grimes:
1. Ramana Maharshi: The Crown Jewel Of Advaita

John Blofeld (Translator):
1. The Zen Teaching of Huang Po: On The Transmission Of Mind*
2. Zen Teaching of Instantaneous Awakening: Chan Master Hui Hai

John J. Prendergast, Peter Fenner, Sheila Krystal (Editors):
1. The Sacred Mirror: Nondual Wisdom and Psychotherapy*

John Myrdhin Reynolds (Translation and Commentary):
1. Self-Liberation: Through Seeing with Naked Awareness*

Junpo Denis Kelly Roshi and Keith Martin-Smith:
1. The Heart of Zen: Enlightenment, Emotional Maturity, and What It Really Takes for Spiritual Liberation

Keith Dowman (Translation and Commentary):
1. Original Perfection: Vairotsana's Five Early Transmissions*
2. Spaciousness: The Radical Dzogchen of the Vajra-Heart – Revised Edition*
3. Natural Perfection: Longchenpa's Radical Dzogchen
4. Maya Yoga: Longchenpa's Finding Comfort and Ease in Enchantment
5. The Flight of the Garuda – Revised Edition

Kennard Lipman and Merrill Peterson (Translation and Commentary):
1. You Are the Eyes of the World: Longchenpa*

Llewellyn Vaughan-Lee:
1. For Love of the Real: A Story of Life's Mystical Secret*
2. Light of Oneness
3. Darkening Of The Light: Witnessing the End of an Era

Meher Baba:
1. God Speaks
2. Discourses

Mu Soeng:
1. Trust In Mind: The Rebellion of Chinese Zen*

Neale Donald Walsch:
1. Conversations with God: Books 1-4
2. Communion with God
3. Home with God: In A Life That Never Ends

Nisargadatta Maharaj:
1. I Am That*
2. The Experience of Nothingness: Talks on Realizing the Infinite
3. Consciousness and the Absolute: The Final Talks of Sri Nisargadatta Maharaj
4. Beyond Freedom: Talks With Sri Nisargadatta Maharaj
5. I Am Not The Body: Discovering the Truth Beyond Bondage

Padmakara Translation Group:
1. Longchenpa: Finding Rest in the Nature of the Mind – The Trilogy of Rest, Volume 1
2. Longchenpa: Finding Rest in Meditation – The Trilogy of Rest, Volume 2
3. Longchenpa: Finding Rest in Illusion – The Trilogy of Rest, Volume 3*

Paramahansa Yogananda:
1. Autobiography of a Yogi*
2. God Talks With Arjuna: The Bhagavad Gita – Royal Science of God-Realization
3. The Second Coming of Christ: The Resurrection of the Christ Within You
4. Paramahansa Yogananda's SRF Lessons for Home Study

Paul Brunton:
1. The Short Path to Enlightenment: Instructions for Immediate Awakening*

Paul Levy:
1. The Quantum Revelation: A Radical Synthesis Of Science And Spirituality*

Peter Samsel (Editor):
1. A Treasury of Sufi Wisdom: The Path of Unity

Ram Dass (with Rameshwar Das on #1 and #2; with Stephen Levine on #3):
1. Being Ram Dass
2. Polishing The Mirror: How to Live from Your Spiritual Heart
3. Grist for the Mill: Awakening To Oneness
4. Still Here: Embracing Aging, Changing, and Dying
5. Paths to God: Living the Bhagavad Gita (audio)
6. The Ram Dass Audio Collection (audio)
7. Love, Service, Devotion, and the Ultimate Surrender (audio)
8. Experiments in Truth: A Collection of Classic Lectures from the '60s to the '90s (audio)

Rasha:
1. Oneness

Richard J. Hooper:
1. The Essential Mystics, Poets, Saints, And Sages: A Wisdom Treasury*

Robert Lanza with Bob Berman (And Matej Pavšič on #2):
1. Biocentrism: How Life and Consciousness are the Keys to Understanding the True Nature of the Universe
2. The Grand Biocentric Design: How Life Creates Reality

Robert Wolfe:
1. Emptiness: Robert Wolfe on the ultimate teaching of ajata/sunyata*
2. One Essence: The Nondual Clarity of an Ancient Zen Poem

Roy Melvyn (Translator #1 and Editor #2):
1. The Lost Writings of Wu Hsin: Pointers to Non-Duality in Five Volumes*
2. The Essential Nisargadatta*
3. I As*

Rupert Sheldrake:
1. Science and Spiritual Practices: Transformative Experiences and Their Effects on Our Bodies, Brains, and Health

Rupert Spira:
1. The Nature of Consciousness: Essays on the Unity of Mind and Matter
2. Being Aware of Being Aware
3. The Transparency of Things
4. The Intimacy of All Experience

Soko Morinaga:
1. The Ceasing of Notions*

Stephen Hirtenstein:
1. The Unlimited Mercifier: The Spiritual Life and Thought of Ibn 'Arabi*

Steve Taylor:
1. The Leap: The Psychology Of Spiritual Awakening*

Tenzin Gyatso – His Holiness the 14th Dalai Lama:
1. The Universe In A Single Atom: The Convergence of Science And Spirituality
2. My Spiritual Journey: Personal Reflections, Teachings, and Talks

Thomas Cleary (Translator and Editor):
1. The Sutra Of Hui-Neng: Grandmaster Of Zen – With Commentary on the Diamond Sutra
2. Rational Zen: The Mind of Dogen Zenji

Thomas Merton:
1. The Asian Journal of Thomas Merton*
2. New Seeds of Contemplation*
3. Mystics and Zen Masters
4. The Wisdom of the Desert
5. The Way Of Chuang Tzu

Toshihiko Izutsu:
1. Sufism and Taoism: A Comparative Study of Key Philosophical Concepts
2. Toward a Philosophy of Zen Buddhism
3. Creation And The Timeless Order Of Things: Essays in Islamic Mystical Philosophy

Wayne Dyer:
1. The Shift: Deluxe Edition (movie)
2. There's a Spiritual Solution to Every Problem
3. Wisdom of the Ages

William C. Chittick:
1. Ibn 'Arabi: Heir to the Prophets
2. The Self-Disclosure of God: Principles of Ibn 'Arabi's Cosmology
3. The Sufi Path of Knowledge: Ibn Al-Arabi's Metaphysics of Imagination

Help thy brother's boat across and lo! Thine own has reached the shore.

~ Hindu Proverb

Appreciative Accolades

Grace Happens was written during a forty-day/night personal retreat at the Diamond Mountain Retreat Center in the SE Arizona Chiricahua Mountains. Their staff was helpful in every way, and the area's quietude and magical vibe beautifully held the space for the book to come into creation. The entire original manuscript manifested extemporaneously, effortlessly arising out of the nowhere and into the now here! All that said, there are those who made forever-appreciated contributions to my life – and consequently to this book – who therefore must be acknowledged.

No book of mine could be written without giving loving thanks to my mom Evelyn, dad William, and stepdad John. I wish all of you could have remained in the body long enough to have held it in your hands. The same is true for my two amazing nephews, Scott and Adam. You both have so many remarkable talents, along with sincere concern for others. Leave it all on The Playing Field guys! Please…don't depart this world with any of the beautifully unique music within you still unplayed! I also want to give a big ol' shout-out to my beautiful sister, Marilyn Peterson, and to Dr. David Peterson, her wonderful lifelong soulmate and husband. During the period between The Kiss and the writing of this book, they twice heartily welcomed me into their home to "sit a spell" and provided more kindness, generosity, and love than I am able to adequately express. I love you both!

Much loving gratefulness to all my dear and amazing friends (platonic and intimate) throughout this life. Thank you so very much for being there with me and, knowingly or not, being my upa gurus.

My everlasting love and well-wishes to Deep Garcha and the Bundyji's for adopting me into their spiritual family, and to Dr. Harvey Cheatham for his honesty when it counted most.

Unceasing indebtedness to Meher Baba and his Center in Myrtle Beach, and to the Self-Realization Fellowship's Atlanta Center and Hidden Valley Ashram in Escondido – all spiritual havens for me.

During my time as operations manager for SRF's Hidden Valley Ashram, I discovered that Brother Devananda and I shared a mutual interest in fine art photography. While my preferred photographic subjects were landscapes, nature, and wildlife, his area of expertise was portraiture. I was privileged to view the many images he had, and without a doubt his collection of SRF monastic portraits was the finest I had and have ever seen. Brother Devananda graciously offered to make some portraits of me and I eventually took him up on his offer, with the stipulation that they be processed in my preference for black and white. The image on the back cover is one of the portraits he made and I want to thank him here for it, as well as for all the fun we had during our time serving together at HVA.

My sincere thanks to Ms. Kay Ostrenko for her encouragement to share my awakening with the world, as well as to Mr. Eli "Flow" Recht for the same, along with his indispensable editing of this manuscript. This book would not be what it is without Eli's extraordinary insights and efforts.

I wouldn't be here now without the dear souls who helped see me through the awakening process. You all know who you are, and I will forever be thankful for your service, understanding, and love. With this, there was no one more important than Mr. Robert Merrill – I love you Brother!

Namo Namah to The Divine Hand:
The Ineffable Loving Doer and Non-Doer of All Things.

Printed in Great Britain
by Amazon